The Sexuality of Christ in Renaissance Art and in Modern Oblivion

THE SEXUALITY OF CHRIST
IN RENAISSANCE ART
AND IN MODERN OBLIVION

LEO STEINBERG

A Pantheon/October Book
New York

The entire work first appeared in the Summer 1983 issue of *October*.

Library of Congress Cataloging in Publication Data

Steinberg, Leo, 1920-
    The sexuality of Christ in Renaissance art and in modern oblivion.

    Bibliography: p.
    Includes index.
    1. Jesus Christ—Art. 2. Jesus Christ—Humanity. 3. Jesus Christ—
Physical appearance. 4. Art, Renaissance. 5. Art, Modern. I. October.
II. Title.
N8050.S74 1984   704.9′4853′094   83-19520
ISBN 0-394-53580-4
ISBN 0-394-72267-1 pbk.

Manufactured in the United States of America

Layout and display typography designed by Naomi Osnos

To Phoebe Lloyd,
companion of all my thought
while I worked on this book,
I offer it in dedication.

CONTENTS

ACKNOWLEDGMENTS

The present essay was originally delivered as a Lionel Trilling Seminar at Columbia University, New York, on November 19, 1981, the discussants being Julius S. Held and John W. O'Malley, S.J. Professor Held's thoughtful comments (prepared for that first occasion, not for this longer version) are answered to the best of my powers in some of the later Excursuses. The response read by Professor O'Malley is herewith published, with his permission, as an envoi.

Many have earned my gratitude: Jack Freiberg, connoisseur of the city of Rome; Dr. Charlotte Lacaze, indispensable bridge to French museums and libraries; Adam Jacobs, my man in Munich; Ruth Campbell, friend and loyal reader of Latin; Bruce Barton, artist-designer and peruser of Pepys; Dr. Marie Tanner, who, in her undergraduate days, steered me to safety through red-tape entanglements; Arthur Danto and Richard Kuhns of Columbia University; Dr. Elfriede Knauer, Georg Knauer, and Paul Watson of the University of Pennsylvania; Alan Shestack of the Yale University Art Gallery; Dr. George Szabo, Curator of the Lehman Collection at the Metropolitan Museum of Art; Dr. Michael Conforti of the Minneapolis Institute of Arts; and Dr. Ralph Sussman for his great heart and skill.

During the years spent on this work, teaching at the University of Pennsylvania, I was blessed with a triple succession of research assistants—young friends then and now. Their names, before long, will honor our profession: John Cunnally; Jack Greenstein; Kevin Salatino.

Next, I must thank my telephone; at the speed of a wish, it would bring me the stintless erudition of Wayne Dynes of Hunter College, New York; the solution to a Latin crux from Eugene F. Rice of Columbia; the inspiriting voice and careful ear of Lisa Miller; or, from John Hollander, one passionate sentence that would show him at home at an address I was groping to reach, assuring me of habitable quarters ahead.

My heavy debt to O'Malley is one I bear with serenity. It is, of course, to his work, and to his courtesies in furnishing rare source materials, that I owe my acquaintance with the sermons preached before Renaissance popes. These sermons are studied in O'Malley's *Praise and Blame in Renaissance Rome,* a book which won the American Historical Association's Marraro Prize as "the outstanding work of the year on any phase of Italian culture or history." I shared the Association's enthusiasm, and conveyed it to the author, along with the suggestion that the art of the Renaissance more than confirmed the conclusions he had drawn from the sermons. O'Malley replied by return mail—in words often recalled to rally faltering confidence.

The bold decision to devote an entire issue of *October* to a topic somewhat remote from the magazine's usual interests was made by Rosalind Krauss, Annette Michelson bravely assenting. I do admire their fortitude. And I was in luck with Douglas Crimp of *October:* a superb editor, he overlooked nothing, and the dross that remains is my cussedness.

*

Re-reading the above, I marvel at the persona engendered by the influence of the form. The writer presents himself as one surrounded and cushioned by friends. He is, he says, "blessed," "in luck," "serene" even in his obligations. Not a word about grievances, or about offenses received and inflicted. Who would suspect a curmudgeon behind such handsome avowals? But perhaps this is what they are good for. By their virtue, ill-humor is temporarily purged, and the author is given a glimpse of the person he might have become, had he formed the habit of privately closing each day with such notations as are called for by the publishing of acknowledgments.

The Sexuality of Christ in Renaissance Art and in Modern Oblivion

Heure de nostre

Eus in adiutorui meu
intende Dne ad adiuua
dum me festina Gloria

Em creator spiritus mentes
tuorum uisita imple superna

gratia que tu creasti pectora Me

The first necessity is to admit a long-suppressed matter of fact: that Renaissance art, both north and south of the Alps, produced a large body of devotional imagery in which the genitalia of the Christ Child, or of the dead Christ, receive such demonstrative emphasis that one must recognize an *ostentatio genitalium* comparable to the canonic *ostentatio vulnerum,* the showing forth of the wounds. In many hundreds of pious, religious works, from before 1400 to past the mid-16th century, the ostensive unveiling of the Child's sex, or the touching, protecting or presentation of it, is the main action (Figs. 1, 2). And the emphasis recurs in images of the dead Christ, or of the mystical Man of Sorrows (Fig. 3). All of which has been tactfully overlooked for half a millennium. Hence my first question — whether the outgoing 20th century is late enough to concede that the subject exists.   I*

My second objective is to propose plausible theological grounds for the genital reference in the works under review — such as are illustrated in Figs. 4-6. Sooner or later someone is bound to notice what the Madonna's left hand in these paintings is doing; to prevent it is not in our power. The question is in what spirit — whether in ribaldry or in reverence, frankly or nervously — the discovery is to be made, and made public.   II

My third concern is didactic. At the risk of belaboring what is obvious, I must address myself to the many who still habitually mistake pictorial symbols in Renaissance art for descriptive naturalism. To take one example: At the sight of an infant Christ touching the Virgin's chin, they will admire the charm of a gesture so childlike, playful, affectionate. They are not wrong, but I think

*   Indications of sources are given in the footnotes. Full references for abbreviated bibliographic citations appear on pp. 204-06. The List of Illustrations (pp. 207-17) provides full captions for the works reproduced. Roman numerals in the margins refer to correspondingly numbered Excursuses in the back pages. To these I have relegated collateral matter, including additional illustrations, expanded quotations and related source material, as well as polemics and digressions I could not resist. Some of the longer Excursuses strike me now as unseasonable interruptions. I suppose they are best read as an epilogue.

Fig. 1. Illumination from the Hours of Philip the Good, *Presentation in the Temple,* 1454-55.

Fig. 2. Andrea del Sarto, *Tallard Madonna,*
c. 1515.

Fig. 3. Andrea del Sarto, drawing for a
Pietà, c. 1520.

Fig. 4. Bartolommeo di Giovanni, *Madonna
and Child,* c. 1490.

Fig. 6. Annibale Carracci Shop, *Madonna and Child with Saints,* 1608–09, detail.

they are satisfied with too little. For the seeming artlessness of what I shall call the chin-chuck disguises a ritual form of impressive antiquity. It is first encountered in New Kingdom Egypt as a token of affection or erotic persuasion (Fig. 124). In Archaic Greek painting the gesture is given to wooers, and it occurs more than once in the *Iliad* to denote supplication (Figs. 125, 126).[1] In Late Antique art, the caress of the chin is allegorized to express the union of Cupid and Psyche, the god of Love espousing the human soul (Fig. 7). And the gesture proliferates in medieval art into representations both of profane lovers and of the Madonna and Child (Figs. 8, 9, 127). Thus no Christian artist, medieval or Renaissance, would have taken this long-fixed convention for anything but a sign of erotic communion, either carnal or spiritual. By assigning it to the Christ Child, the artist was designating Mary's son as the Heavenly Bridegroom who, having chosen her for his mother, was choosing her for his eternal consort in heaven. The chin-chuck, then, betokens the Infant Spouse (a

III

1.   *Iliad,* I, 501–02; VIII, 370–71; X, 454–55.

Fig. 5. Veronese, *Presentation of the Cuccini Family to the Madonna,* 1571, detail.

Fig. 7. Hellenistic bronze statuette, *Cupid and Psyche.*

Fig. 8. Romanesque, *Herod and Salome,* cloister capital from St. Etienne, Toulouse, c. 1140.

phrase I take from St. Augustine[2]) — whether the action appears naturalized on earth, or enskied (Figs. 10–12).

In decoding such ostensible genre motifs as the chin-chuck, our charge is to remain undeceived by their verisimilitude. If the depicted gesture was made to look common, imputable to any mother's child, the intent was not to diminish but, on the contrary, to confirm the mystery of the Incarnation. Lifelikeness posed no threat, because these Renaissance artists regarded the godhead in the person of Jesus as too self-evident to be dimmed by his manhood. What they did not anticipate was the retroactive effect that four centuries of deepening secularism would have on the perception of Renaissance art. They did not foresee that the process of demythologizing Christianity would succeed in profaning our vision of their sacred art; so that now, most modern viewers are content to stop at the demythicized image—a human image drawn to all appearances from the natural world, far afield from the mysteries of the Creed. Could it be that Renaissance artistry, striving for

2.   St. Augustine speaks of "His appearance as an Infant Spouse, from his bridal chamber, that is, from the womb of a virgin"; Augustine, Sermon IX, 2 (Ben. 191); *Sermons,* p. 109. See also Sermon X, 3, pp. 115–16, for the theme of the Infant Spouse, the Virgin's womb as bride chamber, and the Incarnation of the Word "by a marriage which it is impossible to define."

Fig. 9. Simone Martini, *Madonna and Child,* c. 1321–25.

Fig. 10. Marco Zoppo, *Madonna and Child,* c. 1470.

Fig. 11. Barent van Orley, *Madonna and Child with Angels,* c. 1513, detail.

Fig. 12. South Netherlandish, *Madonna and Child,* c. 1500.

truthful representation, became too competent for its own good? Rapt in the wonder of God's assumed human nature, Renaissance artists will have produced work whose winning naturalism was rendered in retrospect self-defeating. Wherever, in humanizing their Christ, they dared the most, we now see nothing out of the ordinary; as though the infant Christ or the adult's corpse were mere pretexts for exhibiting common humanity.

Accordingly, at the sight of a dead Christ touching his groin (Figs. 3, 109ff.), we are told not to wonder because dying men often do this—as if the alleged frequency of the posture in male human corpses justified its allocation to Christ on sacred monuments.[3] Similarly, a picture such as Veronese's *sacra conversazione* (Fig. 80)—four amazed saints gathered about a blithe sleeper —elicits the explanation that "it's what baby boys do." And the outrage of Hans Baldung Grien's *Holy Family* woodcut (Fig. 13) is shrugged off on the grounds that "it's what grandmothers do." Perhaps; but how comes it that the only baby in Western art so entertained is the Christ?

The Baldung Grien woodcut shows the Christ Child subjected to genital manipulation. How should this curiosity be perceived? Shall we hurry past it with stifled titters, or condemn it as scandalous? No matter what the response, one feels that St. Anne's gesture, fondling or testing her grandchild's penis, is a liberty without parallel in Christian art. Yet the action is staged in solemnity, and as the central motif of a work that does not seem scurrilous in intention. One remains at a loss for alternatives, wanting an appropriate context. The thing demands explanation, or at least some explaining away.

Explaining away has been tried. Until the 1981 Baldung Grien exhibition in Washington and New Haven, it was the recourse of the foremost Baldung scholar Carl Koch. Koch interpreted St. Anne's gesture in the light of the artist's known interest in folk superstition—witness Baldung's fascination by witches. But, he continued, Baldung displays "even deeper insight into arcane popular customs believed to possess magic powers. Thus, under pretext of representing the pious companionship of the Holy Family, he dares make the miracle-working spell pronounced over a child the subject of a woodcut composition."[4]

This is all we were told. The nature of this supposed spell, whether fecundative or apotropaic, was not divulged. But Koch's purpose was unmistakable: to forestall any suspicion of impudence on Baldung's part. We were urged instead to applaud the artist's inquiry into secret peasant beliefs, his anticipation of modern anthropological attitudes. In his woodcut, the grandam's gesture, so

---

3.   For the motif of the dead Christ touching his groin, and its subsequent imitation in recumbent tomb effigies, see pp. 96–104 below, and Excursuses XXXVII and XXXVIII.
4.   Carl Koch in Staatliche Kunsthalle Karlsruhe, *Hans Baldung Grien,* exh. cat., Karlsruhe, 1959, pp. 17 and (summary) 241.

Fig. 13. Hans Baldung Grien, *Holy Family,* 1511.

8

far from being prurient or frivolous, was to be understood as a record of Baldung's fieldwork among the folk. Meanwhile, the woodcut's overt Christian subject was reduced to the role of a cover. Apparently, the gesture portrayed would have been too indelicate to stage in a peasant setting, visited on some nameless child; but with the Christ Child anything goes.

IV

An alternative mode of evasion argues the case in reverse: St. Anne's conduct, we hear, is not an arcanum discovered in folk superstition, but a silly genre motif—no further explanation required. We are asked to recall that the practice of admiring and handling a male infant's genitals was formerly common in many cultures, so that Baldung would have represented no more than a routine occasion in a typical household. Philippe Ariès actually cites Baldung's woodcut to document what he calls the once "widespread tradition" of playing with a child's privy parts.

V

What is involved here is a misunderstanding of a critical truth: that naturalistic motifs in religious Renaissance art are never adequately accounted for by their prevalence in life situations. Ordinary experience is no template for automatic transfer to art. There are many things babies do—crawling on all fours, for instance, before they start walking—which no artist, however deeply committed to realism, ever thought of imputing to the Christ Child. For the infant Christ, in Renaissance as in medieval art, is like no other child, whether he sits up to give audience, or rehearses the Crucifixion; whether he hands the keys of the kingdom to Peter, or snatches a makeshift cross from his playmate St. John. He engages in actions, such as eating grapes, or perusing a book, from which common babies desist. And long before normal toddlers learn to put round pegs in round holes, he deftly slips a ring on St. Catherine's finger. In short, the depicted Christ, even in babyhood, is at all times the Incarnation—very man, very God. Therefore, when a Renaissance artist quickens an Infancy scene with naturalistic detail, he is not recording this or that observation, but revealing in the thing observed a newfound compatibility with his subject.

This rule must apply as well to the palpation of the Child's privy parts. The question is not whether such practice was common, but how, whether common or not, it serves to set Mary's son apart from the run of the sons of Eve. Thus we still have to ask what Baldung thought he was doing when he offered the Infant's penis to the grandmother's touch.

I answer, provisionally, that the presentation centers on an ostensive act, a palpable proof—proving nothing less than what the Creed itself puts at the center: God's descent into manhood. And because grandmother Anne guarantees Christ's human lineage, it is she who is tasked with the proving (cf. Fig. 16). Observe that while the Child's lower body concedes its humanity, the arms reach for the Virgin, the hand of the Infant Spouse grasping her chin. Meanwhile, a contemplative Joseph looks on. Book laid aside, he watches the revelation direct, the first man to behold it with understanding.

VI

There is something here that we are expected to take for granted—here as in all religious Renaissance art: that the divinity in the incarnate Word needs no demonstration. For an infant Christ in Renaissance images differs from the earlier Byzantine and medieval Christ Child not only in degree of naturalism, but in theological emphasis. In the imagery of earlier Christianity, the claims for Christ's absolute godhood, and for his parity with the Almighty Father, had to be constantly reaffirmed against unbelief—first against Jewish recalcitrance and pagan skepticism, then against the Arian heresy, finally against Islam. Hence the majesty of the infant Christ and the hieratic posture; and even in the Byzantine type known as the Glykophilousa, the "Madonna of Sweet Love," the Child's ceremonial robe down to the feet. In Otto Demus' words: "The Byzantine image . . . always remains an 'image,' a Holy Icon, without any admixture of earthly realism."[5] But for a Western artist nurtured in Catholic orthodoxy—for him the objective was not so much to proclaim the divinity of the babe as to declare the *humanation* of God.[6] And this declaration becomes the set theme of every Renaissance Nativity, Adoration, Holy Family, or Madonna and Child.

VII

VIII

*

I have learned much from John O'Malley's recent book, *Praise and Blame in Renaissance Rome*—a masterly study that deals for the first time with the sermons delivered at the papal court between the years 1450 and 1521. O'Malley quotes this admonition to preachers from a late 15th-century author (Brandolini): "Whereas in earlier times men had to search for the truth and dispute about it, in the Christian era men are to enjoy it."[7] The preacher is not to waste words persuading believers to belief. His office is to stir men to gratitude and delight. The sermons, accordingly, dwell on the boon conferred by the Incarnation; to which the Christian's proper response is admiration and praise.

Now, "what man praises most especially in God are his works and deeds." Of these, the first was the act of Creation; but his second great "deed" was his becoming flesh and dwelling on earth. And the sermons affirm that God's first accomplishment was surpassed in the second, since the former had proved corruptible through man's sin, but the latter, which redeems from corruption, is good forever.[8]

---

5.   Otto Demus, "The Methods of the Byzantine Artist," *The Mint,* no. 2 (1948), p. 69.
6.   The English word "humanation," obsolete since it was ousted in the 17th century by "incarnation," deserves a place in the active vocabulary; it has at least some of the force of the German *Menschwerdung.*
7.   O'Malley, *Praise and Blame,* p. 70, n. 97, gives the original Latin; on the needlessness of persuading believers to belief, see also his p. 76.
8.   Ibid., pp. 138–39.

"The theology of the Western Church," writes O'Malley, "has generally tended to pinpoint the redemptive act in Christ's death on the cross, or in the conjunction of his suffering, death, and resurrection."[9] The more surprising to hear the Renaissance preachers emphasizing the preeminence of the Incarnation. "That emphasis," O'Malley continues, "wants to view all the subsequent events of Christ's life as articulations of what was already inchoately accomplished in the initial moment of man's restoration, which was the incarnation in the Virgin's womb. . . . Whatever injury man and the universe had suffered in the Fall was healed . . . when the Word assumed flesh."

Shall this insight stop at the work of the preachers? It seems to me—and O'Malley concurs—that the "incarnational theology" which he finds in the Renaissance sermons is immanent in earlier and contemporaneous Renaissance art. So much of this art is a celebration; so much of it proclaims over and over that godhood has vested itself in the infirmity of the flesh, so as to raise that flesh to the prerogatives of immortality. It celebrates the restoral which the divine power brought off by coming to share man's humanity.

And this supreme feat of God, superior even to the primordial act of Creation, is perpetually manifest in the Incarnation, that is to say, here and now in this armful of babyflesh.[10] The wonder of it, and its constant reaffirmation—this mystery is the stuff of Renaissance art: the humanation of God; the more "superwonderful" (St. Bonaventure's word) the more tangible you can make it.

Thus is the realism of Renaissance painting justified in the faith. The rendering of the incarnate Christ ever more unmistakably flesh and blood is a religious enterprise because it testifies to God's greatest achievement. And this must be the motive that induces a Renaissance artist to include, in his presentation of the Christ Child, even such moments as would normally be excluded by considerations of modesty—such as the exhibition or manipulation of the boy's genitalia (Figs. 1, 5, 14). Returning once more to the action in Baldung's woodcut (Fig. 13): if this sort of conduct was routine in Renaissance families, no representation of it would be made, except only in the imagery of the Christ Child, since no other child born of woman needed to have its ordinary humanity brought home and celebrated. Whence it follows that the central action in

9.   Ibid. The following from St. Bonaventure may serve as a standard traditional formulation: "Man has been freed from death and from the cause of death by the most efficacious means: the merit of the death of Christ" (*Breviloquium*, IV, 9, p. 173). The relative ranking of the Resurrection above the miracle of the Incarnation in Eastern theology is explicit in these words of Photius, the 9th-century Patriarch of Constantinople: "Wondrous was the manger at Bethlehem which received my Lord . . . as He had just emerged from a virgin's womb. . . . Yet a far greater miracle does the tomb exhibit; . . . in the latter is accomplished the end and the purpose of God's advent . . ." (Homily X, 7, pp. 209–10). Clearly, the issue here is not one of essential creed. It is not a question of doctrine, but of choice of rhetorical emphasis.
10.   In the words of St. Bernard, "God himself is in this babe, reconciling the world to himself" (*Song of Songs,* Sermon II, 8, p. 14).

Fig. 14. Bartolommeo Montagna, *Holy Family,* c. 1500.

Baldung's print could be at the same time trite and unique; reflective of vulgar practice and special to Christ. We apprehend the event because it is commonplace; and condone its depiction because it touches Christ. And the same principle holds for the self-touching posture of the corpse following the descent from the cross: the artists who introduced the motif understood it as human; they depicted the gesture because its performance was God's.

The image, then, is both natural and mysterial, each term enabling the other. But this reciprocal franchise is peculiar to the Catholic West, where the growth of a Christward naturalism in painting is traceable from the mid-13th century. Of course, the West held no monopoly on the affirmation of Christ's humanity. Every right-thinking Christian, whether Latin or Greek, artist or otherwise, confessed that the pivotal moment in the history of the race was God's alliance with the human condition. But in celebrating the union of God and man in the Incarnation, Western artists began displacing the emphasis, shifting from the majesty of unapproachable godhead to a being known, loved, and imitable.[11] Where the maker of a Byzantine cult image enthroned the incarnate Word as an imperial Christ, satisfied that the manhood of him was sufficiently evident in his filiation from Mary, the art of the West sought to

11.   "That he might be known and loved and imitated" is the formula proposed by St. Bonaventure; quoted in Excursus VII.

Fig. 15. Francesco Botticini, *Madonna and Child with Angels,* c. 1490.

realize that same manhood as the common flesh of humanity. Realism, the more penetrating the better, was consecrated a form of worship.

Yet it remains to ask how a direct demonstration of the incarnate God's human nature justifies a select sexual accent. Christ's manhood, yes, by all means, but why these particular means? Why should there exist even one Christian painting, such as Botticini's *Nativity* tondo in Florence (Fig. 15), where angels vent their joy at God's human birth by bestrewing his pudenda with flowers? Two thousand years earlier, Heraclitus had said: "If it were not Dionysus for whom they march in procession and chant the hymn to the phallus, their action would be most shameless."[12] What then is it in the Christian mystery of the Incarnation that could move its Renaissance celebrants to such venial "shamelessness"? The question leads to three theological considerations that bear ineluctably on Christ's sex.

12.   Hermann Diels, *Die Fragmente der Vorsokratiker,* fragment 15.

*

The eternal, by definition, experiences neither death nor generation. If the godhead incarnates itself to suffer a human fate, it takes on the condition of being both deathbound and sexed. The mortality it assumes is correlative with sexuality, since it is by procreation that the race, though consigned to death individually, endures collectively to fulfill the redemptive plan.[13] Therefore, to profess that God once embodied himself in a human nature is to confess that the eternal, there and then, became mortal and sexual. Thus understood, the evidence of Christ's sexual member serves as the pledge of God's humanation (Fig. 16).

13.   For the conjunction of mortality and fecundity as the defining terms of the human condition, see, for example, St. Gregory as quoted by Bede: "Although God deprived man of immortality for his sin, he did not destroy the human race on that account, but of his merciful goodness left man his ability to continue the race" (Bede, *A History of the English Church and People*, I, 27, 7).

Fig. 16. Cavaliere d'Arpino, *Madonna and Child with St. John, St. Anne and the Magdalen*, 1592–93.

Fig. 17. Ambrogio Lorenzetti, *Madonna del Latte,* c. 1325.

Other modalities of this pledge come to mind, notably the Christ Child's dependence on nourishment; for the iconic type of the nursing Madonna did not enter the repertory of Christian art because painters saw mothers breastfeed their children, and not merely to display the Madonna's humility, as suggested by Millard Meiss, but to attest once again the truth of the Incarnation. This is why the Virgin gives suck even in formal sessions, as when she sits to St. Luke for her portrait. This is why the nursling is so often depicted turning his face to alert our attention (Figs. 17, 18); or, more incongruously, with his mouth engaged and eyes forward, striding toward us (Fig. 141); or even *sub specie aeternitatis,* moon-cradled above the clouds, still owning his erstwhile need (Fig. 143). The image of the *Maria lactans,* popular since the mid-14th century, assured the believer that the God rooting at Mary's breast had become man indeed; and that she who sustained the God-man in his infirmity had gained

Fig. 18. Masolino, *Madonna and Child,*
c. 1423-24.

infinite credit in heaven. We do not suppose that every painter of a nursing Madonna meditated the underlying theology — the meaning of the subject was plain: Christ has to eat. His taking food, initially as an infant and lastly again at Emmaus, tendered the living proof that the substance assumed by the Trinity's Second Person, whether aborning or raised from death, was human flesh subject to hunger.

As for the sexual component in the manhood of Christ, it was normally left unspoken, suppressed originally by the ethos of Christian asceticism, ultimately by decorum. In theological writings the matter hardly appears, except, as we shall see, in connection with the Circumcision. The admission of Christ's sex occurs commonly only by indirection or implication. Thus the humanity taken on by the Word in Mary's womb was said to be — in the locution current from St. Augustine to the 17th century — "complete in all the parts   XI of a man."[14] From the preacher or theologian, no further anatomic specification was needed.

But for the makers of images the case stood otherwise. We have to consider that Renaissance artists, committed for the first time since the birth of Christianity to naturalistic modes of representation, were the only group within Christendom whose métier required them to plot every inch of Christ's body. They asked intimate questions that do not well translate into words, at least not without disrespect; whether, for instance, Christ clipped his nails short, or let them grow past the fingertips. The irreverent triviality of such inquisitions verges on blasphemy. But the Renaissance artist who lacked strong conviction on this sort of topic was unfit to fashion the hands of Christ—or his loins. For even if the body were partly draped, a decision had to be made how much to cover; whether to play the drapery down, or send it fluttering like a banner; and whether the loincloth employed, opaque or diaphanous, was to reveal or conceal. Only they, the painters and sculptors, kept all of Christ's body in their mind's eye. And some among them embraced even his sex in their thought—not from licentiousness, but in witness of one "born true God in the entire and perfect nature of true man, complete in his own properties, complete in ours."[15]

My second consideration pertains to the Christ of the Ministry. When they visualized Jesus adult and living, artists did not, as a rule, refer to his sex—except perhaps in the manner chosen at certain times to render Christ's nudity at the Baptism. For the rest, the sexual reference tends to polarize at the mysteries of Incarnation and Passion; that is to say, it occurs either in Infancy scenes or in representations of Christ dead or risen. Here the oeuvre of Andrea del Sarto is paradigmatic. Twice does it summon us to see Christ place his hand in his groin—once as a laughing child, and again, with disturbing likeness, in a drawing for a *Pietà* (Figs. 2, 3). The crucified God is one with the frolicking infant; end and beginning agree.

Between these poles lies the earthly career of Jesus of Nazareth. And that he, the Christ of the Ministry, was ever-virgin no sound believer may doubt.

XII

XIII

14. "Made up of all the members . . . ," writes St. Augustine (*City of God,* XXII, 18). For Leo the Great and the Council of Chalcedon, see n. 15 below. Originally, such expressions had no genital connotation; but they came to serve euphemistically when such reference was intended, as when the Renaissance preacher Cardulus, referring to the circumcised member, speaks of Christ's body as *"omnibus membris expressum"* (*Oratio de circumcisione,* fol. 89).

The "all" came to mean "nothing excluded"—not even what modesty would suppress. The equivalent modern euphemism is the word "altogether" used as a noun (example cited in *Webster's Third International:* swimming in the altogether).

15. *Totus in suis, totus in nostris;* from the *Tome* of Pope Leo the Great (449; see Bettenson, *Documents,* p. 70). See also the definition of the nature of Christ promulgated at the Council of Chalcedon: "at once complete in Godhead and complete in manhood . . . of one substance with the Father as regards his Godhead . . . of one substance with us as regards his manhood; like us in all respects, apart from sin" (ibid., p. 72).

"A man entirely virginal," says Tertullian. St. Methodius (3rd century) dubs him Arch-virgin and bridegroom, whose success in preserving the flesh "incorrupt in virginity" is to be viewed as the chief accomplishment of the Incarnation. St. Jerome calls Christ "our virgin Lord,"—"a virgin born of a virgin"; and explains that "Christ and Mary . . . consecrated the pattern of virginity for both sexes." Photius (9th century) urges "those not yet married [to] offer virginity; for nought is so sweet and pleasing to the Ever-Virgin." The doctrine draws scriptural support from the passage in Matthew (19:12), where Christ commends those who have made themselves "eunuchs for the sake of the kingdom of heaven."

XIV

Needless to say, this precept was not meant to be taken literally; it was not to be misconstrued as a plea for physical disability or mutilation. Virginity, after all, constitutes a victory over concupiscence only where susceptibility to its power is at least possible. Chastity consists not in impotent abstinence, but in potency under check. In Christological terms: just as Christ's resurrection overcame the death of a mortal body, so did his chastity triumph over the flesh of sin. It was this flesh Christ assumed in becoming man, and to declare him free of its burden, to relieve him of its temptations, is to decarnify the Incarnation itself.[16] It follows that Christ's exemplary virtue and the celebration of his perpetual virginity again presuppose sexuality as a *sine qua non*.

XV

My third consideration concerns Christ in the character of Redeemer. His manhood differs from that of all humankind in one crucial respect, which once again involves the pudenda: he was without sin—not only without sins committed, but exempt from the genetically transmitted stain of Original Sin. Therefore, applied to Christ's body, the word "pudenda" (Italian: *le vergogne;* French: *parties honteuses;* German: *Schamteile*—"shameful parts") is a misnomer. For the word derives from the Latin *pudere,* to feel or cause shame. But shame entered the world as the wages of sin. Before their transgression, Adam and Eve, though naked, were unembarrassed; and were abashed in consequence of their lapse. But is it not the whole merit of Christ, the New Adam, to have regained for man his prelapsarian condition? How then could he who restores human nature to sinlessness be shamed by the sexual factor in his humanity? And is not this reason enough to render Christ's sexual member, even like the stigmata, an object of *ostentatio?*[17]

16.　　Hebrews 4:15 speaks of Christ as "one tempted in all things like as we are, [yet] without sin." St. Augustine makes the three temptations resisted by Christ the types of all human temptation: lust of the flesh, lust of the eyes, and pride of life.

17.　　Christ's necessary exemption from genital shame follows from the theological definition of shame as the penalty of Original Sin. As the German Renaissance theologian Conrad Braun explained it to his generation: "Blameless nudity [*sane nuditas*] . . . is that which Adam and Eve had before sin . . . nor were they confounded by that nudity. There was in them no motion of body deserving of shame, nought to be hidden, since nothing in what they felt needed restraining. But after sin, whatever in the disobedience of their members caused shame (whereat they

Modesty, to be sure, recommends covered loins; and the ensuing conflict provides the tension, the high risk, against which our artists must operate. But if they listened to what the doctrine proclaimed; if even one of them disdained to leave its truth merely worded, wanting it plain to see in paint or marble; if such a one sought to behold Christ in a faultless manhood from which guilt was withdrawn, that is to say, as a nakedness immune to shame; if one such Renaissance artist held his idiom answerable to fundamental Christology so as to rethink the doctrine in the concretion of his own art; then, surely, conflict — if not within himself then with society — was unavoidable. He would be caught between the demands of decorum, lest the sight of nobly drawn genitalia further inflame the prurience of human nature, and the command, deeply internalized, to honor that special nature whose primal guiltlessness would be disgraced by a "garment of misery."[18]

We are faced with the evidence that serious Renaissance artists obeyed imperatives deeper than modesty — as Michelangelo did in 1514, when he undertook a commission to carve a *Risen Christ* for a Roman church (Fig. 19). The utter nakedness of the statue, complete in all the parts of a man, was thought by many to be reprehensible. It is hardly surprising that every 16th-century copy — whether drawing, woodcut, engraving, bronze replica, or adaptation in marble — represents the figure as aproned (Figs. 20, 21);[19] even now the original statue in Sta. Maria sopra Minerva stands disfigured by a brazen breechclout. But the intended nudity of Michelangelo's figure was neither a licentious conceit, nor a thoughtless truckling to antique precedent. If Michelangelo denuded his *Risen Christ,* he must have sensed a rightness in his decision more compelling than inhibitions of modesty; must have seen that a loincloth would convict these genitalia of being "pudenda," thereby denying the

---

blushed . . .), to the disobedience of sin alone was this imputed. . . . So that man, disobedient to God, would feel his disobedience in his very members" (*De imaginibus . . . adversus Iconoclastas,* in *D. Conradi Bruni opera tria nunc primum aedita,* Mainz, 1548, p. 51; also in Paola Barocchi, ed., *Trattati d'arte del cinquecento,* II, Bari, 1961, p. 601, n. 1). The teaching is, of course, Augustinian. "We are ashamed," wrote St. Augustine, "of that very thing which made those primitive human beings [Adam and Eve] ashamed, when they covered their loins. That is the penalty of sin; that is the plague and mark of sin; that is the temptation and very fuel of sin; that is the law in our members warring against the law of our mind; that is the rebellion against our own selves, proceeding from our very selves, which by a most righteous retribution is rendered us by our disobedient members. It is this which makes us ashamed, and justly ashamed" (*On Marriage and Concupiscence,* II, 22, p. 291).

But in the incarnate Word — "whom sin could not defile nor death retain" (St. Leo, *Tome;* Bettenson, *Documents,* p. 70) — flesh did not war against spirit; no bodily member was "disobedient." In the words of Pope Honorius I, writing in 634 to the Patriarch of Constantinople (Denzinger, *Sources,* p. 99): "our nature, not our guilt was assumed by the Godhead." Ergo, no shame.

18. Gregory of Nyssa's term for the fig leaves adopted by our First Parents; see Excursus XIII.
19. The known copies of Michelangelo's *Risen Christ,* excepting only our Fig. 20 and a drawing by Guido Reni at Windsor, are reproduced in Charles de Tolnay, *Michelangelo: The Medici Chapel,* Princeton, 1948, figs. 236–42.

Fig. 19. Michelangelo, *Risen Christ,* 1514–20.

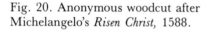

Fig. 20. Anonymous woodcut after
Michelangelo's *Risen Christ,* 1588.

Fig. 21. Jacob Matham after
Michelangelo's *Risen Christ,* 1590s.

XVI   very work of redemption which promised to free human nature from its
Adamic contagion of shame.[20]

That Michelangelo conceived his figure of Christ *all'antica* is evident; the
common charge that he did so to the detriment of its Christian content does not
cut deep enough. We must, I think, credit Michelangelo with the knowledge
that Christian teaching makes bodily shame no part of man's pristine nature,
but attributes it to the corruption brought on by sin. And would not such
Christian knowledge direct him to the ideality of antique sculpture? Where but
in ancient art would he have found the pattern of naked perfection untouched
by shame, nude bodies untroubled by modesty? Their unabashed freedom
conveyed a possibility which Christian teaching reserved only for Christ and
for those who would resurrect in Christ's likeness: the possibility of a human
nature without human guilt.

Yet the nakedness of Michelangelo's marble differs significantly in one
respect from the nudity of antique statues: those ancients continued nude as

20.   The resurrected, both male and female, shall not be ashamed in heaven. This is self-evident
to Thomas Aquinas (as it is to Augustine; see Excursus XI). St. Thomas writes: "Though there
be difference of sex there will be no shame in seeing one another, since there will be no lust to in-
vite them to shameful deeds which are the cause of shame" (*Summa theologiae,* Suppl. q. 81, art. 3).

they had been immemorially; Michelangelo's monumental Christ stood newly denuded. The former are innocent, prelapsarian in the sense that they precede Christian shame; the latter overbears shame in the person of Christ resurrected. I shall be told, perhaps, that the word "prelapsarian" applied to pre-Christian paganism is theologically preposterous; and so it is. But it reflects a cherished persuasion of Renaissance humanists. We find a striking expression of their belief in the *Hieroglyphica* of Pierio Valeriano. Setting out to discuss the ancient symbolism of the human pudenda, Valeriano excuses his subject with the following exordium: "Antiquity, being less vicious, philosophized more plainly and frankly about each and every thing; nor was there at that time anything in the human body which was considered disgraceful [*turpis*] either by sight or name. However, with the development of bad customs, many things had to be declared foul both in deed and in speech. . . ."[21]

Note that Valeriano's periodization consigned the "development of bad customs" to post-antiquity — just as Vasari ascribed the degeneracy of art to the Christian age. The preceding phase was designated "less vicious" (*minus vitiosa*), therefore rightly unencumbered by shame. Christians of a more theological bent would have attributed pagan shamelessness to moral idiocy, postlapsarian ignorance. But neither Valeriano nor Michelangelo saw ignorance shine in the works of the ancients; nor evidence of Original Sin. This is why Michelangelo in his most Christian moments could look to antiquity for the uniform of the blessed. Whatever paganism informed his *Risen Christ* was there as the form of a Christian hope — the eschatological promise of sinlessness concretely embodied.

I am inclined to read the same promise in a startling invention of the 15th century that has never yet been described, though it recurs often enough: the motif of the infant Christ, in childlike innocence, earnestly or in play, pulling his dress aside to expose his sex. It was surely the honest charm of the action that earned it a welcome in both Flanders and Florence, and endeared it to artists as diverse as Roger van der Weyden and Antonio Rossellino (Figs. 22, 23). The same spirited demonstration: a droll little boy chuckling, lifting his bib, invites us to see — the morosest of iconographers might wish to protect such a frisk from the pall of theology.[22] Yet the subject is Christ. And in making the Child's self-display the crux of a devotional image, the deep-thinking Roger was assuredly meditating his subject and thinking Christ. Nor can I believe even the elegant Rossellino unmindful of his protagonist's character. He too

---

21.   Valeriano, *Hieroglyphica*, XXXIV, pp. 245–46 — a work first published in 1556, but more than half a century in the making.
22.   The sculptor of the masterly terracotta group in London (Fig. 23) is identified as Antonio Rossellino in Pope-Hennessy, "The Virgin with the Laughing Child." The author does not remark on the Child's self-exposure and attributes its laughter to the "unreflecting" temper of childhood.

Fig. 22. Roger van der Weyden, *Madonna and Child,* c. 1460.

Fig. 23. Antonio Rossellino, *Virgin with the Laughing Child,* c. 1465–75.

meant Mary's Child for no less than the Incarnation. What these artists relished in the motif was, I submit, its reconcilement of sexual exposure with innocence. For as the first effect of Paradise lost was the punishing shame of the pudenda, so the acceptable sign of restoral is the uncovering of the New Adam, in token of Eden regained.

*

These, then, are my three initial considerations. The first reminds us that the humanation of God entails, along with mortality, his assumption of sexuality. Here, since the verity of the Incarnation is celebrated, the sex of the newborn is a demonstrative sign.

In the second consideration, touching Christ's adult ministry, sexuality matters in its abeyance. Jesus as exemplar and teacher prevails over concupiscence to consecrate the Christian ideal of chastity. We have no call to be thinking of private parts.

But we do again on the third turn. Delivered from sin and shame, the freedom of Christ's sexual member bespeaks that aboriginal innocence which in Adam was lost. We may say that Michelangelo's naked Christs—on the cross, dead, or risen—are, like the naked Christ Child, not shameful, but literally and profoundly "shame-less."

*

The candor of Michelangelo's naked Redeemer consummates a development traceable through two and a half centuries of devotional art. I reproduce a sampling of representative instances. But I should feel defeated were these works taken as illustrations of texts, or of theological arguments. On the contrary: the pictures set forth what perhaps had never been uttered. They are themselves primary texts, and the truisms I have recited were extrapolated from them as their precondition. To put it another way: it is not that the pictures and sculptures parallel any preformed sexual Christology, but that this wants to be formulated to render the works accessible in their wholeness, with their deep content intact. Were it not for the imagery of Fra Filippo Lippi, Bellini, and Michelangelo, of Roger van der Weyden and Schongauer, of Andrea del Sarto and Veronese, my theological considerations could not and need not have been entertained. Without the austerity of these works, without their grave beauty and religious conviction, no theology involving Christ's sexual member can exist without scandal.

Scandal is surely silenced by the authority of the many 15th-century paintings whose action centers on the Madonna's exposure of the Child's sex. The theme can be traced to the mid-1300s (Fig. 24), an outgrowth more likely of popular devotion than of dogmatic theology. Yet the effect achieved is consistently ceremonious. Gentile da Fabriano's Berlin altarpiece of about 1415 (Fig. 25) enthrones a Virgin whose gaze rests on the viewer as she holds the boy's mantle aside to exhibit his loins. Nothing of pleasantry here; her action is meant as a revelation.

The exposure motif recurs in scores of otherwise familiar Renaissance paintings. In the Filippo Lippi in Baltimore (Fig. 26), a wistful Madonna fingers the Infant's sash—a veil of a fabric so sheer that the symbolic character of the action becomes unmistakable. In Zanobi Machiavelli's panel (Fig. 173), the godhood of the Infant Spouse, expressed in the bounty of his embrace, is complemented by the bared lower body.[23] In several altarpieces by Antoniazzo Romano (Figs. 27, 41), the sacramental exposure of the Child's sex underlies a gesture of blessing. The subject throughout is simply the Incarnation, the marriage of godhead with human nature.

Most remarkable, given the hieratic solemnity of the occasion, is the studied genital exhibition in a masterwork of the Quattrocento—Francesco del Cossa's *Pala dei Mercanti,* dated 1474 (Fig. 174). Throning between the patron saints of Bologna, the Virgin retracts the little boy's shift and spreads his thighs: she has born God complete in all the parts of a man.[24]

*

Everyone knows that by 1400 the Christ Child in Western painting has shed Byzantine garb to appear more or less naked. We approve the undress in certain narrative situations, such as the bathing of the newborn by midwives.[25] What ought to surprise us is the Child's nakedness at affairs of state—as when, in the manuscript of a funeral oration for a defunct Milanese duke, the accompanying illumination shows the departed at heaven's court genuflecting before the Madonna and Child (Fig. 28); and even on this high state occasion, September 3, 1402, the infant King of Kings crowning the new arrival wears his birthday's attire. Here and through most of the Quattrocento, the permissiveness of the Child's dress is proportioned to the formality of the moment—the pomp culminates in undress. Like a prince on parade, God wears the armor wherein his victory had been won.

23.   The Zanobi Machiavelli panel is here reproduced in the version at the Yale University Art Gallery from a photograph taken before its ruthless "cleaning" in 1957–58. There is another version in the Pallavicini Collection, Rome (reprod. in Berenson, *Italian Pictures, Florentine,* II, fig. 810). The iconography in both pictures—and in the New Haven picture before restoration and after—is constant.

24.   No available black-and-white photograph is sharp enough to do justice to the revelation.

25.   The motif of the newborn Christ bathed by midwives, derived from apocryphal Infancy gospels, is Early Christian; it became a staple of Byzantine Nativity imagery; see Schiller, *Iconography,* I, pp. 64–65.

Fig. 24. Vitale da Bologna, *Madonna and Child,* c. 1345.

Fig. 25. Gentile da Fabriano, *Madonna and Child with Saints,* c. 1415, detail.

Fig. 26. Filippo Lippi, *Madonna and Child,* c. 1445.

Fig. 27. Antoniazzo Romano, *Madonna and Child with Saints,* 1488, detail.

Fig. 28. Michelino da Besozzo, illumination, *Christ Crowning Duke Giangaleazzo Visconti in Heaven,* 1403.

And yet, the progressive denuding of the infant Christ in proto-Renaissance art is commonly ascribed only to a general interest in the nude figure, an interest said to be spurred by the model role of antiquity and by a new enthusiasm for the natural world. Are not such explanations evasions, escapes into generalities? Their effect, if not their purpose, is to relieve the investigator of his embarrassed perception of scandal on sacred ground. It is as though these showings were receivable only as provocations to be resisted by diffusing attention; for to see them Christ-centered might admit an averted side of religion, a disturbing connection of godhead with sexuality. Better seek safety in naturalism, an approved goal and all-purpose instrument of explanation by which any twinge of anxiety is put to rest. The viewer will gladly learn that if innumerable Renaissance altarpieces show the Infant radically divested and so exhibited, no tedious symbolism need be assumed. After all, many artists, like parents, like doting kin, must have beheld a nude child with unbuttoned affection, delighting in its cheerful physique without second thoughts. And besides, in those far-off days it was the general custom to have the little ones run around naked. These and similar dodges are what one hears. But to repeat: naturalism, addressed to the Christ, could be indulged only if it was compatible with the subject, or better still, furthered the subject. No Renaissance artist was so addicted to skin as to ignore whom he stripped.

The pictures tell us to reverse the priorities. Their chronology demonstrates that the conspicuous display of the privates, instead of resulting incidentally from the Child's total nudity, is more likely the motive that promoted this nudity. And the initial impulse must have derived from that pervasive medieval metaphor which localized Christ's divine nature symbolically in his upper body, his manhood beneath the girdle. The body assumed by the godhead was a hierarchic system, like the macrocosm itself.

XVIII

The notion goes back to the Church Fathers, to St. Augustine and to St. Cyril of Jerusalem (315–86), who declares that "the head means the Godhead of Christ, the feet his manhood. . . ." In the 10th century, when Pope Leo VI described a mosaic of Byzantine type on the vault of a Roman church, he explained that "the half-length figure, by excluding the lower part of the body, laid emphasis on the divine or higher nature of Christ. . . ."[26] Similar Byzantinizing bust portraits must have been on the mind of the 13th-century Bishop William Durandus when he wrote in his once famous book: "The Greeks make use of images, it is said, painting them only from the navel upwards, and not below it, in order to remove all occasion for foolish thoughts."[27] Note that the bishop's justification of the portrait *en buste* is speculative and ascribed to the Byzantine Greeks by hearsay. But as his book passed through no less than forty-four printed editions between 1459 and 1500, his opinions became near canonic. Thus it is no surprise to find the above passage solemnly quoted by another censorious writer on ecclesiastical art—in 1570, at the height of the Counter-Reformation: after a lapse of three hundred years, Durandus is joined by the stern Johannes Molanus in associating the representation of the lower body in sacred figures with impropriety.[28]

---

26.   Cyril of Jerusalem, *Catechesis*, XII, 1, *Pat. Gr.*, 33, col. 726. For the quotation from Leo VI, see R. H. Jenkins and Cyril Mango, "The Date and Significance of the Tenth Homily of Photius," *Dumbarton Oaks Papers*, 9–10 (1956), p. 132. Further relevant sources are cited in Excursus XVIII.

27.   William Durandus, *Rationale divinorum officiorum*, I, 3, 2: "Graeci etiam utuntur imaginibus pingentes illas, ut dicitur, solum ab umbilico supra, et non inferius, ut omnis stultae cogitationis occasio tollatur." "The half-length portrait icon . . . the devotional image *par excellence*"—variously called the *thoracicula*, *effigies a pectore superius*, or *imago ab umbilico supra*—is eloquently discussed (but without further reference to "foolish thoughts") in Ringbom, *Icon to Narrative*, pp. 39ff.

28.   Molanus, *De historia ss. imaginarum et picturarum*, II, 42, p. 120. Cf. Cardinal Federigo Borromeo's *De pictura sacra*, VI (Milan, 1625): "The Greeks themselves, being respectful of decency and modesty . . . when painting the most holy Virgin, displayed the higher part of the divine body, the rest being wrapped by a covering" ("Graeci ipsi servientes honestati, et modestiae . . . cum Sanctissimam Virginem pingerent, superiorem tantummodo divini corporis partem ostendebant, reliqua tegumento involvebantur"; ed. C. Castiglione, Sora, 1932, p. 10).

Now Molanus, as spokesman for the Counter-Reformation, was inveighing against certain trends he deplored in the art of his time; in his text, the Durandus quotation follows upon a rebuke of artists who depict the infant Christ naked. "Surely," he writes, "if they would but consult ancient pictures, they would clearly see in them the child Jesus decently and honorably depicted [*decenter et honeste depictum*], and would perceive that they had themselves greatly degenerated from the innocence of their ancestors." I suspect that Durandus, three centuries earlier, had written from similar scruples, for if he too warned against showing the lower body, this is precisely what artists in his day, the latter half of the 13th century, were beginning to do.

From about 1260 onward, Italian paintings of the Madonna and Child draw attention to Christ's lower limbs. In Tuscany, Coppo di Marcovaldo and Guido da Siena raise the Child's Byzantine robes to flash the legs (Figs. 29, 158, 159). And bare-leg motifs thenceforth persist in Italian painting for fifty years — yielding only to an increased dosage of nudity. What could have caused such protracted trifling? Does it need explanation? It apparently moved Bishop Durandus to demur on grounds of decorum, much as latter-day churchmen have been moved to denounce rising hemlines. But in exposing the Christ Child's bare knees, long before genual anatomy was understood, painters such as Coppo and Guido were neither emulating antique models nor stooping to wantonness. Though the bishop — like all proper prelates fearful of novelty — misprised their mood, the painters were, in fact, seeking to balance the two natures of Christ by shifting the iconic emphasis to his manhood; locating the latter, as ancient symbolism directed, in the inferior parts of a body preconceived as a hierarchical system.

By about 1310, we see four motifs evolving concurrently. First of these is a gradual move toward total nudity. As early as the mid-14th century — notably in French and Bohemian painting (Figs. 30, 31) — Christ can appear wholly nude. Thereafter, the Child's nakedness is a legitimate option, both north and south of the Alps.

Second: the replacement of the Child's stately robes by a diaphanous veil or transparent chemise (Figs. 32, 33, 35, 36, 161).

Third: the accent on the Child's groin by a directional siting of the Madonna's hand. The motif seems to develop in the circle of Giotto (Fig. 33). In Taddeo Gaddi's polyptych of 1355 (Fig. 34), the Child's garment comes apart at the groin, its disorder graced by maternal consent. Outright exposure is not yet felt to be necessary; the prevention of it by the mother's solicitude provides focus enough (Fig. 35).

Fourth: an improvised loincloth formed by a fringe of the Virgin's veil (Figs. 36, 160, 162). This is not an emergency measure for propriety's sake, but a forward reference to the Passion. At the Nativity, we read in a popular medieval text (the *Meditations* of the Pseudo-Bonaventure), the Virgin, before laying the Child in the manger, "wrapped Him in the veil from her head." Then

Fig. 29. Coppo di Marcovaldo, *Madonna del Bordone,* 1261.

Fig. 30. Bohemian illumination, *Adoration of the Magi,* c. 1360–70.

Fig. 31. Bohemian, *Madonna and Child with Emperor Charles IV and Saints,* 1371, detail.

Fig. 32. Maso di Banco, *Madonna and Child Enthroned*, c. 1350, detail.

Fig. 33. Giotto Shop, *Madonna and Child Enthroned*, c. 1320.

Fig. 34. Taddeo Gaddi. *Madonna and Child Enthroned,* 1355.

Fig. 35. Andrea di Bartolo, *Madonna and Child with Fourteen Saints,* c. 1405–10.

Fig. 36. Nardo di Cione, *Madonna and Child with Four Saints,* c. 1355.

again, at the Crucifixion, "saddened and shamed beyond measure when she sees Him entirely nude, [when] they did not leave Him even his loincloth, she hurries and approaches the Son, embraces Him, and girds Him with the veil from her head."[29] Mary's grief at the naked humiliation of her condemned son marks a poignant moment in the most famous of 15th-century French Passion plays.[30] And the anguish of the shamed mother enters the dramatizations invented by painters. Though they knew it to be Mary's role to acquiesce in the Passion, they made the nakedness of her Son the single affliction against which she takes action. Her intervention is implied, antecedently, in a *Crucifixion* panel at the Walters Art Gallery, Baltimore, by the so-called Barna da Siena, where she, alone among her attendant women, lacks the sheer kerchief—whose lace-edged border we recognize in the loincloth worn by the Crucified. Elsewhere her intervention is rendered explicit: she appears draping Christ's loins on a page of the Holkham Bible; in a 14th-century Catalan altarpiece; in the upper right corner of a late 15th-century Westphalian panel (Figs. 37, 38 left, 39).[31] The conclusion seems inescapable that the mother's transparent veil festooning the Child in 14th-century icons is more than an ineffectual modesty token. The veil serves as omen; it aggrieves the Child's nudity by premonition.[32] Beyond the proleptic allusion to Christ "despoiled of his garments," it intimates a joining of first and last moments in the spirit of Job—"Naked came I from my mother's womb and naked shall I return" (Job 1:21). Nakedness becomes the badge of the human condition which the Incarnation espoused.

29.   Pseudo-Bonaventure, *Meditations,* pp. 33, 333.
30.   Arnoul Gréban, *Le Mystère de la Passion,* lines 24650–24683. The dialogue between Jesus and Mary marks the progress of the Passion to come. In the crescendo of griefs, his abasement to total nudity on the cross comes at a point near the climax. "[Notre Dame]—Mourez donc comme meurent les barrons! [Jésus]—Je mourrai entre deux larrons. [Notre Dame]—Que ce soit sous terre, dans le silence! [Jésus]—Ce sera haut sur la croix. [Notre Dame]—Vous serez au moins habillé? [Jésus]—Je serai attaché tout nu. [Notre Dame]—Attendez d'avoir atteint la vieillesse! [Jésus]—En la force de ma jeunesse."
31.   In our Fig. 37, the legend above the Virgin's raised arm reads: "Coment la mere ihesus volupat son courechef entour ses membres" ("How the mother of Jesus wraps her kerchief about his limbs"); see W. O. Hassall, *The Holkham Bible Picture Book,* London, 1954, pl. XVI. In two earlier folios, the *Nailing to the Cross* (fol. 31v) and another *Crucifixion* (fol. 32), the Christ is completely nude and without genitalia (Hassall, pls. XIV, XV). For the Catalan *Crucifixion* (Fig. 38 left), see Meiss, *French Painting,* pp. 125–26, who associates the panel with the *Meditations* text. Note that the *Crucifixion* images in the Catalan polyptych form a narrative sequence. As in the Holkham Bible, the Christ carrying the cross wears a long robe; in the following panel, nailed to the cross, he appears—unlike the draped thieves—stark naked, while the Virgin at the foot of the cross holds her kerchief in readiness, her left index pointing its destination. In the ensuing *coup de lance* panel, Christ's loins are draped.
32.   In Mantegna's San Zeno Altarpiece in Verona, the Virgin's veil falls from her head to pass diaphanous across the Child's naked loins. For similar instances of prolepsis involving the Virgin's veil, see Figs. 26, 36, 160, 162, 195.

Fig. 39. Westphalian, *Disrobing of Christ,* c. 1490, detail.

Fig. 37. English illumination from the Holkham Hall Bible, *Crucifixion,* c. 1325–30.

Fig. 38. Master of St. Mark (Catalan), *Crucifixion* panels, 1355–60.

Fig. 40. Jacopo Bellini, *Madonna of Humility with Donor,* c. 1441.

Fig. 41. Antoniazzo Romano, *Madonna and Child with Donor,* 1474–79.

The timing of these developments, beginning around 1260, suggests that they came in response to the spread of Franciscan piety with its stress on Christ's human nature, its vow of poverty in imitation of Christ, and its slogan "naked to follow the naked Christ" (*nudus sequi nudum Christum*). For all their innocence of anatomy, the pictures we are considering reach out to Christ's nakedness as to a still-distant goal. Their uncovered legs, their see-through garments and gestures of *ostentatio* assure us that what we are witnessing in Italian painting of the later Dugento, and in European art of the 14th century, has as yet nothing to do with any resurgent interest in antique statues; nor with the kind of naturalism that would assimilate the apparel of Mary's Child to the dishabille of the children next door. To say it once more: it was not the aesthetics of the nude figure that gave us the nudity of the Child Christ and, as a dubious bonus, the exposure of his privy parts. It appears rather that this nudity was

Fig. 42. Cosimo Rosselli, *Madonna and Child with St. Anne and Four Saints*, 1471.

urged by symbolic considerations, and that many artists came to regard the In-carnate's sex as a necessary exhibit. Hence, by the 15th century, the frequent avoidance of simple nudity *all'antica* in favor of a dramatized nakedness choreographed as an active withdrawal of garments. Such dramatization of nudity in high art is profoundly *unclassical*. Only an impulse arising from within Christian strictures can account for those numerous 15th-century paint-ings in which the Madonna unveils the Child or decks its loins with attention-gathering ceremony (Figs. 24–26, 40–43, 173). And only a strong religious conviction could have brought forth those many images in which the unveiling takes form as a self-revelation (Figs. 22, 23, 44–46, 49, 170). Surely the men who painted these pictures, inventing ever-new variations on the exposure motif, knew what they were about — though I can find no reference to the mat-ter in contemporaneous writing, nor in the oblivion of subsequent literature.

Fig. 43. Filippino Lippi, *Mystic Marriage of St. Catherine,* 1501, detail.

Fig. 44. Burgundian, *Madonna and Child,* c. 1490.

Fig. 45. Benedetto da Maiano, *Madonna and Child,* c. 1480–90.

Fig. 46. Domenico Ghirlandaio (?), *Madonna and Child*.

Fig. 47. Hans Baldung Grien, *Nativity,* 1523.

Fig. 48. Hans Baldung Grien, *Venus and Cupid,* 1525.

By the 16th century, the motif becomes more insistent. In a Piero di Cosimo altarpiece, a splendidly unabashed boy brandishes the Madonna's scarf as a resource that might have done something for modesty, had he so wished (Fig. 171). Hans Baldung's painting of 1523 (Fig. 47) shows the radiant Child of the Nativity intent on performing a self-exposure not unlike the more practiced self-revelation which the painter elsewhere attributes to the goddess of love (Fig. 48). Again and again we see the knowing boy parading his nakedness. Indeed, the young God-man is made to flaunt his sex by means normally associated with female enticement. In their exquisite teasing of swags of gossamer about the hips, only the eroticized figures of Venus, Lucretia, or Fortuna rival the infant Christ; as though their showings and his involved a comparable manifestation of fateful loins.

Or consider Jan van Hemessen's *Madonna and Child* at the Prado, dated
1543 (Fig. 49): the Virgin sits low on the ground in the traditional posture of a
Madonna humilitatis, demure in her mystic character as the bride of her Son.
The boy's glance of mature masculine admiration culminates in the ritual touch
of her chin, so that all his upper body bespeaks the warmth of the Heavenly
Bridegroom. Yet the Virgin, as the mother of the "God born in the flesh" (St.
Augustine), proves that flesh with the fingers of her left hand. And her right
spreads his limbs as the Child withdraws his covering in sign of his assumed
manhood.

Fig. 49. Jan van Hemessen, *Madonna and Child,* 1543.

40

To the themes of the Child unveiled by the mother, and of the Child self-exposed, we need to add the important theme of cooperation—conspicuous in a group of *Madonnas* ascribed to Verrocchio or his school. In the picture at Frankfurt (Fig. 50), the naked Christ stands statue-like on a quilted pillow, raising his hand in benediction. His podium appears to be the sill of a high loggia or window, a hazardous perch for a little boy. Yet it is not his safety that concerns the Madonna so much as the delicate bunting about his hips: it depends from her right hand and from his left—and the management of it is the picture's central event, gravely enacted, like the holding up of a cloth of honor. Again, in a panel of c. 1470 at the Metropolitan Museum (Fig. 51), the Virgin, advancing both hands, fingers the fine-spun fabric, of which the blessing Christ sustains one end. And in a terracotta relief at the Bargello, the left hands of both mother and Child hold the flaps away from his loins. The indwelling thought is not to be thought away. In all these works, the tasking of the Child's double gesture—precociously blessing and urging his nakedness—serves to discriminate the two natures whose union in Christ hypostasizes the Incarnation.

It is not possible to do justice to the prodigality of these showings—in the North no less than in Italy. The means used are few, but they were meant to fascinate by their functional ambiguity: the shirt or swaddling in disarray; the

Fig. 50. Verrocchio, *Madonna and Child,*
c. 1470.

Fig. 51. Verrocchio Shop, *Madonna and Child,* c. 1470.

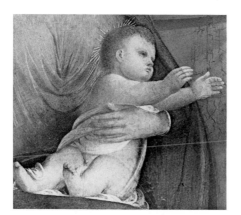

Above left: Fig. 52. Roger van der Weyden,
Madonna and Child, c. 1460.

Above right: Fig. 53. Giovanni Bellini,
Madonna and Child, c. 1470.

Fig. 54. Bramantino, *Madonna and Child with
Saints,* c. 1518, detail.

flinching loincloth, the distracted mantle, negligent and permissive; the fabrics
fussed so as not to hinder the showing; and—in some of the world's noblest
paintings—the calculated near-miss (Figs. 52–54, 144, 177–82).

Do they become less religious, less Christian, when their genital focus is
recognized? To us, the intent of these paintings is assured by their formal
austerity and moral certitude. Their goal is pre-fixed, their aim steady: tirelessly,

XXI

42

they confess the mystery of the dual nature of Christ, and the leasing of his humanity to mortal suffering. This is why so often in these 15th-century icons, the disclosure of the Child's sex participates in a mystic or tragic vision that forbids the least inkling of playfulness. Such is the Montefeltro Altarpiece by Piero della Francesca; or Cosimo Rosselli's grand altarpiece in East Berlin, dated 1471 (Fig. 42); or the never sufficiently known work of Bramantino (Figs. 54, 141). And such is Schongauer's engraving of the Christ Child as *Salvator Mundi* (Fig. 55). What led this master—along with Mantegna and others of the 15th and early 16th centuries—to conceive the world's ruler in solitude under the form of the Child? Only the dwelling on the sufficiency of God's humanation, only the "incarnational theology" characteristic of Renaissance thought, could have assigned the government of the world and its redemption to the Infant who had yet to achieve the Passion and Resurrection.

Schongauer's engraving is of small scale, but designed to be well considered. Its patent symbols are a cruciform nimbus, the orb of empire in one hand, a saving benediction administered by the other; and a fluttering mantle—a ceremonial pallium that nearly covers the groin—makes a punctual detour to disclose that the Child is sexed. Not a whim, not a sportive flourish, but a demonstration of Christ's human nature. In Schongauer's vision, the exposed member counts for no less than the array of salvific attributes.[33]

Fig. 55. Schongauer, *Christ Child as Salvator Mundi*, c. 1480.

33.   Schongauer's motif of the priestly robe parted for studied exposure is not uncommon in Northern art; see also Fig. 56; the Campin shop *Madonna and Child with Saints* in the Washington National Gallery; and three paintings by Hans Holbein the Elder, two in private collections (Norbert Lieb and Alfred Stange, *Hans Holbein der Ältere,* Berlin, 1960, figs. 1 and 32), and the altarpiece of 1499, now in Augsburg, Staatliche Gemäldegalerie (ibid., fig. 37). The nude Infant holding the orb of universal empire occurs in several engravings by the Master E.S., notably the *Einsiedeln Madonna* (Lehrs 81) and the *Madonna Enthroned with Eight Angels* (Lehrs 76). For the parted cloak, cf. his *Christ Child with New Year's Greeting* (Lehrs 50).

Fig. 56. Alsatian, *Madonna and Child with St. Anne,* 15th century.

Glance next at the *Virgin Adoring the Sleeping Child* of 1483 by Francesco Bonsignori, a close follower of Mantegna (Fig. 57). The Infant's shift rides up to the midriff, but the gloom of the picture discourages smiling. Nothing here that is wayward or casual. Nor is it in unconcern for her baby's health that Bonsignori's Madonna leaves it lying bare-bottomed on a cold stone. For the slab beneath the Child's body is of that same marble which supports Mantegna's *Dead Christ* (Fig. 58), to wit, the Stone of Unction—according to legend, a red stone streaked with white by the Virgin's indelible tears. While the nimbed head of the Child rests against an uprighted cushion, his sacrificial manhood, symbolized in his lower body, invites the Passion. And over his exposed genitalia, the Madonna's hands loom like a canopy, a ciborium. It is as though the very structure of such images of foreboding intimated a tragic, anatomically localized vulnerability.[34]

34.   The "ciborium effect" may be yet another symbolic formula. The earliest example known to me is a composition by Roger van der Weyden which, significantly, includes the Child's self-exposure (Fig. 22). A later North Italian instance is an altarpiece by Lorenzo Lotto, the *Virgin Enthroned with Saints,* c. 1540–46, Ancona, Sta. Maria della Piazza: here again the "canopy" of the Virgin's hands over the genitals of the Child forms the core of the compositional structure.

Fig. 57. Francesco Bonsignori, *Virgin Adoring the Sleeping Child,* 1483.

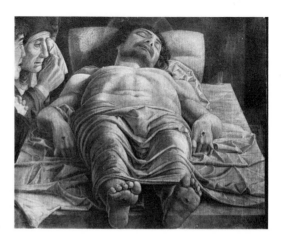

Fig. 58. Mantegna, *Dead Christ,* before 1506.

Post-Renaissance Christians, from the latter 16th century onward, were to see something shocking in all of this; and though custodians of art often felt daunted by the prestige and the commodity value of major old masters, offending parts were painted out wherever feasible. As modern Christianity distanced itself from its mythic roots; as the person of Jesus was refined into all doctrine and message, the kerygma of a Christianity without Christ;[35] as the content of the old holy pictures was diverted to pious folklore—their whole glory vested in the supposedly civilizing effect of their art—the exposure of genitalia, no matter whose, became merely impudent. No longer was it conceivable that Christianity had once, during that Renaissance interlude, passed through a phase of exceptional daring, when the full implications of Incarnational faith were put forth in icons that recoiled not even from the God-man's assumption of sexuality.

Normative Christian culture—excepting only this Renaissance interlude—disallows direct reference to the sexual member. In religious art as in standard discourse the thing is unmentionable and undepictable. "For the sake of propriety," wrote St. Jerome, "the organs of generation are called by other names"; and nearly twelve centuries later, the humanist educator Luis Vives (1492-1540) pronounced the male member "improper because of lechery and dishonor."[36] Therefore, if it must be referred to, let it be by periphrasis, euphemism, or substitution. The object itself is taboo, incompatible with common decency, to say nothing of reverence. In this respect Christian culture lies at the furthest remove from cultures whose ritual imagery not only acknowledged the phallus, but empowered it to symbolize something beyond itself; as is done wherever phalli function as amulets; as was done in the ancient Mediterranean, when phalli were placed on tombs, or borne in procession; as was still done in the Bacchic mysteries of Hellenistic and Roman times in which, as M.P. Nilsson has shown, the phallus as "principal symbol" stood for "the life-giving power . . . promising immortality."[37] There exists perhaps no more poignant proof of Renaissance openness to ancient mystery symbolism than the

35. The project of a Christianity without Christ is discussed in Rudolf Bultmann's *Kerygma and Myth,* p. 23: "It might well appear as though the event of Christ were a relic of mythology which still awaits elimination. This is a serious problem, and if Christian faith is to recover its self-assurance it must be grappled with. For it can recover its certainty only if it is prepared to think through to the bitter end the possibility of its own impossibility or superfluity. It might well appear possible to have a Christian understanding of Being without Christ, as though what we had in the New Testament was the first discovery and the more or less clear expression, in the guise of mythology, of an understanding of Being. . . ."

36. Epistle XXII, 11; St. Jerome, *Letters,* pp. 143-44; and Vives, *Dialogues* (1571), quoted in Ariès, *Centuries of Childhood,* p. 109.

37. Martin P. Nilsson, "The Dionysiac Mysteries of the Hellenistic Age," *Acta Instituti Atheniensis Regni Sueciae,* Lund, 1957, pp. 44-45. That 16th-century scholars were fully aware of the subject is proved in Montaigne's *Essays,* III, 5 (1588), in the paragraph beginning "In most parts of the world that part of the body was deified. . . ."

willingness of profound Christian artists to place this interdicted flesh at the center of their confession of faith.

But what constitutes the connection? Is the *ostentatio genitalium* in Renaissance images of the Christ Child in any sense cognate with the phallic cults of antiquity? Of the voluminous literature dealing with the subject of "penile display," very little, if any, bears directly on the present inquiry.[38] To students of cultures, or of individual psychology, the phenomena of genital exhibition are familiar either as symbolic modes of aggression, or as forms of fertility worship. Neither one nor the other operates in the images under discussion — unless by inversion of traditional connotations.

In traditional symbolism, the male organ tends to signify power. Latin writers treated the *mentula* "as exciting fear, admiration and pride. It was a symbol of power which might present a threat to an enemy."[39] The mid-12th-century poet Bernardus Silvestris empowered it further. In his marginally Christian but enormously influential allegory, *De mundi universitate,* the penis battles Lachesis and renews the threads cut by the Fates.[40] The poem recounts the creation of the world and reaches its climax in the formation of man, concluding in praise of the sexual organs: "Unconquered, the nuptial weapons fight with death, they restore nature and perpetuate the race." To which the Christian — at least before the doctrine of Original Sin was reformulated by the Council of Trent — might respond: Yes, they perpetuate the race, those vaunted organs; but as disobedient members, warring against the spirit. And since they labor in lust,[41] sin also is by them perpetuated, and with it, the guerdon of sin — the dying of each. But the organ of the God-man does better. By dint of continence, through the willed chastity of the Ever-virgin, it obviates the necessity for procreation since, in the victory over sin, death, the result of sin, is abolished. In such orthodox formulation, the penis of Christ, puissant in abstinence, would surpass in power the phalli of Adam or Dionysus. And it is perhaps in this sense that the old connotation of the phallus as anti-death weapon is both adapted to the Christ context and radically converted.

But such conversion is precisely characteristic of Christological symbolism, and we may claim that Christ's genitals contrast with the Bacchic

---

38.   On the subject of penile display (including phallic ornaments worn as late as the 19th century from Naples to Japan), see Daniel Rancour-Laferriere, "Some Semiotic Aspects of the Human Penis," *Quaderni di studi semiotico,* 24 (September-December 1979), pp. 37–82, with ample citation of further literature.

39.   J. N. Adams, *The Latin Sexual Vocabulary,* New York, 1982, p. 77.

40.   See the chapter devoted to Bernardus Silvestris' *De mundi universitate* in Economou, *The Goddess Natura,* esp. pp. 71 and 158.

41.   Thus Pope Innocent III (1198-1216), *On the Misery of the Human Condition:* "Everyone knows that intercourse, even between married persons, is never performed without the itch of the flesh, the heat of passion, and the stench of lust. Whence the seed conceived is fouled, smirched, corrupted, and the soul infused into it inherits the guilt of sin . . ." (trans. D. Howard, New York, 1969, p. 8).

phallus as the mystic Lamb contrasts with any fiercer heraldic beast; as the crown of thorns contrasts with conventional kingly regalia; the *arma Christi* with the paraphernalia of a knightly escutcheon; or as the sign of the cross contrasts with the Roman eagle. From Roman militarism Christianity did take the device of the standard, or trophy of victory. But where the Roman sign elevated a bird of prey, the Christian trophy holds up the scaffold on which a man condemned underwent crucifixion. In this instance, the conversion is all-apparent from the change in symbolic form. The difficulty in recognizing a comparable conversion in the instance of penile display arises from the similarity of the sign, so that the novel meaning must be sought in the context alone. But that context is part of the common creed. The sexual member exhibited by the Christ Child, so far from asserting aggressive virility, concedes

Fig. 59. Joos van Cleve, *Holy Family,* c. 1515–20.

Fig. 60. Jacob Jordaens, *Holy Family,* c. 1620–25.

instead God's assumption of human weakness; it is an affirmation not of superior prowess but of condescension to kinship, a sign of the Creator's self-abasement to his creature's condition. And instead of symbolizing, like the phallus of Dionysus, the generative powers of nature, Christ's sexual organ — pruned by circumcision in sign of corrupted nature's correction[42] — is offered to immolation. The erstwhile symbol of the life force yields not seed, but redeeming blood — in the words attributed by the poet Crashaw to the Christ Child in his Circumcision — "the first fruits of my growing death." We perceive a similar bond to the Passion in a painting by Joos van Cleve, where the coral cross of a rosary screens and jewels the privy parts (Figs. 59, 60).[43]

42. For the legitimacy of the word "pruning" in the present context, see Excursus XXIV. The word also occurs in Calvin's discussion of circumcision, *Institutes of the Christian Religion,* IV, xiv, 21.
43. The cut lemon at the Child's foot in Joos' picture may — like the wormwood laid to the dug of Juliet's nurse (*Romeo and Juliet,* I, 3) — allude to the Child's imminent weaning as to a grief to come. The prominent knife suggests further aggression.

consequence never to be forgotten: the Son of God, says Bede, "submitted to circumcision as decreed by the law. . . . He who was without any stain of pollution . . . did not reject the remedy by which the flesh of sin is made clean." Why, then, did he submit? Firstly, says Bede, "that he might commend to us the necessary virtue of obedience by an outstanding example. . . . Likewise also he submitted himself to the waters of baptism, by which he wished the people to be washed clean of the filth of sin . . . undergoing it himself, not from necessity, but . . . to set an example. . . . Purification, both by the law and by the gospel, none of which he stood in need of, the Lord did not despise and did not hesitate to undergo."[50] It is this doctrine of the Circumcision as a painful ordeal, not due yet obediently suffered, that will enable St. Bonaventure, centuries later, to designate as Christ's Passion his entire life even from its beginning.

Bede himself ends on the familiar eschatological note — the circumcision as the type of that ultimate cleansing "from all stain of mortality." We look forward, he says, to

> our true and complete circumcision, when, on the day of judgment, all souls having put off the corruption of the flesh . . . we will enter the forecourt of the heavenly kingdom to behold forever the face of the Creator. This is prefigured by the circumcision of the little ones in the temple of the Lord in Jerusalem. . . . The time of this most longed-for entrance . . . is that eighth day on which the circumcision is celebrated. [Moreover] the daily practice of virtues . . . is our daily circumcision, that is, the continuous cleansing of the heart, which never fails to celebrate the sacrament of the eighth day . . . so-called because it exemplified the day of the Lord's Resurrection. . . .[51]

Thus, by the end of the 7th century, and long before its emergence as a common subject of art, the Circumcision of Jesus in Christian thought has become manifold — initiatory, exemplary, sacrificial, eschatological. Nor can we grasp its psychological complexity without bearing in mind what Origen in the early 3rd century had called "the disgrace which is felt by most people to attach to circumcision."[52] Origen here expressed an attitude held not only by ancient pagans, but traditionally endemic in Christendom — Erasmus includes circumcision among the Jewish customs on which "we cry shame."[53] Perhaps this explains why Christian artists did not represent the physical effect of circumcision when the subject was a revered figure, David or Christ. They

XXIV

50.   Bede, *In die festo circumcisionis domini,* cols. 54A, 55A.
51.   Ibid., cols. 56B, 56D, 57D.
52.   Origen, *On First Principles,* IV, 3, 3, p. 293.
53.   Erasmus, "Dulce bellum inexpertis," in *Adages,* trans. M.M. Phillips, Cambridge, Mass., 1964, pp. 335–36.

resisted the mark of it as an imperfection: and as we read in the fourteenth Epistle of St. Jerome, "when anything is made less, it cannot be called perfect."[54]

It is on this note that St. Bernard (12th century) begins his first Sermon on the Circumcision.

> Already diminished by assuming our flesh, Christ further lessens himself by receiving the circumcision. God's Son had abased himself one degree beneath the angels in taking on human nature, and this day, by accepting the remedy for our corruption, he descends a thousand times lower still.

In an impassioned apostrophe, designed to confirm the conclusion already reached four centuries earlier by Bede, Bernard demands:

> How could circumcision have been needful to thee, who hadst neither committed sin, nor contracted its stains? . . . Is the physic, then, for him who ails not? Is it the physician in lieu of the patient who requires the medicine?

He speculates:

> He might, without difficulty, have preserved his flesh in its integrity, he who had issued without doing injury from a virginal womb. It would not have been hard for the Child to repel from his body the wound of the circumcision, since even in death, he easily kept it free from corruption.[55]

This and much else in the sermon is Bernardine rhetoric. But in what follows, Bernard makes an original contribution of far-reaching consequence to our subject — indeed, to the one subject worthiest of a Christian Doctor's vocation: the discovery within Scripture of ever-new proof that God became man. Bernard discerns, apparently for the first time, a necessary relation between the two events celebrated on January 1; and perceives that their correlation precisely reflects the union of godhead with human nature. Citing St. Luke's account that the Child, on the day of its circumcision, received the name ordained by the angel of the Annunciation — the name Yeshua interpreted as "salvation" — Bernard exclaims:

> Great and marvelous mystery! The Child is circumcised and is called Jesus. What connection is there between these two things. . . . But in this you may recognize him who comes to be mediator between God and man. . . . The circumcision is proof of the true

---

54. Jerome, *Letters,* p. 65.
55. *Oeuvres de St. Bernard,* pp. 375–76.

humanity he has assumed, while the name given to him . . . re-
veals . . . his majesty. He is circumcised as a true son of Abraham,
he is called Jesus as a true Son of God.[56]

"Proof of his true humanity." In Bernard's vision of the redemptive
scheme, the Circumcision has become crucial. It bears the incarnate God's
answer to humanity's prayer—as we learn by considering this other Bernardine
text, wherein is described mankind's desolation before the advent of Christ.
There lived in those days, says the preacher, good men of faith. But though
they had the assurances of the Prophets, they languished and "longed for the
more powerful assurance that only [Christ's] human presence could convey."
Bernard represents them as pleading: "If the mediator is to be acceptable to
both parties . . . then let him who is God's Son become man, let him become
the Son of Man. . . . When I come to recognize that he is truly mine, then I
shall feel secure in welcoming the Son of God as mediator. Not even a shadow
of mistrust can then exist, for after all he is . . . my own flesh."

The "shadow of mistrust," the vestige of unbelief that could have thwarted
the boon of the Incarnation itself, lifts at the God-man's bleeding in his Circumcision. Those first oozings guarantee Christ's humanity; they are his cre-
dentials as acceptable champion—proof incontrovertible that the Incarnation
was real.[57]

We must add a few words from St. Thomas Aquinas. His departures
from St. Augustine, and from his contemporary St. Bonaventure, need not
concern us, but he does, as usual, set out the entire tradition—dropping
nothing and adding much. Moreover, Renaissance Rome honored him beyond
any other medieval figure, and his expositions became quasi-canonic at the
papal curia long before they were declared normative for the Church.[58]

Discussing the Old Testament rite of the circumcision, Thomas adduces
three reasons for the choice of the member circumcised, and two for the choice
of the day:

There are three reasons which justify the circumcision of the organ
of generation. First, because it was a sign of that faith by which

56.   Ibid., p. 376.
57.   The above quotation is taken from St. Bernard's second sermon on the Song of Songs (II,
6, p. 12). We shall hear its argument restated with ever-mounting enthusiasm by later preachers
(see pp. 62–63).
58.   Heiko A. Oberman has shown how far from universal was the acceptance of St. Thomas'
authority within "the pregnant plurality of fourteenth-century thought"; and how broadly
"Aquinas failed to appeal to philosophers and theologians well into the fifteenth century" ("Fourteenth-century Religious Thought: A Premature Profile," *Speculum*, 53 [1978], pp. 80–93).
O'Malley does not dispute these findings, but his concern is with the papal Rome of the Renaissance. And he has uncovered surprising evidence that the veneration of St. Thomas, the honoring of his doctrine on a level with the teaching of the Church Fathers, was a Renaissance cult,
established in mid-15th-century Rome (O'Malley, "The Feast of Thomas Aquinas").

Abraham believed that the Christ would be born of his seed. Second, because it was a remedy for original sin which is transmitted through the act of generation. Third, because it was ordered to the diminishing of fleshly concupiscence which thrives principally in those organs because of the intensity of venereal pleasure.[59]

As for the choice of the day, there are, says Thomas, "two reasons for fixing the eighth day for circumcision." The literal reason is "the delicate condition of the infant before the eighth day" and its increasing sturdiness thereafter, which arouses a corresponding increase in parental love, and with it a growing reluctance to subject it to so grim an ordeal. But the figurative reason for the choice of the day points, he says, to "the following mystery: that in the eighth period of time, the time of the resurrection, on the eighth day, spiritual circumcision will be accomplished by Christ. . . ."[60]

Finally, when Thomas sets forth the reasons "why Christ should have been circumcised," he finds not one, two, or three reasons, but seven:

First, to show the reality of his human flesh against the Manichee who taught that he had a body which was merely appearance; against Apollinarius who said that the body of Christ was consubstantial with his divinity; and against Valentinus who taught that Christ brought his body from heaven. Second, to show approval of circumcision which God of old had instituted. Third, to prove that he was of the stock of Abraham who received the command about circumcision as a sign of the faith which he had in Christ. Fourth, to deprive the Jews of a pretext for not receiving him had he been uncircumcised. Fifth, to commend the virtue of obedience to us by his example; and so he was circumcised on the eighth day as was prescribed in the Law. Sixth, that he who had come in the likeness of sinful flesh should not spurn the customary remedy by which sinful flesh had been cleansed. Seventh, to take the burden of the Law upon himself, so as to liberate others from that burden. . . .[61]

St. Thomas interprets the Circumcision of Christ as a redemptive act; wherein he follows Bede following Ambrose. And he follows St. Bernard in pronouncing it the first proof of Christ's true human nature.

*

One potential objection to the foregoing review must be dealt with before we proceed: how relevant is all this abstruse theology to the work of Renais-

59. *Summa theologiae,* III, q. 70, art. 3, resp. 1.
60. Ibid., resp. 3.
61. Ibid., q. 37, art. 1, responsio.

sance artists? Are we to believe that they sat up nights reading Bede, Bernard, and Thomas Aquinas?

There are two answers. First, that most of these theological notions were not then as rare as modern oblivion has made them; they were the stuff of the sermons to which all Christendom was exposed, artists included. The theology of the Church Fathers and Doctors resounded continually from the pulpits. Secondly, the gist of the above arguments was broadcast in two steady best sellers of the late Middle Ages and Renaissance. I have in mind, to begin with, the *Meditations on the Life of Christ* by the Pseudo-Bonaventure — a work of naive sentimental piety, composed shortly before 1300 and aimed at the common reader. Chapter VIII treats as follows of Christ's Circumcision.

XXV

> Today our Lord Jesus Christ began to shed His consecrated blood for us. From the very first, He who had not sinned began to suffer pain for us, and for our sins He bore torment. Feel compassion for Him . . . for perhaps He wept today. . . . Today His precious blood flowed. His flesh was cut with a stone knife. . . . Must one not pity Him? . . . The child Jesus cries today because of the pain He felt in his soft and delicate flesh, for He had real and susceptible flesh like all other humans. . . .[62]

Observe that the Child's divinity is not argued — a title such as "our Lord" asserts it sufficiently. What must be insisted on is the tenderness of the God-man's flesh, vulnerable and hurting. The argument that the Circumcision authenticates the Incarnation is being conveyed to the plebs.

The other best seller to which I referred is the *Golden Legend,* compiled in the late 13th century by the Dominican Archbishop of Genoa, Jacopo da Voragine. For nearly three hundred years, the *Legenda aurea* served as the standard compilation of the lives of the saints, and as a source book for every Renaissance painting with a hagiological theme. The structure of the work follows the liturgical year, and the entry for January 1 informs us that Christ allowed himself to be circumcised "to show that he had assumed true human flesh; so as to destroy the error of them who would say that he had taken on a phantasmal and not a true body. To confute their error, he wished to be circumcised and emit blood, for [in the phrasing of William Caxton's translation of 1483] a body phantastic shall shed no blood."[63]

---

62. Pseudo-Bonaventure, *Meditations,* pp. 43–44.
63. Voragine, *Golden Legend,* p. 34. I take this occasion to remark that the readiest available English version of the work — *The Golden Legend of Jacobus de Voragine,* translated and adapted from the Latin by Granger Ryan and Helmut Ripperger, Arno Press, New York, 1969 — is quite useless to any serious reader with a historical sense. The translators' claim in the Foreword that "deletions are few, and changes in the text still fewer," is not borne out by comparing their digest with the original. (Voragine's eight-page chapter on the Circumcision of Christ dwindles in their edition to a page and a half.) Textual changes are as frequent as they are gratuitous. (Voragine

Thus once again, in this most popular Renaissance reading, the genuineness of the Incarnation is put to proof in the sexual member. More than that: the wounding of it initiates the salvation of humankind, for the archbishop says further: "On this day he began to shed his blood for us . . . and this was the beginning of our redemption." Then, after citing three subsequent effusions of the precious blood (at the Agony in the Garden, the Flagellation, and the Nailing to the Cross), Voragine comes to the fifth and last shedding—"when his side was opened [with a lance] and this was the sacrament of our redemption, for then out of his side issued blood and water"[64]—the blood and water which, in Augustine's wording, "we know to be the sacraments from which the Church is built up." In Voragine's formulation, the first and last wounds received are not yet placed in immediate apposition, but they appear as the terminal points of an ordained cycle. Linking beginning and end, the knife's cut to the gash of the lance, we trace a passage on the body of Christ from man to God; the sexual member broaching the mortal Passion, the breast yielding the gift of grace. Put into words, the anatomical consequence of Voragine's formula comes as a shock—that Christ's redemptive Passion, which culminates on the cross in the blood of the sacred heart, begins in the blood of the penis.

We are educated to shrink from such thinking. But it is Christian thinking—implicit in doctrine, explicit wherever in Renaissance art Christian teaching is brought face to face with its own metaphoricity. The coupling of Christ's last and first wounds—a verbal figure to bridge a lifespan of three decades—becomes topical in 15th- and 16th-century Passion pictures that guide the trickle of gore from the breast back to the groin: a blood hyphen between commencement and consummation (Figs. 63–65, 96, 98, 184–87).[65] On this integrity of the Passion enduring under the multiplicity of its incidents, the painters linger much as St. Bonaventure had done, and as two English poets of the 17th century were to do. Both Milton and Crashaw throw the trajectory of Christ's Passion from Circumcision to Crucifixion, from the knifed member to the speared heart. I quote from Milton's sonnet, "Upon the Circumcision," 1634:

XXVI

---

has Christ assume *veram carnem humanam,* and there is no reason, unless the original is felt to be too too solid, to translate "true human flesh" as "human form.") Nor are we heartened by these confessions at the end of the Foreword: "Most of the omissions have been long and highly involved theological passages, which we felt rather encumbered than enhanced the book as a whole. . . . Occasionally, too, we have eliminated passages in which repetitions were multiplied . . . or where the stories told would have offended rather than inspired the reader of today."

64.   Voragine, *Golden Legend,* p. 34.

65.   In a sermon preached in 1493 in the papal chapel, the preacher Cardulus (see p. 64 below) interprets Christ's penultimate words on the cross—"Consummatum est" ("it is finished")—as referring to the cessation of circumcision. Interesting in the present context, but perhaps no more than ingenious rhetoric adapted to the occasion, since the sermon was delivered on the Feast of the Circumcision.

Fig. 64. Henri Bellechose, *Retable of Saint Denis,* 1416.

Fig. 63. Jean Malouel, *Pietà*, c. 1400.

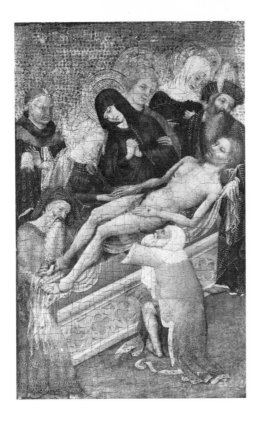

Fig. 65. Dijon School, *Entombment,* c. 1400.

> . . . he, that dwelt above
> High-throned in secret bliss, for us frail dust
> emptied his glory, even to nakedness;
> . . .
> And seals obedience first with wounding smart
> This day; but oh! ere long,
>   Huge pangs and strong
>   Will pierce more near his heart.

Crashaw's sonnet of the same year — "Our B. Lord in his Circumcision to his Father" — begins:

> To thee these first fruits of my growing death
> (For what else is my life?) lo I bequeath.

It ends:

> These Cradle-torments have their towardness.
> These purple buds of blooming death may bee,
> Erst the full stature of a fatall tree.
> And till my riper woes to age are come,
> This knife may be the speares *Praeludium.*

Like Renaissance paintings of the brooding Christ Child, Crashaw's poem foreshortens duration. The newborn savior, nesting omnipotence in the condition of vulnerability, surrenders to his first stigma the life-giving organ. Eight days old, the manful God lives in the instantaneity of beginning and end, hosts a yet distant death and overleaps the time lapse while submitting to time's regiment. This is more than a case of divine prescience. As in the prolepses of Renaissance painting, as in the "incarnational theology" of the preachers, Christ's death is conceived as wholly infolded in his miracle birth. Not that the Passion and Resurrection are denied their necessity, but they are regarded — I am quoting O'Malley — as "articulations of what was already inchoately accomplished" in the Incarnation.[66] And this must be why we find Renaissance preachers contemplating the redemptive work of God's infant body much as Renaissance painters did, that is to say, with the same dismissal of squeamishness, the same enthusiasm, the same sense of fulfillment.

The evidence is spread wide in the sermons preached during the 15th century on the Circumcision of Christ. Their essential message is still the message of the Church Fathers and Doctors. The arguments of Augustine, Ambrose, Bede, Bernard, Aquinas, Bonaventure, and Jacopo da Voragine are voiced again, sometimes in renovated latinity, but unfailingly to affirm traditional teaching. New in these orations is their festive tone, their choice of emphasis, their congratulatory zeal and unabashed exultation.

What shall be said of this Circumcision, "which pertains to the salvation of mankind and your immortality," demands a Ciceronian humanist (who died in 1431, and whose undated oration was composed for delivery by a Franciscan friar). "What shall be said about this first holy shedding of blood . . . this most precious blood which today our Lord spills for us for the first time. . . . He wished to be circumcised that he might extinguish the flames of our detestable lusts. . . ." By the voluntary gift of his blood, we are told, Christ has prevailed over the devil. And the oration congratulates him as a victor, whose triumph is compared with the military triumphs of ancient Rome. In the Feast of the Circumcision, "we celebrate the day in which our victor brings back to us the first trophies of the victory over our perpetual foe."[67]

Even more pertinent to our subject are the sermons preached at the Vatican on the Feast of the Circumcision. Declaiming at Solemn Mass before the pope — *coram Papa inter missarum solemnia* — the preachers revel in the exegetic tradition, and rejoice in directing their eloquence to Christ's sexual member.

Of the 164 sermons O'Malley has studied, some in manuscript, others in incunabula, ten were preached on January 1, and the message they bear is con-

---

66. O'Malley, *Praise and Blame*, p. 138. The familiar prolepses in Renaissance scenes of the Infancy — their stark allusions to the Passion and Resurrection — are surely the pictorial equivalent of the incarnational soteriology of the preachers.
67. See the summary of Gasperino Barzizza's unpublished oration in O'Malley, *Praise and Blame*, p. 84.

sistent: the Circumcision of Christ, wherein the Incarnation is verified, the Passion launched, and the Resurrection presaged, is the pledge and commencement of human salvation—"the symbol of Christ's Passion and its beginning."[68] Thus in a published sermon delivered c. 1460 by Giovanni Antonio Campano:

> Today he began to open for us the door and to make accessible the entry to life. At the moment the boy was circumcised, the weapons for our salvation appeared for the first time in the blood of that infant.

Bernardino Carvajal, preaching in 1484 before Sixtus IV, wants the feast celebrated "as though the Lord were circumcised today, so that we may have the primordial beginning of his Passion confirmed in us."

So again in Antonio Lollio's oration of 1485:

> Today is opened for mankind the book of the Circumcision, the first volume of the most bitter Passion. Here issues the first blood of our redemption. . . .
> Today we begin to be saved, Holy Father, for we have Jesus . . . who today has chosen to spill his blood for the sake of man whom He created. . . . For until this most holy day, which is not unjustly set at the head of the year, we were all exiles. . . . Let us enter through the gate which circumcision has opened for us, and which today lies open even wider through baptism. . . . Let us venerate this most sacred day of the circumcision, which we can call the gate that opens the way to Paradise.

XXVII

And Battista Casali, preaching before Julius II in 1508:

> Rightly the Church decreed the celebration of this day of life which is the forecourt of our redemption and a sure compact of salvation between Christ and mortals.

The Circumcision extolled in these sermons is more than a gateway, forecourt, or even "first volume." It is the *sine qua non* of mankind's redemption. Campano (c. 1460) declares that:

> It would not have been enough for Christ to be born for us had he not begun to shed that divine blood in which our salvation reposes.

68. Quotations from the six circumcision sermons adduced on pp. 62–64 are taken from: Lollio, *Oratio circumcisionis,* fols. 1, 2, 5v; Campano, *De circumcisione,* fols. 85v, 87; Carvajal, *Oratio in die circumcisionis,* fols. 8, 8v; Casali, *Oratio in circumcisione,* in O'Malley, "Casali," p. 280; de Bagnariis, *Oratio de nomine Iesu,* fol. 1; and Cardulus, *Oratio de circumcisione,* fol. 88v.

This notion of the insufficiency of the Incarnation alone — which we encountered earlier in St. Bernard — recurs again in the oration of Antonio Lollio.

> Nor would it have sufficed for Christ to be born for wretched mortals, if (after eight days were fulfilled) he had not undertaken, while still a boy, to spill his blood by being circumcised.

The logic is sound; since the Incarnation draws its effectiveness from responsive faith, it would have forfeited that effectiveness, had it been open to legitimate doubt:[69] without proof of blood, the flesh assumed by the godhead might have been thought merely simulated, phantom, deceptive. Such indeed were the pestiferous doctrines advanced more than a thousand years earlier by Docetists and Gnostics, those who held Christ's assumed body to have been spiritual, not carnal, so that he only appeared to be suffering.

Against these long-buried heresies our preachers discharge the full spleen of their rhetoric. Each conjures up ancient errors which, by one ruse or another, denied Christ his veritable humanity. Campano points triumphantly to Christ's Circumcision to confound the aberrations of Apelles (2nd century), Valentinus (2nd century), Manichaeus (3rd century), Apollinarius (4th century), etc. — names long ago execrated, heresies utterly crushed and disproved, their very memory preserved only in the diatribes of the champions of victorious orthodoxy. The early apologists (such as Clement, Tertullian, and St. Irenaeus) had roundly refuted them; Aquinas in his encyclopedic way had recorded them; now our Renaissance orators exorcize them for rhetorical effect. It is remarkable to hear preachers of the late Quattrocento raise up the old heresiarchs so as to overwhelm them again and again by the power of Christ's Circumcision. Thus Bernardino Carvajal (1484, before Sixtus IV):

> By circumcision he showed himself to be truly incarnate in human flesh. Whereat Manichaeus, Apollinarius, and Valentinus poured forth heresies, Manichaeus ascribing to Christ a fantastic body, Apollinarius a divine, Valentinus a celestial; which clearly excludes the natural pain in the circumcised flesh of the Lord. But surely, if blood was flowing, there was pain, aggravated in the infant flesh. Truly therefore the human flesh of Christ has been most fully demonstrated by his circumcision.

Lollio's sermon of the following year opens in pugnacious apostrophe of these same hapless heretics:

---

69. See the passage from St. Bernard, quoted above, p. 55, where it is argued that God's descent to companionship with mankind, though foretold by the Prophets and fervently longed for, would not have availed unless man was convinced that the body assumed in the Incarnation was true human substance.

> Today we declare war on thee, Manichaeus! . . . Prayerful and
> stripped for contest we enter the decisive palestra, eager to wrestle
> with Apelles and Manichaeus, confident, with God's help of winning
> rich spoils and the triumph of victory.

Outraged at the slanders that would have made Christ's agonies vain, the
preacher exclaims:

> O Basilideans, who deny that Jesus suffered . . . look upon the cir-
> cumcised boy, hardly come into the light. . . . O Apellites, who say
> that Jesus was an illusory man, hear the voice of the crying boy, and
> believe now that he suffered an inflicted wound. O iniquitous
> Sedechians, look . . . on Jesus the firstborn of Mary, who is
> rendered bloody today. . . . Look upon the boy of eight days
> brought here today to be circumcised. O Valentinians, O Alexan-
> drians, O Manichaeans . . . and all you heretics and proclaimers of
> false doctrine — spew out now the old dudgeon [*fermentum*] . . . and
> consider the clemency of the boy Jesus who, in need of milk and the
> nurse, afflicted his most holy and pure flesh with the pain of cir-
> cumcision.

The above was evidently accounted a *tour de force;* Poliziano dubbed
Lollio's sermon "a golden oration." In its verve and theatrical genius and the
elegance of its Latin, it must have seemed fairly exceptional. No wonder that
more humdrum performances, covering the same ground year after year, encouraged what O'Malley calls an "almost ineradicable" inclination to talk during the sermons. In the year following Lollio, the cardinals, if they listened,
would have heard from de Bagnariis that "the incarnate Word . . . suffered circumcision in order to . . . shatter the errors of diverse future heretics whom he
foresaw"; and that "Christ underwent circumcision in order to demonstrate the
truth of his human flesh."

Not all of the sermons delivered on January 1 came to be printed; and
though all had to be written out and submitted for prior clearance, not all have
survived. But the next Circumcision sermon, preached after 1493 before Alexander VI by Franciscus Cardulus, tells us once more that the heretics are
routed by the event of this day, since "the human flesh of Christ has been most
fully demonstrated by his circumcision." And the preacher proceeds:

> He did not offer his body to be wounded in order that the substance
> of his true flesh be denied by the impiety of heretics. . . . It is good
> to overturn the profitless opinions of incorrigible men . . . [Fol-
> lowed again by a roster of loathed Gnostic names].

And finally, on a note which Renaissance art makes familiar:

Who would doubt that he had a real body derived from his mother —
a body that had all its members [*omnibus membris expressum*]. Who . . .
could maintain that to be simulated which is fondled [*attrectatur*],
taken in the hand, receives a wound, feels pain?[70]

Not twenty years separate these protestations from the fond grandmother
of Baldung's woodcut (Fig. 13), or from the self-touching Child of Andrea del
Sarto (Fig. 2). In the pictures as in the sermons, the argument for the authenticity of Christ's manhood (his godhood needing no argument unless before
infidels) draws its invincible strength from the Child's sexual member.

*

We have imagery better known and more discreet than the audacities of
Baldung and Andrea del Sarto to assure us that incarnational symbolism in
Renaissance painting hovered about the Child's groin. I have in mind the common rendering of the Adoration of the Magi. These pictures project a Christology of which the rhetoric of the pulpit is but an echo. Their central subject is
the marvelous proof offered to the Three Kings: God, come to dwell humanly
among men, exposes his frailest member — whether to the knife, the touch, or
the steadfast gaze of the faithful — in order to dispel mistrust of his Incarnation
forever.

The Child's nakedness in Renaissance representations of the Epiphany is
so commonplace that we tend to leave it unquestioned. But it is at least rea-
sonable to wonder why a loving mother would expose her newborn's skin to the
nipping air so soon after Christmas; or why the incarnate God should be unclothed while receiving the homage of the kings of the earth. St. Augustine had
not yet visualized it that way. "He, weak in his infant limbs, wrapped in infant's
swaddling clothes, was adored by the Magi," he wrote.[71] And medieval artists
quite properly kept the Child covered. It was the art of the 14th century that
began to reverse the tradition (Fig. 31); and by the 15th century, the Child's
nudity at the levee had become *de rigueur*.

The thoroughness of the change is borne in on us when we realize open-
eyed what Ghirlandaio is showing in his famous tondo of the *Adoration* (dated
1487) in the Uffizi (Fig. 66). At the heart of a populous scene, the eldest Magus
kneels before the Madonna and Child. The Virgin's right hand retains one infant knee, her other hand lifting his flimsy cover. And the old King reaches
reverently to touch with two sanctified fingers the loincloth which the boy holds
aside in deliberate showing. The pictorial action, the portentous event, the

---

70. Cardulus, *Oratio de circumcisione,* fol. 89. Cf. fol. 86v — Christ underwent circumcision "to
show himself to mortals in the flesh" (*ut se mortalibus incarne monstraret*).
71. St. Augustine, Sermon XIX, 1 (Ben. 200); *Sermons,* p. 160.

Fig. 66. Domenico Ghirlandaio, *Adoration of the Magi,* 1487, detail.

epiphany, is the exposure to the worshipper of the Child's groin. This, according to Ghirlandaio, is what the Wise Men traveled to see. The revelation to the Magi, who knew beforehand that a God had been born, is the demonstration *ad oculos* that he was born "complete in all the parts of a man." And if we recall that the subject of the picture, the Feast of the Epiphany, falls six days after the Feast of the Circumcision, we may suspect a revelation, too, of the Child's prompt consent to self-sacrifice—in Lollio's words (1485) "while still in a tender state, wishing to dissolve our sin with his blood."[72]

72.   Lollio, *Oratio circumcisionis,* fol. 2.

Of course, Ghirlandaio is not alone in understanding the meaning of the Infant's exposure at the Epiphany. The Northerners understand it no less than Ghirlandaio's compatriots (Figs. 67, 68, 188; 69, 70, 189–91). And once we also have grasped it, we begin to see what before was prohibited—the clear focus of the adorer's glance. Though the motif of the King's steady gaze on the Child's genitalia is remarkably common, it remained unseen because it was improper to notice and could not be conceptualized without shame. Yet the object of the old King's regard is daylight clear in such works as Mantegna's *Adoration of the Magi* (Fig. 70; cf. the painting from which the engraving derives), or in Bruegel's *Adoration* in London (Fig. 71). This latter deserves special attention, since the great showing is here rendered momentous by being tracked on a commanding diagonal. The action starting from lower left involves the Magus' stare, the Child's crotch and smile, the Virgin's bounteous bosom, the respectful hat of St. Joseph, and the whispered confidence at his ear. If the effect is part comic, so much the better. This is, after all, a happy occasion; the humanation of God, none happier since the creation of light.

XXVIII

Fig. 68. Jan van Scorel, *Adoration of the Magi,* c. 1530–35.

Fig. 67. Tyrolean, *Adoration of the Magi,* c. 1440.

Fig. 69. Botticelli, *Adoration of the Magi,*
c. 1470, detail.

Fig. 70. Mantegna School, *Adoration of the
Magi,* c. 1475–80.

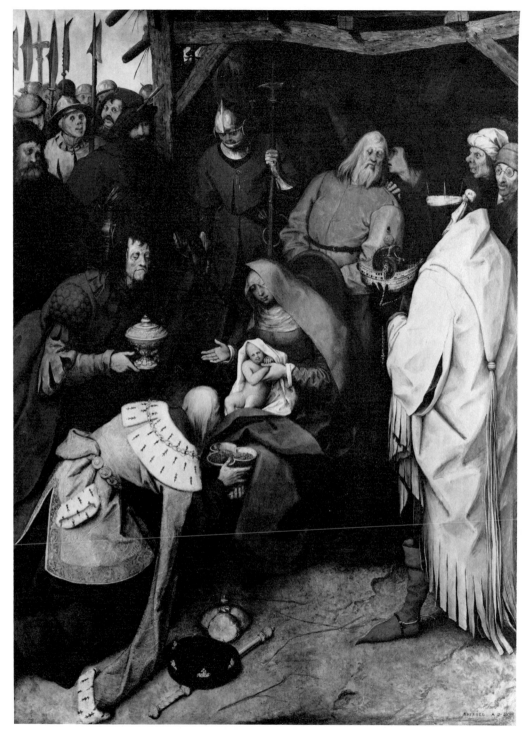

Fig. 71. Pieter Bruegel, *Adoration of the Magi*, 1564.

Fig. 72. Giovanni Cariani, *Madonna and Child with Donor,* 1520.

Fig. 73. Sebastiano del Piombo, *Holy Family
with Saints and Donor,* c. 1505–10.

Whether any of these pictures of the *Adoration* intend a reference to the foregone Circumcision is not ascertainable. We see only that they show the infant exposing his nakedness like one conferring a boon; we are unsure whether the message is — "Look, I your Creator have come to share your humanity"; or, in St. Bonaventure's words, "See how I have not delayed to pour out for you the price of my blood."[73] The message, in either reading, is a summons to the believer's faith. And it is surely in response to this summons that the Adoration became a model for the gaze of private Venetian donors wishing to testify — as the Magi had done — to their faith in the Incarnation (Figs. 72, 73).[74]

*

The Incarnation of the Trinity's Second Person is the centrum of Christian orthodoxy. But we are taught that the godhead in Christ, while he dwelled on earth, was effectively hidden — insufficiently manifest for the Devil to recognize, obscured even from Christ's closest disciples (Mark 8:27–30; Matt. 16:13–20), apparent only to a handful of chosen initiates and a few beneficiaries of his miracles.[75] By the testimony of Scripture, the manhood in Christ, though free from ignorance and sin, was otherwise indistinguishable — not because the protagonist of the Gospels assumed a deceptive disguise (like a godling in pagan fable), but because he took real flesh in a woman's womb and endured it till death.

This much Christendom has professed at all times. Not so Christian art. For when a depictive style aims at the other-worldly; when the stuff of which human bodies are formed is attenuated and subtilized; when Christian representations of Christ, dismayed by the grossness of matter, decline to honor the corporeality God chose to assume — then, whatever else such art may be after, the down-to-earth flesh of the bodied Word is not confessed. It is arguable from a stylistic viewpoint — at least in retrospect and from a Renaissance vantage — that the hieratic Christs of Byzantine art are better adapted to Gnostic heresies than to a theology of Incarnation; for, to quote Otto Demus again, "The Byzantine image . . . always remained a Holy Icon, without any admixture of earthly realism." But for those Western Christians

---

73. St. Bonaventure, *Tree of Life*, p. 129.

74. Cf. also Giovanni Bellini's *Madonna and Child with Saints and Donor* (Louvre) and Andrea Previtali's *Madonna and Child with Donor* (Padua, Museo Civico).

75. Cf. the Gnostic Gospel of Thomas, Saying 91: "They said to him, 'Tell us who You are so that we may believe in You.' He said to them, 'You read the face of the sky and of the earth, but you have not recognized the one who is before you'" (*Nag Hammadi Library*, p. 128). As to the hiddenness of Christ's divine nature during the Ministry, the propagandistic trend of the canonic Gospels seems to create somewhat of a problem. The working of the redemptive plan required that the devil be tricked into thinking Jesus mere man, hence deserving of death. But of the demons whom Jesus exorcized, most were sensitive to his other nature. What then made the devil so sluggish?

who would revere the Logos in its human presence, it was precisely an "admix-ture of earthly realism" that was needed to flesh out the icon. And because Renaissance culture not only advanced an incarnational theology (as the Greek Church had also done), but evolved representational modes adequate to its ex-pression, we may take Renaissance art to be the first and last phase of Chris-tian art that can claim full Christian orthodoxy. Renaissance art—including the broad movement begun c. 1260—harnessed the theological impulse and developed the requisite stylistic means to attest the utter carnality of God's humanation in Christ. It became the first Christian art in a thousand years to confront the Incarnation entire, the upper and the lower body together, not ex-cluding even the body's sexual component. Whereat the generations that followed recoiled, so that, by the 18th century, the Circumcision of Christ, once the opening act of the Redemption, had become merely bad taste. When Goethe reports on Guercino's *Circumcision of Christ,* a painting he admired in the artist's birthplace at Cento in mid-October 1786, he speaks of it in the simper of polite conversation: "I forgave the intolerable subject and enjoyed the execu-tion."[76] And a standard modern reference work by Louis Réau explains that the Circumcision dropped out of Christian iconography because of the subject's "indecency."[77] Both authors unwittingly abrogate the special status of the body of Christ—the exemption of Christ's nakedness from the mores of Christen-dom.

We are left with a cultural paradox: Renaissance artists and preachers were able to make Christian confession only by breaking out of Christian restraints.

*

One gesture in paintings of the Madonna and Child offers its meaning direct; and it graces some of the most cherished creations of Renaissance art. I refer to pictures—among them several by Giovanni Bellini (Figs. 74, 199)—wherein the sex of the Christ Child takes emphasis from the mother's protecting hand. In movements of sublime tenderness deeper than modesty, Mary's hand shields—and converts into symbol—her Son's vulnerable humanity. This "pro-tection motif" seems commoner in Italian painting (Figs. 75-77), but it is found as well in Germany and the Netherlands (Figs. 193, 194). In Isenbrandt's *Rest on the Flight into Egypt,* the boy seizes the proffered grape that forebodes the Pas-sion, while the Virgin screens his groin with the flat of her hand (Fig. 78). And a Hans Baldung woodcut (Geisberg 85; c. 1515-17) presents the Madonna is-suing from the gates of heaven while pressing protective fingers on the Child's genitals.

XXIX

76. "Ich verzieh den unleidlichen Gegenstand und erfreute mich an der Ausführung" (*Itali-enische Reise*).
77. Louis Réau, *Iconographie de l'art chrétien,* II/II, Paris, 1957, p. 260.

Fig. 76. Lorenzo Lotto, *Holy Family with Donors,* c. 1526-30.

Fig. 74. Giovanni Bellini, *Madonna and Child*, c. 1475–80.

Fig. 75. Cosimo Rosselli, *Madonna and Child with the Infant St. John.*

Fig. 77. Palma Vecchio, *Holy Family with the Magdalen,* c. 1516–17.

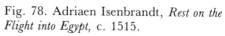

Fig. 78. Adriaen Isenbrandt, *Rest on the Flight into Egypt,* c. 1515.

Fig. 79. Bruges School illumination, *Adoration of the Magi*, c. 1480–1500.

The motifs of exposure and of maternal protection survive in abundance. Less frequent are pictures from the late 15th and 16th centuries that show the privy parts touched by the boy himself—whether in sleep, bashfulness, or ostension. This curious category includes an *Adoration* page from a Bruges Book of Hours (Fig. 79), Andrea del Sarto's *Tallard Madonna* (Fig. 2), Sodoma's *Holy Family* at the Villa Borghese (Fig. 203), a Titianesque *Sacra Conversazione* (Fig. 202), and Veronese's *Holy Family with St. Barbara and the Infant St. John* (Fig. 80)—a short list, but long enough to make the items on it other than idiosyncratic.[78] Under what impulse were such pictures created? how were they meant to be understood? and, being misunderstood (presumably as excesses of irreverent "realism"), how is it that they were preserved?

At the mention of Veronese's name, art historians are likely to suspect irreligion. Veronese's insouciance before the tribunal of the Inquisition in 1573 is notorious; and some might want to charge the Child's gesture in St. Barbara's presence to the artist's supposed worldliness, his penchant, perhaps, to make

78.   A few further instances: the triptych of the *Madonna and Child with Saints* by Ludovico Urbani, 1474, Recanati, Museo Diocesano; an engraving by the Master of St. Sebastian, c. 1480, depicting the Virgin and Child in a design for a pax (Lehrs 10); Denis Calvaert's *Mystic Marriage of St. Catherine* panel of 1590 in the Capitoline Museum, Rome.

mockery of the sacred. But Veronese was an intelligent man; and like every intelligent artist, he respected his subject; and like most great artists he could not help but rethink it. Now suppose that his subject was simply the Word made flesh—the First Principle and Almighty Power become to all appearances an ordinary man-child. "Ordinary," says Veronese, except to those who even now confess the Child's inapparent divinity in its very consent to be human. And is not this what the picture shows? The artist has staged a tableau of the marvelously banal, a domesticized *sacra conversazione,* wherein the Child, doing what babies do, moves the surrounding figures to staggered reactions of pensiveness, impetuous curiosity, devotion, surprise. In clockwise order: the Virgin pressing her breast; St. Joseph peering; St. John, too, gazing centerward as he kisses the Infant's toe; and St. Barbara with the palm branch she wins for her martyrdom in that same Infant's cause. Not for a moment can we imagine this crew unmindful of the dormant godhood in their midst; or less than stirred by its humanness. These witnesses at the cradle are admitted to an intimacy more awesome than infantile masturbation.[79] As the sleeper touches the fount where the first drops of all-healing blood are to issue, they learn that the boy's divinity wills the Passion of its assumed body; and they are seeing this willingness expressed in a mode consonant with the infant body assumed.

Some such awareness of authentic religious meaning may explain the repeated copying of Veronese's picture—known to us in no less than five versions.[80] But before long, as incarnational realism yielded to better manners, the work's meaning was lost and the motif became unacceptable. Gian Antonio Guardi's copy in Seattle (Fig. 205) beggars the bystanders' awe by removing its cause; it inserts a cloth under the Child's active hand—in lieu of a stark revelation, a modest *cache-sexe.* And of the recently cleaned version in Baltimore, the museum catalogue reports that "the only area of extensive overpaint was the addition of drapery between the Child's legs" (Fig. 204). Then, discussing the composition, the text observes, not unperceptively: "Attention should be paid to a rare compositional feature—the absence of a focal point."

Even more astonishing (because one cannot naively dismiss the action as a naturalistic motif) is Veronese's *Presentation of the Cuccini Family to the Madonna* (1571; Figs. 5, 81). As the Theological Virtues present the family of the donor, the Virgin presents the Child—her right hand, his foot, her left, his sex. The

79.   Only in comic-erotic imagery does infantile masturbation become a subject for art—as in the sixth plate of *The Erotic Drawings of Mihály Zichy* (1827–1906), New York, 1969. Had Veronese depicted the Infant alone, its likeness to Zichy's contented baby would be remarkable. But the comparison proves that Veronese's whole meaning resides in the varied reactions of the attendant saints.

80.   The known versions of Veronese's picture are discussed in *Italian Paintings XIV–XVIIth Centuries from the Collection of The Baltimore Museum of Art,* ed. Gertrude Rosenthal, Baltimore, 1981, pp. 179, 182–85. A painting by Antonio Carneo inserts the Veronese Child into an even more elaborate figural context (Fig. 207).

companion to this majestic painting—originally on a facing wall in the Cuccini Palace in Venice—was a *Christ Bearing the Cross.* Gloss as you will the Virgin's gesture in the *Presentation,* it demands to be understood in a Christological context.

Rarest among Infancy scenes that refer sexually to the manhood of Christ are images of the Child with the penis erect. They survive in sufficient number to show that 16th-century painters and patrons thought the motif not inappropriate. Yet, for obvious reasons, this troubling phenomenon has not been reported, and notice of it even now is likely to start every skeptical impulse; as it did in this writer, before close confrontation with Alvise Vivarini's altarpiece of 1504 in the Leningrad Hermitage (Figs. 82, 208) removed the last doubt. Here again is a *sacra conversazione* of somber mood; yet the Child's member—discreetly shadowed and barely perceptible in black-and-white reproduction—is rendered in satyr-like elevation. And so it appears again in the Perino del Vaga *Holy Family* tondo in Liechtenstein (Fig. 83).[81] Such emblematic virility, even

81.   For a good reproduction in color of the Leningrad Vivarini, see B. Asvarishch et al., *The Hermitage,* Leningrad, 1977, pl. 5. Another example of the motif that escaped overpainting is Girolamo del Pacchia's *Holy Family with Infant St. John,* c. 1530, formerly London, Duke of Westminster; reprod. in Berenson, *Italian Pictures, Central,* III, fig. 1559.

Fig. 82. Alvise Vivarini, *Madonna and Child with Saints,* 1504.

Fig. 83. Perino del Vaga, *Holy Family*, c. 1520.

in private shadow, does seem exceptional. But more lifelike versions of infant erection (a baby's penis stiffens and levels without change of size) turn up in iconic *Madonnas* by Holbein the Elder, Giovanni Bellini, Cima da Conegliano, Perugino, Marco Palmezzano, Francia, Pacchia, Correggio, and Raffaellino dal Colle (Figs. 84–87); and thereafter in the work of some Northern Mannerists. Andrea del Sarto contrasts the Christ Child's stiffer member with that of St. John—a differentiation which suggests the likeliest reason for the motif: it demonstrates in the Infant that physiological potency without which the chastity of the man would count for nought.

XXX

Fig. 84. Cima da Conegliano, *Madonna and Child*, c. 1500–10.

Fig. 85. Perugino, *Madonna and Child*, c. 1500.

Fig. 86. Correggio, *Madonna of the Basket,*
c. 1523–25.

Fig. 87. Raffaellino dal Colle, *Madonna and
Child with the Infant St. John,* c. 1530.

Whether presently common or scarce, such symbolic images cannot be written off as aberrations. Our museums hang countless old pictures expurgated for precisely this sort of detail. One deft brushstroke or two would take the naughtiness out of a Renaissance icon and fit it for modern walls. Few offenders escaped. How many Renaissance pictures contained motifs that now strike us as scandalous we shall never know. What astounds us is that they existed at all, and that any came through unscathed after running gauntlets of censorship from the mid-16th to the mid-20th century.

XXXI

*

One small group of pictures poses a more difficult problem. Is it conceivable that Christian artists would assign the erection motif to the figure of the dead Christ?[82] The loins of these figures are, of course, draped; but it had long been the special pride of Renaissance painters to make drapery report subjacent anatomic events. Even the infant erection was sometimes betrayed only by the heave of the loincloth; of which outstanding examples are Correggio's *Madonna di S. Giorgio* in Dresden (Fig. 88), several *Madonna and Child*

82.   The fallacy of naturalism as a general-purpose explanation has been so often attacked in this essay that I shall not try to refute it here, where the folklore of hanged men's erections seems particularly irrelevant.

Fig. 88. Correggio, *Madonna di S. Giorgio,* 1530–32, detail.

Fig. 89. Jan van Scorel, *Madonna and Child
with Donors,* c. 1527–29, detail.

Fig. 90. Jacques de Gheyn, *Madonna and
Child with the Infant St. John,* c. 1590–93.

Fig. 91. Willem Key, *Pietà,* after 1530.

panels by Jan van Scorel (Fig. 89)[83] and an astonishing engraved roundel by Jacques de Gheyn after Abraham Bloemaert (Fig. 90), its mystical circumscription bespeaking the joys of heaven.[84] Could a like signal emanate from the dead Christ? What, for instance, are we to make of the *Pietà* by Willem Key (Munich and Karlsruhe; Fig. 91)—a picture known in two versions and believed to have been begun by Quentin Massys? Shall we construe the turbulence of the loincloth as an inflation of vacant folds, or are we bound to interpret these surfaces as reactive to forms beneath, insinuating a phallic tumescence? The latter, since we cannot be sure, seems an unholy notion. Yet the problem is posed again in the famous *Pietà* etching by Jacques Bellange (Fig. 92), and again in a late 16th-century anonymous Flemish *Christ as Victor over Sin and Death* (Fig. 93). Finally, a positive answer becomes compelling when we

83.   Three other Van Scorel panels display the same motif; see Friedländer, *Early Netherlandish Painting,* XII, no. 329 (Berlin), no. 332 (Kassel), no. 413 (Lisbon).
84.   The engraving (Hollstein 334) dates from the early 1590s. Its circumscription reads: "Dear Jesu, how sweet the delights, How everlasting the comforts, Constant and unalloyed, wherewith You solace our souls. This world has not the like; it mingles sorrow with joy and knows nought that endures ("Quam dulces semper lusus, quam propria semper, Et syncera animis confers solatia JESU. Talia non hic mundus habet, qui tristia miscet, Laetis, et solidi quicquam promittere nescit").

Fig. 92. Jacques Bellange, *Pietà,* c. 1615.

Fig. 93. Flemish, *Christ as Victor over Sin and Death,* c. 1590–1600.

Fig. 94. Ludwig Krug, *Man of Sorrows,* c. 1520.

compare certain images of the mystical Man of Sorrows, dating from 1520–32, where phallic erection is unmistakable. Among these is a rare engraving by Ludwig Krug (Fig. 94), impressions of which can have survived only by being locked away in print cabinets seldom disturbed.[85] And there are three paintings of the subject by the young Maerten van Heemskerck—the predella of one inscribed "Ecce Homo" (Figs. 95–97). An anonymous variant, painted on glass and cruder in quality, adds the four beasts of the Evangelists, the ox in bull-like charge at the center (Fig. 98).[86]

Are these works sacrilege or still affirmative Christian art? And if we incline to admit them, then how, under what rationale? We expect no certainties here, no texts or supportive documents to spell out intentions. Mystery in such 16th-century pictures is duly veiled. But our quandary we can analyze with some precision: whether to keep denying the existence of the erection motif or to acknowledge its presence; whether to dismiss the motif as gross foolishness or to grant it symbolic value; and, finally, whether to reject its symbolism as alien or to allow a possible, if irregular, compatibility with the subject.

XXXII

Let me assume that the ithyphallic motif in these images of the mystical Man of Sorrows was mysteriously meant. One might conjecture that Heemskerck's symbol simply inverts the archaic biblical euphemism of "flesh" for penis. At the original institution of circumcision, the Lord of Genesis (17:13) says: "My covenant shall be in your flesh." Heemskerck's paintings would reverse that trope by representing the risen flesh in the roused sexual member. It is no far cry from one to the other—no straining leap of imagination to equate penile erection, reciprocally, with flesh vivified.

As a symbol of postmortem revival, the erection-resurrection equation roots in pre-Christian antiquity: it characterized Osiris, the Egyptian god of the afterlife, represented with his restored member out like a leveled lance.[87]

---

85.   Cf. the unusually explicit genital reference in Ludwig Krug's two surviving woodcuts— *The Fall of Man* and the *Expulsion from Eden* (c. 1515; Geisberg 890 and 891). The artist is evidently concerned with the role of the sexual organ in redemptive history.

86.   The Amsterdam Rijksmuseum preserves yet another version of Heemskerck's *Man of Sorrows* (no. A1306), but this panel does not appear to be autograph.

87.   The elements of the Osiris myth, as they came down to the Renaissance through Plutarch and Diodorus Siculus, may be summarized as follows: a beneficent ruler, Osiris was betrayed and murdered by the evil Seth-Typhon, and his body dismembered (the event is depicted in one of Pinturicchio's frescoes in the Vatican Borgia Apartments). Isis, his loyal consort, reassembled the scattered parts of the body, remade the unretrieved phallus, and established it as an object of special worship. Osiris is resuscitated, procreates after death, and his cult comes to be identified with the phallic rites of Dionysus-Bacchus. Plutarch (*Moralia*, 371) gives the myth a metaphysical interpretation: "In the soul, Intelligence and Reason, the Ruler and Lord of all that is good, is Osiris, and [in nature] . . . that which is ordered, established and healthy . . . is the efflux of Osiris and his reflected image. But Typhon is that part of the soul which is . . . unruly."

The Renaissance literature on Osiris is discussed in Jean Seznec, *The Survival of the Pagan Gods,* New York, 1953, pp. 21, 26, 228, 238; and in Edgar Wind, *Pagan Mysteries in the Renaissance,* 2nd ed., New York, 1968, pp. 99, 133ff., 174, 300.

Fig. 95. Maerten van Heemskerck, *Man of Sorrows*, c. 1525–30.

Fig. 96. Maerten van Heemskerck, *Man of Sorrows*, 1532.

Fig. 97. Maerten van Heemskerck, *Man of Sorrows*, 1525.

Fig. 98. After Maerten van Heemskerck, *The Trinity with Christ Resurrected*.

And the ithyphallus as emblem of immortality haunts later Mediterranean mysteries honoring Bacchus. The prevalence of such symbolism accounts perhaps for the readiness with which Christian theology associated the penis in its circumcision with resurrection (see pp. 52, 156–57).

In Western literature, the *locus classicus* for our metaphoric equation is Boccaccio's *Decameron*, the tenth tale of the third day, where the sexual arousal of the anchorite Rustico is announced, with blasphemous irony, as "la resurrezion della carne." The context of the novella makes Boccaccio's wording — the resurrection of the flesh following its mortification — an apt and effective pun. But this same "pun," now deeply serious, lurks in the greatest 16th-century representation of the *Raising of Lazarus* — Sebastiano del Piombo's colossal painting in London, composed with the assistance of Michelangelo: Lazarus' loincloth, which in the preparatory drawing dips unsupported between the thighs,

XXXIII

appears in the painting firmly propped from below — a sign of resurgent flesh.[88]

Constant throughout is the conceit of the phallus as a manifestation of power. In an ancient text well known to 16th-century authors, the *Oneirocritica,* or *Interpretation of Dreams,* of Artemidorus, "the penis . . . is a symbol of strength and physical vigor, because it is itself the cause of these qualities. That is why some people call the penis 'one's manhood' [*andreia*]."[89] And the "machismo" of the 16th century gave this sentiment visual expression in a feature of masculine dress unique in Western history: the salient codpiece as a token of prowess and virile fecundity.[90]

Nothing here seems specifically Christian. Yet it is precisely in the Renaissance that this ancient topos surfaces in the most Catholic context — within a sermon on the Circumcision delivered by Battista Casali in 1508, again *inter missarum solemnia,* before Pope Julius II. During a lengthy aside on a commemorative phallic hieroglyph posted on triumphal obelisks by King Sesostris of Egypt, the preacher invokes the male member as the "greatest testimony of fortitude" (*amplissimum fortitudinis testimonium*).[91] In common with his audience of prelates and theologians, Casali takes it for granted that the phallus is reasonably equated with power.

XXXIV

But the supreme power is the power which prevails over mortality. It was for this that the penis — "unconquered weapon" in the contest waged with the Fates, battling victoriously against death — was praised by Bernardus Silvestris (see p. 46). And it is in this sense again that the phallus of Christ resurrected is spoken of in yet another sermon, delivered by Cardulus before Pope Alexander

88.   Obviously, in a picture so large and complex, the topical undulations of Lazarus' loincloth need never be noticed — probably never were. But we are now posing a novel question: whether, in a picture of 1520, the sexual member could participate in resurrection symbolism. And we are shown a positive answer when we follow the roll of the loincloth from thigh to thigh. I entreat speed readers not to dismiss this observation before giving the image careful attention.
      The two surviving studies for the Lazarus group are discussed and reproduced as Michelangelo autographs in Johannes Wilde, *Italian Drawings . . . in the British Museum: Michelangelo and His Studio,* London, 1953, nos. 16–17, pls. xxix–xxx. The attribution is rejected (in my view rightly) in Luitpold Dussler, *Die Zeichnungen des Michelangelo,* Berlin, 1959, nos. 561–62.
89.   Artemidorus, *Oneirocritica,* I, 45, p. 38f. The passage is cited by Valeriano (see p. 186).
90.   Flaunted as an instrument not of pleasure, but of power. Cf. Montaigne's pretended puzzlement in 1588 when the fashion had begun to go out of style: "What was the meaning of that ridiculous part of the hose our fathers wore, and which is still seen on our Swiss? What is the idea of the show we still make of our pieces, in effigy under our breeches; and what is worse, often, by falsehood and imposture, above their natural size?" (*Essays,* III, 5). Striking examples of that "ridiculous" 16th-century fashion are: the squire in Lucas van Leyden's engraving of the *Triumph of Mordecai,* 1515; Parmigianino's *Count of San Secundo* (1533–35; Madrid, Prado); Bronzino's *Portrait of a Young Man* (c. 1535–40; New York, The Metropolitan Museum of Art); Nicolo della Casa's engraving of *Baccio Bandinelli,* 1548; Titian's *Philip II* (1550; Madrid, Prado); François Clouet's portrait of *Henry II* (1559; Florence, Uffizi); Hans Lautensack's engraved portrait of *Georg Roggenbach* (1554; Bartsch 9); and Tobias Stimmer's portrait of *Jakob Schwitzer* (1564; Kunstmuseum Basel). More problematic is the recurrence of the motif in Bruegel's *Peasant Dance,* Detroit Institute of Arts, and in Callot's *Balli di Sfessania.*
91.   O'Malley, "Casali," p. 283.

VI some ten years before Casali's. Discussing the theological question whether or not the circumcised prepuce of Christ was reassumed in the risen body, Cardulus cites opinions both for and against, and reports that those in favor of reassumption regard the restored member as a *signum victoriae* — i.e., the phallus as sign!

Returning now to Heemskerck's outrageous conception of the Man of Sorrows with the *testimonium fortitudinis* in plain evidence, we restate our question: is the erection-resurrection equation in paintings of c. 1530 admissible within the Christian ethos? And now a positive answer no longer seems scurrilous: in the similitude of Christ's body, Heemskerck (like Ludwig Krug and the others) may have attempted a metaphor of the mortified-vivified flesh. To justify his conception, he could have said, or thought, something like this: if it was in the organ of generation and lust that Christ initiated his Passion; and if, in the exegetic tradition, its circumcision on the eighth day prefigures the Resurrection, the final putting away of corruption; then what is that organ's status in the risen body? Or more simply: if the truth of the Incarnation was proved in the mortification of the penis, would not the truth of the Anastasis, the resuscitation, be proved by its erection? Would not this be the body's best show of power? It was surely in this sense that the Heemskerck canvas of 1525 (Fig. 97) was understood by the glass painter who found its seated Man of Sorrows adaptable to an elaborate Resurrection, complete with Trinity, attendant angels, and Evangelists' symbols (Fig. 98). Without change of posture, the Christ in the copy appears to rise from the tomb, as does the horned bull, inserted between Christ's mounting thighs under his member.

I do believe that Heemskerck's images of the Man of Sorrows were conceived with a Christian will and *de profundis;* they impress me as desperate raids on the inexpressible — the unknowable mystery of a god's unmanned body in its resurgence. Nevertheless, they remain deeply shocking. Their vision of a settled Christ, alone in sterile, self-centering masculinity, seems to us — and must have seemed to most artists — a miscarried symbol. And it miscarries on more counts than one. Not only because Heemskerck's sense of human anatomy as a jerked mechanism is here especially chilling; and not only because the precision of the physiological datum, favored by utmost proximity, overwhelms the symbolic purpose. Heemskerck's iconic vision transgresses because the pictorial economy is thrown off balance by the genital symbol. Inordinately affective in psychic impact, it remains exiguous on the scale of the picture — one either misses it, or sees nothing else; so that the failure is ultimately a failure of art.

I have dwelled on this "failure," perhaps unfairly, in order to set up a contrast with a resounding success. By the mid-15th century, an acceptable circumvention of the prohibited member had been devised in Northern art — a diversion that spares what is midmost by fanning out; a potent synecdoche that celebrates the thing covered in the magnificence bestowed on the covering: I mean the enhanced loincloth of Christ on the cross.

Fig. 99. Robert Campin (?), *Crucifixion*, c. 1420-40.

As a compositional artifice, this banner loincloth is an inspired invention. It resolves a pictorial problem posed by conventional *Crucifixion* designs—the problem of vacant flanks in the middle zone of the field between crossbeam and horizon. By means of a gorgeous flutter flaring forth from the center, the blanks are repleted and animated; and so felicitous is the solution that its aptness on grounds other than formal has never been challenged. No one has questioned the wisdom of making such pageantry of a breechcloth; or grudged its tur-

Fig. 100. Roger van der Weyden, *Crucifixion,* c. 1450.

bulence as a wind gauge where no breath is stirring; nor its plausibility in a narrative that calls for the least covering of a victim whose garments are the coveted loot of his executioners.

The full deployment of this invention, as of so many, appears to be due to Roger van der Weyden (Campin perhaps cooperating; Figs. 99, 100). In several of Roger's *Crucifixions,* the spare aprons of the earlier masters unfurl into flying banners, buoyed up by an indwelling breeze where all else is becalmed. By 1500, these streamers winging the sacred loins glorify most German crucifixes (Figs. 101–04, 222–25) — often over-abundantly, as if less were *lèse majesté.* Yet, ostensibly, still a loincloth. Only the inherent metaphoricity of Renaissance realism could exalt this humblest of garments to such efflorescence, and convert the *ostentatio genitalium* decently into a fanfare of cosmic triumph.

XXXV

Fig. 101. Lucas Cranach, *Crucifixion,* 1503.

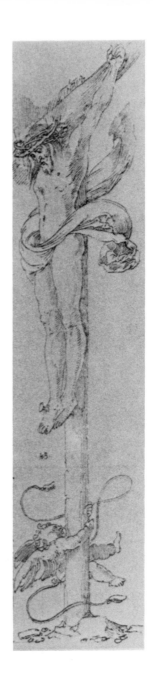

Fig. 103. Master D.S., *Crucifixion,*
c. 1505–10.

Above left: Fig. 102. Dürer, *Christ on the
Cross,* 1505.

Above right: Fig. 104. Hans Baldung Grien,
Christ on the Cross, c. 1515.

In the undisguised form of the *ostentatio,* the groin of the adult Christ is directly touched. Such action is found in four distinct situations. In the first of these — scenes of *Christ Shown to the People* — it is exceedingly rare, but one outstanding instance is a mid-16th-century Italian masterpiece by Moretto da Brescia (Fig. 105). Moretto treats the historic moment of the *Ecce Homo* as an ahistoric devotional image — more like a Man of Sorrows. It is a stern picture: a stairway leads up to a loggia; at its foot lies the cross, less than lifesize, but for an attribute large enough. At the stairhead, a winged weeping angel exhibits the seamless garment of Christ; and the Condemned himself under his crown of thorns, seated low with tied hands, the reed between the fingers of his left hand, while his right presses against the groin. This pressure and the fixity of his outright glance comprise all his action.

Surprisingly constant is the gesture of the self-touch in many-figured scenes of Entombment or Lamentation. That the lay of the hand in these instances is not less than a "gesture" seems to me undeniable, since no stir of limbs in Christ's body, whether doing or suffering, can be other than willed. This much at least the divine nature in the Incarnation ensures. As the incarnate Word deigned to gestate in a virgin womb and exited without giving injury; as Christ ascended the cross and there spread his arms in worldwide embrace; as in his death, laid on his mother's lap, he gently fingers a fold of her garment, and, entombed, will resist corruption, so also his disposition of

XXXVI hands, even in death, is at all times volitional and heuristic. Medieval and Renaissance artists understood that the hands of the dead Christ will not plunge where the living divinity would refrain. Yet in their images of the aftermath of the Passion, Christ's hand falls again and again on the genitals — in small-scale illuminations, in painted altarpieces, in monumental sculptural groups.

The motif can be traced back to the 1330s. In one early instance (Fig. 106), it seems interpretable as a modest safeguard, since the painter has chosen to leave Christ's ample loincloth transparent. (Cf. the "Christus pudicus" in 14th-century *Baptisms,* discussed in Excursus XIV.) Expressions of modesty may still be intended in certain illuminations from the late 14th century, where either the mother or an attendant *pleurante* draws a sheet over the private parts (Figs. 107, 108). Even in 15th-century works, the modesty explanation for the placement of Christ's own hands would remain plausible if the body lacked other covering. But in another early instance of the motif (Fig. 109), the loins of the corpse are draped, as they tend to remain throughout the 14th and 15th centuries; and it must be a motive other than modesty that calls and attracts attention to well-hidden pudenda. Say, rather, that an ostensibly functional gesture is now re-enacted symbolically.

Fig. 105. Moretto da Brescia, *Ecce Homo,* c. 1550.

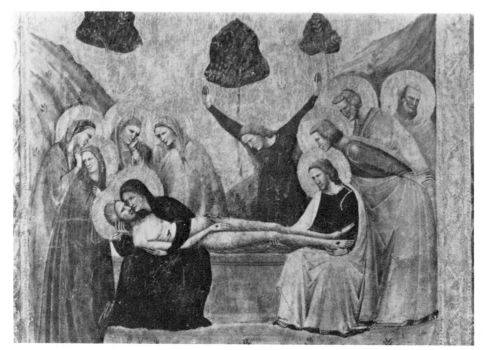

Fig. 106. Rimini School, *Lamentation*, c. 1330, detail.

Fig. 107. Illumination from the Petites Heures of Jean de Berry, *Entombment*, c. 1380–85.

Fig. 108. French illumination, *Lamentation*, c. 1400.

Fig. 109. French, *Entombment,* c. 1330.

Fig. 110. Alberto di Betto da Assisi, *Lamentation,* c. 1421.

This is manifestly the case in such sculptural groups as our Fig. 110, and in Fouquet's illuminations and other contemporaneous manuscripts (Figs. 111, 112).[92] Thereafter, the dead Christ's hand on the loincloth, sometimes tensed to a vital grasp, is found over and over in both Italian and Northern works (Figs. 113, 114, 228–31). We have noted the action as well in a drawing by Andrea del Sarto (Fig. 3), and are probably meant to recognize it in a sketch by Pontormo.[93] Only from the latter 16th century onward does the gesture gradually fade from the repertoire: in the canonic Catholic imagery of the Wierix brothers of Antwerp a self-touching hand is unthinkable, though it survives in

92.   The Fouquet shop *Lamentation* reproduced below (Fig. 112) is a copy of the illumination for Vespers in the Hours of Etienne Chevalier (c. 1452–61, Chantilly, Musée Condé); the *Embalming of Christ,* placed at Compline in the same Hours, again displays the groin-touching gesture.
93.   Florence, Uffizi 300F; see Janet Cox Rearick, *The Drawings of Pontormo,* Cambridge, Mass., 1964, fig. 105.

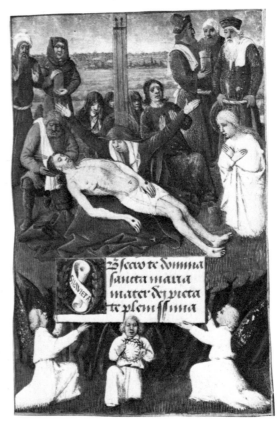

Fig. 111. Guillaume Vrelant (?), illumination, *Entombment,* c. 1454.

Fig. 112. Fouquet Shop illumination, *Lamentation,* c. 1470.

Fig. 113. Master of the Žebrák Lamentation,
Lamentation, c. 1505.

Fig. 114. Jan van Scorel, *Lamentation,* c. 1535–40.

Fig. 115. Ribera, *Entombment,* c. 1630.

rare instances even into the 17th century (Figs. 115, 232, 233). In Ribera's *En-tombment* at the Louvre—of which we know several replicas—Christ's left-handed motion cannot be meant simply to steady the knot of the loincloth; the act is demonstrative and it is grievous, like the dead Christ's showing of his stigmata.[94]

XXXVII

In earlier Renaissance representations of the deposed body, the groin-searching hand occurs as well on a monumental scale. Often in lifesize composite sculptures of the Entombment—in groups known as the Holy Grave, widely disseminated through French, North Italian, and Germanic regions during the 15th and early 16th centuries—this pathetic reach is the last physical act assigned to the Crucified (Figs. 116, 117). The gesture is too pointed and too oft-repeated to disregard, or to dismiss as a veristic portrayal of what dying men are said to do in their throes. Whether normal or not in actual death situations, a dead man's hand cupping his genitals forms no part of standard icono-graphic traditions. We find no such posture on the Dying Gauls of Pergamene

94.   For replicas of Ribera's painting, see Nicola Spinosa, *L'opera completa del Ribera* (Classici dell'Arte, 97), Milan, 1981, no. 38; to which should be added the 19th-century engraving by Joa-quín Luque Roselló (reprod. in Luís Alegre Nuñez, *Real Academia de Bellas Artes de San Fernando: Catálogo de la Calcografía Nacional,* Madrid, 1968, no. 55, fig. 4) and an unrecorded 17th-century (?) painted copy at the Seminary of St. Charles Borromeo in Overbrook, Pennsylvania.

sculpture; nothing like it among the felled combatants of Baroque battle scenes; or in Mathew Brady's Civil War photographs; nor in the thousands of actors and extras who feign death in the movies. Civilian corpses, from plague victims to heroes, likewise avoid the gesture—except only certain tomb figures housed in sanctified spaces. And these are of a date well past the invention of the motif. The gesture in its origin before the mid-14th century is proper only to representations of Christ, and for some sixty years to none other. Only by the end of the 14th century do we see it adapted to representations of Adam, and to high-dying princes and prelates whose tomb effigies rehearse Christ's own posture.

XXXVIII

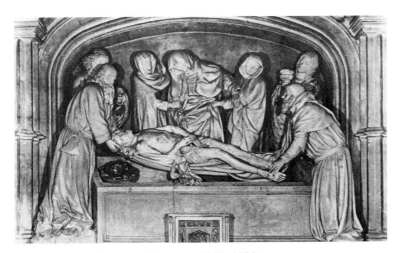

Fig. 116. French, *Entombment,* c. 1450–1500.

Fig. 117. Germain Pilon Shop, *Entombment,* c. 1540–54.

Fig. 119. French, *Pietà,* 15th century.

To me it now seems that the dead Christ touching his groin is visualized in the totality of a promise fulfilled. His Passion completed, he points back to its beginning, much as his blood runs from the last wound back to the first — as if to say, *consummatum est.* In the joining of first and last, the Passion is brought to perfection.[95]

And we need look for no other meaning when we encounter the gesture in Northern Pietà groups of the 15th century (Figs. 118, 119, 234–38). In rare instances, it is the Madonna's hand that rests on the loincloth — in reminiscence perhaps of Mary's role as protectress of Jesus' infancy (Fig. 121). But whether the act is performed by the mother or by the living godhead in the corpse of the Son, or jointly by both (Fig. 120), its sign character is apparent.

95.   An operation is felt to be perfect when the span from beginning to end collapses in unity. Thus St. Bonaventure on the perfection wrought by the Incarnation (*Breviloquium,* IV, 1, p. 144): "What more suitable act of wisdom than to bring the universe to full perfection by uniting the First and the last: the Word of God, origin of all things, and the human creature, last to be made." Cf. also n. 65 above.

Fig. 118. French, *Pietà,* c. 1400.

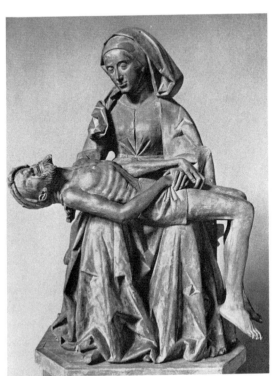

Fig. 120. Upper Bavarian, *Pietà,* c. 1490.   Fig. 121. Flemish, *Pietà,* c. 1510–20.

Fig. 122. After Roger van der Weyden, *Throne of Grace,* 1443.

A sign it remains in a 15th-century Flemish subgroup of the type we know as the Trinity, or Throne of Grace. Normally, in these visionary images, the Second Person is posed upright, indicating with the right hand the last wound received. But the works I have in mind differ from the more common type in directing the Father's left hand to the Son's groin (Figs. 122, 123, 243–46). Like the symbolic "blood hyphen," the two pointing hands span the Alpha and Omega of the Passion, the *ostentatio genitalium* complementing the requisite *ostentatio vulnerum.* We are shown once more that the incarnate Word died as a full-fraught man, triumphant over both sin and death; his sexuality vanquished by chastity, his mortality by Resurrection.

XXXIX

Fig. 123. Swabian, *Throne of Grace with Saints,* c. 1480.

There is something disquieting in these presentations; and this leads me, hesitantly, to a final reflection of the kind I have sought to avoid. It will not have escaped the reader that my discussion has left out of account all psychological considerations; such factors as may operate in the Christological creed itself, and such psychic determinants as may have influenced individual artists. As to the first, I gladly leave it to students of disciplines other than mine. Nor am I inclined to speculate on the inner motives of painters who chose to involve the sexuality of Christ in their iconography. If personal or subconscious drives motivated this or that artist in his approach to the Christ theme, these drives were ultimately subordinated to his conscious grasp of the subject, since the treatment he accorded the subject must be compatible with the liturgical function which the work was to serve—often as a commissioned altarpiece in a place of public worship. And monumental images of the Trinity were certainly destined for altars. Their meaning, as I understand it, was to give visible form to a climactic liturgical moment, the moment of the petition in the rite of the Roman Mass when, at the transubstantiation of the Eucharistic species into the sacramental body of Christ, that body sacrificed is offered to the Father with prayers for its acceptance. The Throne of Grace, as the Apostle called it (Hebrews 4:16), is the idea of the sacrificed Son in his acceptability to the Father. Visualized as the triune godhead enriched by the humanity of the Second Person, it had been a familiar theme since the 12th century.

But what makes the images I am citing rare and psychologically troubling is the Father's intrusive gesture, his unprecedented acknowledgment of the Son's loins. Nothing in received iconography sanctions it; and common intuition proscribes it. Joyce's Stephen Dedalus speaks of the steadfast bodily shame by which sons and fathers are sundered.[96] He perceived their severance, the distancing of their persons through shame of body, as the way of all flesh. And precisely this shame caves in now before our eyes. Natural distance collapses in this coalition of Persons wherein the divine Father's only-begotten is (as theology has it) a virgin, virginally conceived; enfleshed, sexed, circumcised, sacrificed, and so restored to the Throne of Grace; there symbolizing not only the aboriginal unity of the godhead, but in its more dramatic, more urgent message, a conciliation which stands for the atonement, the being-at-one, of man and God. For this atonement, on which hinges the Christian hope of salvation, Northern Renaissance art found the painfully intimate metaphor of the Father's hand on the groin of the Son; breaching a universal taboo as the fittest symbol of reconcilement. Such a symbol can only have sprung from an artist attuned to the deep undertow of his feelings. And it would not surprise me if its originator turned out to be, once again, Roger van der Weyden. It is perhaps more surprising that a handful of painters, engravers, and carvers understood the metaphor well enough to adopt and to imitate it — before everybody was educated into incomprehension. But this incomprehension — the "oblivion" to which the title of this essay refers — is profound, willed, and sophisticated. It is the price paid by the modern world for its massive historic retreat from the mythical grounds of Christianity.

*

A few words more. The field I have tried to enter is unmapped, and unsafe, and more far-reaching than appears from my present vantage. Much of what I have said is conjectural and surely due for revision. I can hardly claim, as St. Bernard does in closing his eighty-second sermon on the Song of Songs: "We need have no regrets for anything we have said; it is all supported by unquestioned and absolute truth." But I have risked hypothetical interpretations chiefly to show that, whether one looks with the eye of faith or with a mythographer's cool, the full content of the icons discussed bears looking at without shying. And perhaps from one further motive: to remind the literate among us that there are moments, even in a wordy culture like ours, when images start from no preformed program to become primary texts. Treated as illustrations of what is already scripted, they withhold their secrets.

96. *Ulysses,* Episode IX (Random House ed., p. 205): "They are sundered by a bodily shame so steadfast that the criminal annals of the world, stained with all other incests and bestialities hardly record its breach."

EXCURSUSES

I. Whether the subject exists

The terms "Christ" and "sexuality" are normally felt to be irreconcilable, and rightly so; sin, absent in one, but incriminating the other, keeps them apart. Therefore, the claim that they do come together in Renaissance painting arouses vigorous disbelief. And if the proof is said to reside in the pictures, the hearer assumes that those pictures must be exceptional. Such initial resistance gives way—as I have found repeatedly in private sessions with skeptics—only to the cumulative impact of number. This is why no less than 123 pictures are reproduced in the text of this essay and as many again in the back pages, with many more cited in reference. How such superfluity is received depends less on the person than on the progress of persuasion. Readers in their skeptical phase will think half a hundred instances still too few. And once conviction has taken hold, more than six is too much.

But the glut of the evidence is essential. It helps establish the subject as one concerned not with idiosyncrasies, but with a major phenomenon in historic Christianity. The present archive of Renaissance images wherein the emphasis on the genitalia of Christ is assertive and central runs near a thousand; and it keeps expanding, because the material abounds.

II. Whether the subject ought to be publicized

More surprising than the forthright treatment of the *ostentatio* motif in the works reproduced is the fact that they escaped subsequent censorship. Normally, such passages in Renaissance pictures would have been retouched sooner or later: a loincloth insinuated under the mother's hand sufficed to convert a demonstrative act into a posture of common modesty. Down to the 1930s, dealers, collectors, and public museums felt bound to expurgate paintings that would otherwise have seemed unfit to exhibit (see Excursus XXXI below). Apparently, the offending features were viewed either as marks of irreligion on the part of the artist, out of place where the subject was sacred; or else, as if the characters represented had been caught off-guard in awkward moments of privacy. Either way, it was wrong to look—which explains why anyone giving the matter his full attention falls under instant suspicion. Can his motives be sound? "Why are you interested in this?" is often the first question asked,

110

prompted by fear of that "impious curiosity" which the Doctors of the Church have so roundly condemned. Then let me quote St. Bonaventure addressing a fellow religious: "Imprudent investigations," he writes, "are displeasing to . . . good brothers, and to God, and to his angels. But I would wish that you and I may . . . detest no more than we should, nor things that should not be detested" (*Letter to an Unknown Master,* VIII, 335; quoted in Bougerol, *Bonaventure,* p. 8).

III. On the dignity of the touched chin

What I have summarily called the chin-chuck should be understood to include any reaching for, any touching, fingering, pinching, caressing, cupping, or clasping; so long as the target is constant (Figs. 7–12, 124–28). The hand at, under, or approaching the chin is what counts, and it counts heavily in received iconography.

Fig. 125. Drawing after Archaic Greek shield relief, *Priam before Achilles,* 600–550 B.C.

Fig. 124. Egyptian relief, *Ramses III and Concubine,* XIX Dynasty.

Fig. 126. Archaic Greek vase painting, *Theseus Wooing Ariadne,* 700–650 B.C.

Fig. 127. French mirror case, *Lovers Riding to the Hunt,* c. 1320–40.

Fig. 128. Cologne School, *Madonna with the Sweet-pea Blossom,* c. 1410.

Robert Herrick had serious love play in mind when he wrote: "Love makes the cheek and chin a sphere to dance and play in." But the lines were composed before the mid-17th century, at the expiring end of an ancient tradition. Thereafter, for reasons difficult to assess, the chin-oriented gesture rapidly loses status.

For some years past, I have kept a note of every delivered chin-chuck in my reading: from *Guzman de Alfarache* (1599–1604) and Pepys' *Diary* (1664), through Swift and Fielding and George Eliot to Joyce and Proust. And there is not one in this random haul but conveys some tang of nastiness, coarseness, or condescension. To unpack the collection here would be wasteful. Let it suffice that the chin-chuck as a symbolic form has suffered a gradual debasement since the 17th century. It may still befit children, giving or getting it; but between adults, a chin-chuck administered by man to woman is patronizing, faintly demeaning—and implies something of mockery when the receiver is male. Modern lovers, it seems, do not localize erotic fantasies at the chin; and what had been a mature lovers' gambit in medieval and Renaissance practice has come to look comical. Therefore, any bid to sublimate or to sacralize the chin-chuck motif in the iconography of devotional art must seem misdirected.

And yet, the woman touching the chin of a man may be, in an early 16th-century engraving, the disconsolate Virgin squatting by the corpse of her son (Veit Stosz, Lehrs 3; cf. the mid-14th-century Bohemian *Pietà* by the Hohenfurt Master, Schiller, *Iconography,* II, fig. 605). And the reciprocal chin-chuck observable on French children's playgrounds ("Je te tiens, / Tu me tiens / par la barbichette; / Le premier / qui rira / aura une tapette") may, in medieval art, stand for the highest good, the *summum bonum:* at the

Fig. 129. Upper Rhenish illumination, *Death of the Virgin*, 1250–1300.

Virgin's death, her soul's nuptial union with Christ finds expression in a mutual touching of chins (Fig. 129). The gravity of the gesture in such adult moments has gone unnoticed, perhaps because allocation to the Christ Child had conceptualized it as typical infant behavior.

Emile Mâle (1949) had seen only "winsome childishness" in the young Christ's "caress of his mother's chin" (*aimables enfantillages;* see Excursus XVII); and a major 1972 exhibition catalogue of medieval art still reads the gesture as "illustrating an evolution toward humanization and tenderness" (*Rhin-Meuse: Art et Civilisation 800–1400,* Cologne and Brussels, 1972,

p. 331, no. L6). On the other hand, some recent observers have begun to see the chin-chuck as a functioning part of Christian symbolism (see Steinberg, "Metaphors," pp. 280–83). Hans Wentzel's discussion of the Sponsa-Sponsus image in a 12th-century illustration of Canticles interprets "das Umfangen des Kinns"— the clasping of a woman's chin—as Christ's expression of love for the human soul ("Die ikonographischen Voraussetzungen der Christus-Johannes-Gruppe und das Sponsa-Sponsus-Bild des Hohen Liedes," in *Heilige Kunst: Jahrbuch des Kunstvereins der Diözese Rottenburg,* Stuttgart, 1952, p. 11). And the author of the "Maria-Sponsus" entry in Kirschbaum's *Lexikon* (1970) remarks that, in small French Bibles since the mid-13th century, Song of Songs illustrations depicting the Virgin and Child show the infant embracing the mother, "or united with her in a gesture of tenderness perhaps interpretable in a bridal sense (e.g., the Child touching the mother's chin)"; see Dorothee von Burgsdorff in *Lexikon der christlichen Ikonographie,* ed. Engelbert Kirschbaum, II, Rome, etc., 1970, col. 309.

It is the context of Song of Songs illustrations that provides the clue. The adaptation of the old lovers' ploy to Christian art was, I suggest, mandated by Canticles 2:6 (repeated in 8:3). I refer to the words "his left hand is under my head and his right hand shall embrace me" (*Laeva eius sub capite meo, / Et dextera illius amplexabitur me*).

To these words, the Middle Ages assigned the sublimest role. In the apse mosaic of Sta. Maria in Trastevere, Rome (before 1143), where Christ and the Madonna throne side by side as consorts in heaven, Mary displays a scroll inscribed with this verse. And for St. Aelred of Rievaulx (d. 1167), these same words point the climax of the unitive mystic experience, when soul and God meet directly: "All earthly affections being put to slumber, and all worldly desires and thoughts silenced, [the soul] takes its joy only in the kiss of Christ and rests in his embrace, exulting and saying: 'His left hand is under my head, and his right hand shall embrace me'" (quoted from *Pat. lat.,* 195, col. 673, in Perella, *The Kiss Sacred and Profane,* p. 61).

How was this action visualized, and what did the exegetes make of the text's primary sense? Here we need not be of two minds, for the reading of the verse, then as now, was unequivocal (see Pope, *Anchor Bible,* p. 384: "This verse needs little explication"—it applies ". . . to sexual embrace"). The words were understood to refer to the consummation of physical love as a figure for the spiritual. Origen (d. c. 254), setting the course for all subsequent Christian interpretations of Canticles, weaves back and forth between the literal sense and the mystic:

His left hand is under my head, and his right hand shall embrace me. The picture before us in this drama of love is that of the Bride hastening to consummate her union with the Bridegroom. But turn with all speed to the life-giving Spirit and, eschewing physical terms, consider carefully what is the left hand of the Word of God, what the right; also what His Bride's head is—the head, that is to say, of the perfect soul or of the Church; and do not suffer an interpretation that has to do with the flesh and the passions to carry you away (Origen, *Song of Songs,* p. 200; *Pat. gr.,* 13, cols. 162–63).

Further on, Origen writes: "Here the Church that is the Bride begs her Bridegroom who is the Word of God to support her head with His left hand, but with His right hand to embrace the whole of her, and hold her body fast."

Explicit testimony that the words "left hand under my head" signify coitus comes from Jerome. Expounding a verse in Daniel (2:34), which speaks mysteriously of a "stone cut out of a mountain without hands," Jerome sees in it a prophecy of Christ "born a virgin of a virgin," and adds: "'Hands' is, of course, to be understood of the marital act, as in the verse *His left hand is under my head and his right hand shall embrace me*" (Epistle XXII, 19; Jerome, *Letters,* p. 151). This literal reading holds in the *Expositio in cantica canticorum* of the Venerable Bede, who would have the lovers in a *lectulus,* or small bed (*Pat. lat.,* 91, col. 1105). Likewise in the

114

famous commentary of Honorius of Autun (early 12th century), the first, or literal, reading of the verse has the "true King" reclining on the Bride's couch; which is no sooner said than Honorius proceeds to explain that the nuptial act here refers to the Word's espousal of human nature in the Incarnation, and also to Christ's marriage with the Church (*Expositio in cantica canticorum, Pat. lat.,* 172, col. 585).

St. Bernard, in the fifty-first of his eighty-six sermons on the Song of Songs, is more forthcoming:

"His left arm under my head, his right arm will embrace me". . . . It is clear that the bridegroom has returned for the purpose of comforting the distressed bride by his presence. . . . And because he found that during his absence she had been faithful in good works . . . he returns this time with an even richer reward of grace. As she lies back he cushions her head on one of his arms, embracing her with the other, to cherish her at his bosom. Happy the soul who reclines on the breast of Christ, and rests between the arms of the Word! "His left arm under my head, his right arm will embrace me" (Sermon LI, 5; Bernard, *Song of Songs,* p. 44).

Bernard returns to the theme in the following sermon (p. 49): "her tender bridegroom supports her head on his left arm, as has already been said, that she may relax and sleep on his breast." The reading of the ambiguous Latin *laeva eius* ("his left") as "arm," rather than "hand," enables Bernard to envisage the action as a marital embrace in reclining position. But as he continues he hastens to subtilize what he had just made concrete:

What more are we to think the left hand and the right are for the bridegroom, the Word? Does that which is called the word of man have within it separate bodily parts. . . ? All the more does he who is God and the Word of God not admit diversity of any kind. . . . For he is the wisdom of God, of whom it is written: his wisdom is beyond numbering. But . . . we speak as well as we can of that which we do our best to understand, . . . taught by the authority of the Fathers and the usage of the scriptures that it is lawful to appropriate suitable analogies from the things we know . . . (Sermon LI, 7, pp. 45–46).

Were such "analogies from the things we know" equally suitable to the visual arts? Preachers and exegetes dealing with words had an easier time of it. They could assert that the verse under discussion—at the first of its four levels of meaning—denoted a couple embraced in reclining position in the marital act; then swiftly unsex the image into abstraction. But what dodge was available to an artist who had to present that amorous symbol in a code grounded in physicality; whose Bride had to be drawn concrete, formed as a woman, yet without the umbrage of Jerome's nuptial act, or the Bernardine "lying back with the head cushioned on one of his arms"? In the 12th-century mosaic at Sta. Maria in Trastevere, the seated Sponsa receives Christ's right-armed embrace on her shoulders, but despite the full verse spelled out on her scroll, the left-hand action of Christ is omitted: clearly unfit for representation.

Fortunately, art has other resources. In a 12th-century illumination from Salzburg, the female figure, identified by the *laeva eius* inscription, wafts toward the enthroned Bridegroom, whose left hand gropes chinward along her cheek (frontispiece to an Honorius of Autun manuscript volume, Munich, Bayerische Staatsbibliothek, ms. lat. 4450, fol. Iv; see Reiner Haussherr, *Die Zeit der Staufer,* exh. cat., Württembergisches Landesmuseum, Stuttgart, 1977, I, no. 740, for description and citation of literature).

In the celebrated colored Dutch blockbook of Song of Songs illustrations (1465; Munich, Bayerische Staatsbibliothek), the Bride and Bridegroom, canopied by a banderole bearing the *laeva eius* verse, act out the same scriptural moment, not however in accord with exegetical interpretation, but after an alternative model: the crowned Sponsa rests head and arms on the knees of the seated Sponsus; his right hand embraces her shoulders, his left hand is under her head—at the chin.

In my hypothesis the artists resort to the ancient formula of the touched chin—already allegorized via Cupid and Psyche—to convey the lovers' tryst without the bedding down prescribed in the literal commentary on Canticles. In other words, they use the chin-chuck as metaphor—as a visual text with both literal and mystical connotation. Passing between Christ and the Virgin, the gesture becomes an all-purpose sign for the love bond between Christ and Mary-Ecclesia, between Christ and the soul, the Logos and human nature. Needless to say, not every artist pondered the textual background or the theological implications of the chin-chuck; some assigned it to the right hand instead of the left. But all must have known that they were wielding a symbol, no matter how naturalized in appearance. The following three reproductions (Figs. 130–32) illustrate works dating from c. 1200, c. 1410, and c. 1565. Each is precise in representing the Virgin with Christ's right hand embracing and his chinward left "under her head."

Fig. 131. Master of Heiligenkreuz, *Madonna and Child,* c. 1410.

Fig. 130. French, initial "O" from a Canticles manuscript, *Christ and Ecclesia,* c. 1200.

Fig. 132. Luca Cambiaso, *Madonna and Child*, c. 1565.

IV. Irreligious alternatives

Under the influence of Carl Koch, one other commentary on Baldung's "scandalous" woodcut entered the literature: Jean Wirth's "Sainte Anne est une sorcière," *Bibliothèque d'Humanisme et Renaissance,* 40 (1978), pp. 449–80. Wirth accepts Koch's reading of St. Anne's gesture as a "conjuration," but he does not think it benign. He believes the print to be an instrument of derision, directed against the growing popularity of the cult of St. Anne. That his interpretation puts the Madonna in collusion with a wicked old sorceress gives him no qualm. As he sees it, the two women exploit the inattention of the nodding St. Joseph to play the boy a mean trick that will condemn him for life to enforced chastity. And this hypothesis strikes Wirth as the more plausible, since Jesus did in fact die prematurely, leaving no progeny. ("Les deux femmes lui jouent un mauvais tour qui le condamnera à une chasteté forcée. . . . Comme le Christ est mort prématurément . . . et qu'il ne fut pas gratifié par le ciel d'une progéniture, la seconde hypothèse [the hypothesis of the malignant spell] vient plus naturellement à l'esprit." No wonder Wirth is astonished to find that the artist responsible for this "explicit blasphemy" escaped burning, or even censure.

The glosses of Wirth and Koch are cited here because, until 1981, no others were offered. And the maturer approach embodied in the 1981 Baldung exhibition catalogue (Marrow/Shestack, *Hans Baldung Grien,* no. 21, p. 129) still contends against a naturalism deeply entrenched. One scholar suggested that the Christ Child, as almost the only infant character in Renaissance art, must necessarily be the repository of whatever observations artists make about infant behavior. Another sought to explain St. Anne's forwardness as an "optical illusion"; or as "nothing remarkable, since it is not uncommon for a grandmother to diaper her baby grandchild."

V. Concerning the practice of fondling a man-child's genitalia

In the interest of maximizing fecundity, the great anatomist, Gabriello Fallopio (c. 1523–62) thought it necessary to admonish parents and nurses to "be zealous in infancy to enlarge the penis of a boy" (see A. Comfort, in *The Anxiety Makers,* London, 1967, p. 94). But if such zeal was ever endemic in Western Christendom, it has not been so recorded in visual documents—excepting only and paradoxically in the instance of Christ, the Ever-virgin. And yet Ariès adduces Hans Baldung's woodcut for its supposed documentary value. His (inaccurate) description of it reads as follows: "St. Anne's behavior strikes us as extremely odd—she is pushing the child's thighs apart as if she wanted to get at its privy parts and tickle them. It would be a mistake to see this as a piece of ribaldry" (*Centuries of Childhood,* p. 103). For further discussion of this "widespread tradition" (Ariès), see Lloyd deMause, "The Evolution of Childhood," *History of Childhood Quarterly,* 1 (1974), p. 507, and especially Elizabeth W. Marvick, "Childhood History and Decisions of State: The Case of Louis XIII," in *The New Psychohistory,* ed. Lloyd deMause, New York, 1975, pp. 213–14. The latter paper deals with the infancy of the future Louis XIII, as recorded in the diary of his physician, Dr. Héroard. We learn that when the Dauphin was a year old, he regularly touched and exposed himself, and invited handling, etc. But the record of these proceedings was locked in a doctor's diary; no artist in 1602 would have depicted the Dauphin in such extremity. The question remains: Why the Christ?

VI. More on the Baldung Grien woodcut

Any purely secular reading of St. Anne's forward gesture in Baldung's woodcut must be misguided if only because it defects from the context. That context allows no loose ends. Everything in the artist's design takes part in a coherent symbolic program, from the gravity of the persons depicted to each prop and action: the book and posture of Joseph; the Child's reach for the Virgin's chin; the solicitude of St. Anne and, finally, the dead tree hosting a vigorous vine. This lifeless stump with its undulant contour and its locus at the right margin is close kin to the paradisal tree in Baldung's *Fall of Man* woodcut of the same year (1511). But whereas, in the *Fall of Man,* the Edenic tree was entwined with a serpentine Satan rising in leftward coils, it is a rectifying fresh vine that mounts the dry trunk behind St. Anne. If Baldung knew what he was doing, he also knew that, according to legend, the Tree of Life planted in Eden was predestined to yield its wood to the cross. Thus, in the St. Anne woodcut—whose subject is nothing less than the Incarnation—the vine as reference to the Passion is already in place on the *lignum vitae.* (Cf. on this point, Marrow/Shestack, *Hans Baldung Grien,* no. 21, p. 129, where, however, the vine-Christ equation is somewhat weakened by a further reference to the grape vine as a symbol of St. Anne's fruitfulness. The above catalogue entry included a brief summary of my reading—with premature citation of publication. For a similar symbolic interpretation, see Colin Eisler, "Hans Baldung Grien: An Exhibition Reviewed," *The Print Collector's Newsletter,* 12 [July—August 1981], p. 69.)

VII. Who needs God's divinity proved?

The constant in the orthodox creed is the union of Christ's two natures; but the emphasis shifts, depending on the polemical needs of the moment. Thus the early Church Fathers were emphatic about the divinity in the historical Jesus. St. Augustine confessed that before his conversion he was only thinking of "Christ as of a man of excellent wisdom, to whom no man could be equaled. . . . But what mystery there was in 'the Word was made flesh,' I could not even imagine" (*Confessions,* VII, 19). Elsewhere he writes: "We have refuted the folly of those who . . . refuse to worship [Christ] as God, but whom, nevertheless, they . . . pronounce worthy to be honored as a man far surpassing other men in wisdom" (*Harmony of the Gospels,* II, prologue, p. 102). And again: "This is precisely what constitutes unbelief, that Christ is held to be without any divinity whatsoever" (Sermon IX, 2 [Ben. 191]; *Sermons,* p. 108).

But how was the divinity of Christ argued, how was skepticism to be overcome? Apologists such as St. Irenaeus argued from the saving effect of Christ's ministry and redemptive death upon human guilt, since no one but God could forgive sins against God. (For St. Irenaeus, Clement of Alexandria, and Origen on this point, see Pelikan, *Christian Tradition,* I, p. 155.) The logic is irrefutable: those who consider themselves absolved know absolutely that only a divine agency could have won their acquittal.

Others, notably St. Athanasius (295–373), argued the godhead of Christ from the miracles. The Incarnation was necessary, Athanasius explained, in order to refute three kinds of idolatry: the worship of nature, the worship of demons, and the worship of other men, such as defunct heroes or ancestors. Christ quashed these errors by the miracles he produced in his manhood, in the course of which he subdued nature's laws, routed demons, and rose from the dead, as no man had done before; thereby proving to those who venerated the dead, or demons, or nature, that he lorded over them all.

> Because men had turned away from the contemplation of God . . . and were seeking God in creation and sensible things, and had set up mortal men and demons as gods for themselves; for this reason . . . the Word of God took to himself a body . . . in order that those who supposed that God was in corporeal things might understand the truth from the works which the Lord did through the actions of his body. . . . If their minds were preconceived toward men, so that they supposed them to be gods, yet when they compared the works of the Savior with theirs, it appeared that the Savior alone among men was the Son of God, since men had no such works as those done by God the Word. . . . [For he] cast out every illness and disease from men; from which anyone could see his divinity.

Similarly, Christ confounded the worship of demons by showing that he could put them to flight ("for the fact that he commanded demons and cast them out was not a human deed, but a divine one"); and he dethroned the dead as objects of adoration by himself dying and rising again. Finally, ". . . even at his death . . . the whole creation was confessing that he who was known and suffered in the body was not simply a man, but the Son of God and Savior of all. For the sun turned back, and the earth shook, and the mountains rent . . . and these things showed that Christ who was on the cross was God . . ."

(*De incarnatione,* 15, 18, 19, pp. 171, 179, 181).

These Early Christian arguments for the godhead of Christ derive from Christ's inimitable power—whether it be the power to control the forces of nature, to command demons, or to remit Original Sin. But compare St. Bonaventure. Like St. Athanasius, the great Franciscan (d. 1274) speculates on "the reason why the Incarnation of the Word was necessary":

> When man sinned . . . he fell headlong into weakness, ignorance, and malice. . . . He could no longer imitate divine power, behold divine light, or love divine goodness. The most perfect way for man to be raised out of his misery was for the first Principle to come down to man's level, offering Himself to him as an accessible object of knowledge, love, and imitation. Man, carnal, animal, and sensual, could not know, love, or imitate anything that was not both proportionate and similar to himself. So, in order to raise man out of this state, the Word was made flesh; that He might be known and loved and imitated by man who was flesh. . .
> (*Breviloquium,* IV, 3, pp. 144–45).

Bonaventure worships, but he no longer pleads the godhead of Jesus. Arguments from Christ's power over nature, demons, and death—arguments by which Athanasius nine hundred years earlier had sought to cow skeptics and heretics into submission—are not adduced. The "first Principle," we are told, became man so as to put a model of man's own potential within his reach. Augustine's fear that mere admiration of Christ's human excellence might annul belief in his divinity is no longer a clear and present danger. To the faithful, the grandeur of God is sufficiently manifest in his condescension.

And how, we may ask, would a Renaissance preacher argue the divinity of Christ? The answer seems to be that he would not, because believers do not need persuasion. Michelangelo said as much in a remarkable speech justifying the relative ages of mother and Son in his first *Pietà*. Mary's youthful bloom, he explained, might have been "ordained by the Divine Power to prove to the world the virginity and perpetual purity of the Mother." But, he continued, this was "not necessary in the Son, but rather the contrary; wishing to show that the Son of God took upon himself a true human body subject to all the ills of man, excepting only sin, *he did not allow the divine in him to hold back the human* [emphasis added], but let it run its course and obey its laws. . ." (Condivi, p. 26).

VIII. Dogma as pictorial subject

It may be too early to speak of a trend, but during the past decade or so a fair number of Renaissance images have been significantly retitled. By whatever names they were formerly called, their subjects have come to be recognized as simply the Incarnation. Such is Piero di Cosimo's altarpiece at the Uffizi, which Mina Bacci showed to be not an Immaculate Conception, as used to be thought (*L'Opera completa di Piero di Cosimo* [Classici dell'Arte, 88], Milan, 1976, no. 33, p. 92). Such again is a major altarpiece at La Verna, an enameled terracotta relief by Andrea della Robbia dated 1479, recently published by John Pope-Hennessy. The relief presents the nude Christ Child laid on a grassy mound, attended by the Madonna and angels in various attitudes of veneration. "The Adoration of the Child" would once have seemed the self-evident subject. But Pope-Hennessy reads the majuscule legend in the predella ("VERBUM CARO FATTŪ EST DE VIRGINE MA.")—which, he writes, "informs us, if up to this point we were in any doubt, that the altarpiece represents not the Adoration of the Child, but the Incarnation, the mystery of the word made flesh" ("Thoughts on Andrea della Robbia," *Apollo*, 109 [March 1979], pp. 176–97).

No predella inscription accompanies Fra Filippo Lippi's well-known *Adoration of the Child* in Berlin, painted c. 1460 for the chapel of the Medici Palace in Florence. But this is the work from which the della Robbia relief at La Verna derives, and it encapsulates the doctrine of the Incarnation in yet greater fullness. The setting is a dark forest. From right of center, the kneeling Virgin looks down on the naked Child. Her stature, despite genuflection, is undiminished; her mantle, lit by no natural light, a thin morning blue. And beneath the hem of her tunic lingers the Child's straight foot—Lippi's token of "whenceness," the sign of the Infant as "issue," plained on the florid earth. At the same time, the Child forms the nether pole of the upright Trinity. The dove sheds its rays down the gaping center, and at the summit, God the Father spreads his palms to the Child's measure. Sts. John and Bernard attend as witnesses to the Incarnation.

At least one more painting by Lippi represents the same subject again: the *Madonna and Child with Two Angels* at the Uffizi. A recent analysis by Marilyn Aronberg Lavin reads it, in the symbolic mode of the Song of Songs, as a royal wedding, wherein Christ, through Mary, takes humanity as his bride ("The Joy of the Bridegroom's Friend," pp. 193–210).

A further instance is the late retitling of an altarpiece by Fra Bartolommeo. "Its subject had been misunderstood," we read in the 1982 catalogue of Florentine works in the Louvre (Sylvie Béguin, et al., *Le XVIᵉ siècle florentin au Louvre*, Paris, 1982, no. 11). Dismissing earlier alternative titles ("Annunciation," "Immaculate Conception"), the author informs us that its proper subject is "the Incarnation of Christ." Candidates equally eligible for such renaming—e.g., Botticini's *Madonna and Child with Angels* (Fig. 15), or Michelangelo's *Doni Tondo*—readily come to mind. (The case for the Michelangelo tondo was presented during my A. W. Mellon Lectures in the Fine Arts, May 1982, at the National Gallery of Art, Washington, D.C.; to be published by Princeton University Press.)

Such pictures project a new iconography that is neither iconic nor narrative, nor linked to any liturgical feast. They are historiated emblems designed to enshrine the central mystery of the Creed. As Mina Bacci wrote of the Piero di Cosimo altarpiece at the Uffizi, they are direct "visualizations of the dogma."

The incidence of such pictures and the demand which they presuppose confirm the emergence of a specific theological orientation in the Quattrocento. And their mislabeling in the recent past reflects an unwitting redistribution of emphasis. For when the envisioned dogma is called an Adoration, we are being directed to that which is worshipped, namely the divinity in the Child; whereas the intent of these pictures was to extol the Word's Incarnation.

This does not mean that the godhead in Christ was to be slighted; only that the evidence for it must come through the veil of the flesh, or, as we should say, by way of naturalism. The familiar effect of this requirement was the progressive humanization of the Christ Child in Renaissance art. But this should be seen with its corollary—the imperative to offset that humanization by inventing ever subtler intimations of the Infant's divinity—inventions that deserve to be catalogued, even where their interpreta-

tion remains conjectural. Following is a preview of what such a catalogue might contain.

Discounting insignia, such as the crossed nimbus or the attendance of angels and supernatural portents, our inventory would include signs of instant maturity nothing short of miraculous. For example: a build of Herculean musculature at the outset of life; or a controlled, athletic agility in standing, striding, grasping, etc. Such metaphors of ideality are characteristically Italian. Alternatively, 15th-century Flemish paintings, notably Roger's (Figs. 22, 52, 138), present the Child with distended belly and spindly legs—an apparent debility which connoisseurs with a penchant for diagnostics attribute to rickets; I have heard it said these past forty years that those Flemings painted rachitic babies because they didn't know any better. It is, however, more probable that the condition of Roger's typical Christ Child symbolizes the state of the newborn, by which the precociousness of the Infant is rendered the more amazing. ("The births of living creatures at first are ill-shapen," wrote Francis Bacon.)

We have come to take precociousness in the baby Jesus for granted. His grown-up behavior—the bestowing of blessings, crowns, keys, betrothal rings, and so on—these quaint anomalies are familiar in principle (Figs. 28, 133, 134). But we are continually entertained by the unexpected, as when we find him indicating the right word on a page (in Botticelli's Uffizi *Magnificat*); or when the Blessed Cardinal Giovanni Dominici (d. 1419) suggests that the Child be shown tracing a hem for his mother to sew. ("Iesu profila ed essa Madre tal profilo cuce"; *Regola del governo di cura familiare compilata dal Beato Giovanni Dominici* [1403], ed. Donato Salvi, Florence, 1860, pt. IV, p. 131; englished in Creighton E. Gilbert, *Italian Art 1400-1500: Sources and Documents,*

Fig. 133. Lorenzo Lotto, *Mystic Marriage of St. Catherine,* 1523.

Fig. 134. Cesare Magni, *Madonna and Child with Saints,* c. 1530.

Englewood Cliffs, N.J., 1980, p. 145. An earlier German translation is intriguing, but unfortunately untenable: it would have the Child furnish the drawing which his mother uses as an embroidery pattern; see P. Augustin Rösler, *Kardinal Johannes Dominicis Erziehungslehre . . . ,* Freiburg i. Br., 1894, p. 26—"wie Jesus zeichnet, während die Mutter selbst nach der Zeichnung stickt.")

We come upon more surprises in studying the Child Jesus' diet, his companionships, his playthings, and pastimes (Figs. 78, 135, 136). But most deserving of itemization is the theme of prolepsis—a future tense in the grammar of visual representation whose origins lie in antiquity: an infant Hercules holding the apples of the Hesperides is the figure of him who *will* steal the apples. The phenomenon was noted by Bernard Schweitzer in discussing the helmet of Menelaus, decorated with anachronistic references to the hero's subsequent peregrinations: "The journeys of Menelaus fall into the period after the conquest of Troy. How then could he, on the plains of Ilium, be wearing a helmet which alludes to these travels? But it is a familiar experience, confirmed over and over, that antique art readily used this kind of prolepsis for the characterization of figures" ("Das Original der Pasquino Gruppe," *Abhandlungen der sächsischen Akademie,* 1936, p. 109).

In the iconography of the Christ Child, and most conspicuously in Renaissance painting, the sense of futurity is pervasive—objectively, because Christ's whole destiny is engraved in the Incarnation; subjectively, because the boy is understood to foreknow his death. Upon this theme artists played infinite variations. A (lost) Leonardo cartoon represented—according to a contemporary's account dated April 3, 1501—"the Christ Child seizing a lamb and about to embrace it. The mother . . . catches the Child to

Fig. 135. Style of Joos van Cleve, *Christ Child Eating Grapes,* c. 1515.

draw it away from the lamb, that sacrificial animal which signifies the Passion." The same writer described another of Leonardo's pictures: ". . . a Madonna seated, and at work with a spindle, while the infant Christ . . . looks with wonder at four rays of light that fall in the form of a cross, as if wishing for them" (Fra Pietro da Novellara, writing to Isabella d'Este; see Ludwig Goldscheider, *Leonardo da Vinci,* London, 1943, p. 19).

I see no end to the artists' resourcefulness in the staging of premonition. Instances unfamiliar, or not previously recognized, come in unbidden—like the postcard in yesterday's mail, with its reproduction of Quentin Massys' *Madonna and Child* in Brussels (no. 6647). The picture exhibits again the mysterious anachronism of the Child as beadsman (cf. Fig. 128): the little boy toys with the rosary and halts at one of the five larger beads that symbolize the stigmata. Or, visiting the Yale Art Gallery, notice what

Fig. 136. Quentin Massys, *Madonna and Child,* c. 1500.

may be premonitory—how else should the tendered blessing be understood? In a gesture uncharacteristic of infants, the boy throws out both arms, as he will again on the cross; and the mother catches the movement by hand and wrist, as if to say—"but not yet." This "not-yet" motif, which presents the joy of the Virgin as a privilege preceding her sorrows, remains to be studied; it is surely the narrative content of the Leonardo cartoon cited above, of Michelangelo's *Tondo Taddei* (London, Royal Academy), and of Raphael's *Alba Madonna* in Washington.

All these inventions share the common objective of reconciling incompossible yet consubstantial natures in the person of Christ. One distinguishes two approaches to the same end, drawn from opposite

the Infant is doing in Pinturicchio's *Madonna and Child* (Fig. 137): he looks down at his pet goldfinch, thoughtfully holding its wingtips out at full spread—an image of the Crucifixion produced in child's play. This is hardly a new invention, but perhaps an original variation. In Cima's *Madonna and Child* in London [no. 634], the boy holds the wing-spreading bird by its tail. And I recall seeing a noble 14th-century stone-carved Madonna group from Joigny in the Louvre: as the Child touches his crowned mother's chin, mother and Child between them spread-eagle the bird. (For the wingspread as a recurring Crucifixion symbol, cf. John Donne's poem "The Crosse," and the emblem of the French Ordre de St. Esprit.) Even Correggio's delightful small *Madonna of the Basket* in London (Fig. 86)

Fig. 137. Pinturicchio, *Madonna and Child with Saints,* c. 1490–95.

starting points—either from gloom or from jollity, but each, in its way, Christological. Naturalism here will not answer. Where the Child's spirit is somber, it is not because little Jesus is thought to be moody, peevish, or vexed, but because the young Christ, as conceived by Mantegna, Bellini, or Michelangelo, knows himself born to incipient death; and this despite the fact that the body blooms in full Italianate health. On the other hand, in the vision of Roger van der Weyden, Jesus displays the physical immaturity of the neonate, yet exposes his sex with exacting precision—and smiles (Figs. 22, 138). This glee is a marvel since, according to Aristotle and other ancient authorities, a baby awake does not smile until forty days after birth, when both mother and child are out of danger. The infant's first smile, then, becomes, as Reinach puts it, a formal taking possession of life (Reinach, "Le rire rituel," p. 590). And the neonate's smile is an awesome thing. Pliny reports that one child only since the race came into being smiled on its birthday: Zoroaster—significantly, as Norden points out, the founder of the first soterial religion (Norden, *Die Geburt des Kindes,* pp. 64ff.).

How much of this ancient lore survived through the Middle Ages on a folk level remains to be studied. Since an infant's first smile is an event waited for, cheered and bragged of in every home, it seems not unlikely that the canonic schedule would be remembered, even in 15th-century Flanders. If so, the undeveloped infant anatomy portrayed by Roger and his Northern followers should be seen in the light of the smile which often accompanies it. The physique is the neonate's; the smile, the sign of preternatural origin. At any rate, the prodigy of the smiling newborn is herewith offered as a hypothesis that seems to me preferable to the rachitic, which would have Roger naive

Fig. 138. Roger van der Weyden follower, *Madonna and Child,* after c. 1440.

enough to derive his norm of human infancy from rickety babies.

Assume the conjecture correct, and we are given a telling contrast: the Child raw, callow, ungainly as on the day of its birth, yet smiling as a normal baby would not; or, contrariwise, the Child battening and robust, yet oppressed by foreboding. In both alternatives, a duplex nature.

A word or two more on the laughing Child. Granted that young children make merry, and that this observation intrigued some Renaissance artists. Even in the early Quattrocento, long before they dispose of the requisite skill, they give us half-parted lips with intent to show the Child smiling. By the latter 15th century the problem as a task in naturalistic representation was mastered. But the impulse to depict a child's smile was initially an impulse to ascribe it to Christ. It was an idea about the divine Child's subjective response to humanation that posed the representational problem.

When a laughing Christ Child appears in one of Andrea del Sarto's Madonna groups—clutching his genitals as he points to his mother's breast, or chuckling to see her point to her bosom (Fig. 2)—the painter is telling us that he (unlike Mantegna, Bellini, or Michelangelo) imagines the nursling jubilant at his Incarnation, laughing for the very reason that the heavens rejoice. It is even conceivable that—in the vision of Rossellino, Piero di Cosimo, Raphael, Correggio, or Andrea del Sarto—God enjoys being man, tasting the goodness of his creation and the excellence of human milk. One thing is certain: the hilarity is projected as consonant with, better still, as indicative of the mystery. I doubt that it was ever meant to exhibit "the age-old relationship between the prescient Virgin and the unreflecting Child," as though a babyish want of reflection could overwhelm this Child's other nature (Pope-Hennessy, "The Virgin with the Laughing Child," p. 73, referring to Rossellino's terracotta group, Fig. 23). No Renaissance artist knew a Christ "unreflecting," whether living or dead, *in utero* or in infancy.

The Child's laughter does not enter Renaissance iconography because children frolic, as though it behooved the Christ Child to act only as others do. If he smiles, it is at least thinkable that he was meant to act like the savior child apostrophized in the closing lines of Vergil's Fourth Eclogue. The heavenly child of Vergil's messianic poem had been identified with the Christian Savior since the 4th century. At the end of the poem, the moment of parturition, he is exhorted: "Begin, baby boy, to know thy mother with a smile." For those Renaissance art-ists, Northern or Mediterranean, who conceived their Christ Child as newly born, its instant smile would be—like the imminent smile in the Eclogue—the signal of the birth of a god.

But I know of no text to indicate that artists of the 15th and 16th centuries meant their smiling Christ Child to obey the Vergilian apostrophe. The classic summary of the interpretative tradition of the Fourth Eclogue is Domenico Comparetti, *Vergil in the Middle Ages* [1895], London, 1966, chap. vii, "Vergil as Prophet of Christ." It throws no light on the problem. My suggestion that the human smile of the Christ Child is also a token of its divinity enters our catalogue only as an unproven hypothesis.

IX. God's greater deed

We are not accustomed to place material nature and human salvation on one intellectual track; scientific inquiry and soteriology have been diverging too long. But they were rated together by the Greek Fathers as first and second creation; and the second was adjudged more wonderful than the first (see Danielou, *The Bible and the Liturgy*, pp. 269–70). For St. Augustine, too, the redemption through Christ was a divine feat easily paired with the Creation; his saints, as they enter heaven, sing the ". . . praises of God in that he not only made what was not, but redeemed from corruption what he had made" (*City of God*, XXII, 17). Implicit in Augustine's vision of the Two Cities is the conviction that the City of God, immanent in the world since the coming of Christ, outranks the terrestrial creation. And the 12th-century Augustinian, Hugh of St. Victor, tips the balance decisively; he parallels the distinction between God's works of creation and those of restoration with the relative merits of the elect and the reprobate:

> You must understand that the elect assess the works of God in one way, the reprobate in another. For the elect reckon the works of restoration as superior to those of the first creation, because those were made for bondage, but the former were for our salvation. The reprobate, by contrast, love the works of creation more than those of restoration, because they seek present satisfaction, and not future bliss. The pagan philosophers, in searching out the nature of things with curiosity—that is, in inquiring into the works of creation, have become futile in their thoughts; but Christian sages, by meditating constantly upon the works of restoration, drive every vanity from theirs. The elect, considering their restoration, are kindled with the fire of love divine; the reprobate, with their false love of the loveliness of things created, grow cold in the love of God (*Noah's Ark*, IV, 11, pp. 137-38).

Now we learn from O'Malley (pp. 49, 139) that Renaissance preachers were willing likewise to rank the redemption the greater of the two deeds by which God is known. Yet in Hugh of St. Victor's askesis they might have perceived some ingratitude. For it is one thing to disparage the created world in its fallen condition. But God's decision to dwell creaturely within his creation rectified the created order. And to persist in contemning a world which God reconciled to himself by sharing its substance is to disdain the means employed in the redemption.

How orthodox theology would deal with this argument I am not certain. But it is the contained, inward argument of Renaissance art. Its world (to adapt Bonaventure's formula) is a world "known,

loved, and imitated," a world restored to admirable perfection, a natural order of divine institution and redeemed carnality.

X. The signal at the breast

The nursling eyeing the viewer and calling attention to what he is doing—this extraordinary motif becomes commonplace in Trecento painting and survives amazingly amidst untold variations through more than three hundred years (Figs. 59, 139, 141-43). But its simple

Fig. 139. Carlo di Camerino, *Madonna of Humility with Temptation of Eve.*

Fig. 140. Cima da Conegliano, *Madonna and Child,* c. 1510.

The commentary misses the demonstrativeness of the action, the urgency of its appeal, the sense of a message conveyed, as if to say, "I live with food like you— would you doubt my humanity?"

In art-historical literature, the message has not been received. Puzzled by the Infant's alerting glance in Cima's *Madonna and Child* in Amsterdam (Fig. 140), one scholar mistakes its grave summons for a momentary distraction: "La Madonna sta offrendo il seno al Bambino distratto e rivolto verso di noi. . . ." (Luigi Menegazzi in *Cima da Conegliano. Catalogo della Mostra,* Venice, 1962, no. 74, p. 55). Even the blatant paradox by which the summons is driven home in Bramantino's *Madonna and Child* (Fig. 141) has aroused only perplexity: William Suida found it "strange" ("cosa strana") that "the sturdy

meaning remains to be recognized. Millard Meiss interpreted the Child's hitherward glance while seeming to suck as another instance of the Trecento trend to invigorate the design and narrow the psychological distance between image and viewer.

> The intimacy between the Virgin and Child . . . effects a like intimacy between these figures and the spectator, and this is greatly enhanced by the behavior of the Child. Though nursing, he turns to look directly outward, and the Virgin in most examples does likewise. . . . The turn of the head and glance of the Infant out toward the spectator, while his body faces the Virgin and he presses her breast into his mouth, results in a combination of movements that is one of the remarkable innovations of early Trecento Italian art (Meiss, "The Madonna of Humility" [1936], in *Black Death,* p. 146).

Fig. 141. Bramantino, *Madonna and Child in a Landscape,* c. 1485.

babe is shown in the act of advancing toward the foreground, while sucking, as if in passing, the maternal breast, and gazing with intense self-consciousness at the spectator" (*Bramante Pittore e il Bramantino,* Milan, 1953, p. 67). Nor does Suida notice the simultaneous attention to the Child's loincloth, which must be part of the message: the assumption of both sex and hunger is the Child's twofold offering to the viewer.

Fig. 143. Ribera, *Madonna and Child,* 1643.

Fig. 142. Joos van Cleve Shop, *Holy Family,* c. 1520.

Sexual capability and dependence on food: these are defining traits of the human condition, and their polarity is implied in Renaissance paintings whenever the Christ Child designates or exposes at the same time his penis and the maternal breast (Figs. 2, 144, 145). The polarity is explicit in St. Augustine's sermon for Christmas (Sermon I, 23–24 [Ben. 51]; *Sermons,* pp. 52–56), which links eating and begetting as correlative instruments of survival:

> There are two works of the flesh upon which the preservation of mankind depends. . . . The first . . . has to do with taking nourishment. . . . But men subsist by this support only as far as they themselves are concerned; for they do not take measures for a succession by eating and drinking, but by marrying. . . . Since, then, the human race subsists in such wise that two supports . . . are indispensable, the wise and faithful man descends to both from a sense of duty; he does not fall into them through lust. . . . If these prudent and temperate people were offered the opportunity of living without

130

food and drink, with what great joy would they welcome this benefaction. . . . [The parallel was stated earlier:] If they could be given the opportunity of having children without marital intercourse, would they not embrace so great a privilege with the greatest enthusiasm?

Seven hundred years later, the thought is echoed by Hugh of St. Victor, whose wise man "sorrows even to have to satisfy those needs which the weakness of man's state imposes" (*Noah's Ark,* I, 3, p. 97).

Another six hundred years, and ship-wrecked Gulliver at last finds St. Augustine's ideal of rational, pleasureless procreation nobly realized by the Houyhnhnms (Jonathan Swift, *Gulliver's Travels* [1726], IV, chap. viii).

Fig. 144. Filippo Lippi, *Madonna and Child with Saints,* c. 1435–40, detail.

Fig. 145. Central Italian, *Madonna and Child with Saints* (overpainted), c. 1525–50.

XI. "Complete in all the parts of a man"

Following are three probable instances of indirect reference to the genitals of Christ in standard theology.

(1) An allusion to Christ's sexual member in circumcision may be intended when St. Bonaventure explains that as the infection of lust and corruption in us had "penetrated every part of the body," so Christ "suffered in every part of his body" (*Breviloquium,* IV, 5, p. 172).

(2) The reference is implicit when the mocking of Noah's nakedness (Gen. 9:21–25) is said to foreshadow the Passion—a typology in the 13th-century *Biblia pauperum* that goes back to St. Augustine: "The nakedness of [Noah] signifies the Savior's passion"; and again, "The passion of Christ was signified by that man's nakedness" (*City of God,* XVI, 2).

The genital focus in the analogy gains precision when the scene of the mocking of Noah appears depicted over an altar to which the Christ Child is brought for the Presentation (see the panel by the Master of the Life of the Virgin in the National Gallery, London).

(3) The eschatologies of both St. Augustine and St. Thomas Aquinas make reference to the pudenda of glorified bodies in an argument that necessarily implicates Christ's sexual member. Augustine speculates whether on the Last Day women shall be resurrected as women or in the optimal form of Christ's own masculinity. The question was forced upon him by the Gnostic pronouncement that women, having no place in the Kingdom, must either stay out or change sex. The closing paragraph of the Gospel of Thomas tells it as follows:

> Simon Peter said to them, "Let Mary leave us, for women are not worthy of life." Jesus said, "I myself shall lead her in order to make her male, so that she too may become a living spirit resembling you males. For every woman who will make herself male will enter the Kingdom of Heaven" (*Nag Hammadi Library*, p. 130).

Augustine rules (as will Aquinas, see our n. 20) that women shall rise female as they had lived. The passage deserves quoting in full (*City of God*, XXII, 17):

> For my part, I feel that theirs is the more sensible opinion who have no doubt that there will be both sexes at the Resurrection. . . . For . . . from those bodies vice shall be withdrawn, while nature shall be preserved. Now the sex of woman is not a vice, but nature. And in the Resurrection it will be free of the necessity of carnal intercourse and childbearing. How-

ever, the female organs shall remain adapted not to the old uses, but to a new beauty, which, so far from provoking lust, now extinct, shall excite praise to the wisdom and clemency of God.

The "new beauty" to which, in Augustine's fantasy, the female organ shall be adapted was, I suspect, suggested to him by the conventional obliteration of the rima in Hellenistic and Roman sculpture. Meanwhile, we note that the argument arises entirely from St. Paul's dictum that the resurrected will be "conformed to the image" — or "shaped into the likeness" — "of the Son of God" (Rom. 8:29; cf. Eph. 4:13). It is this promise which raises the issue whether those who had lived as women would resurrect with a female or, like Christ, with a male organ.

I add a fourth instance, drawn from somewhat marginal eschatology. In the debate whether Christ resurrected in a body still circumcised or with foreskin restored, the proponents of the former alternative argue that the Jews on the Last Day "would see him as the brother whom they had not received, and against whom they had contended most cruelly" (Carvajal, *Oratio in die circumcisionis*, fol. 9v).

XII. The necessary nudity of the suffering Christ

Nothing less than a sense of necessity on the part of Renaissance artists can account for developments such as the following:

In Trecento Italy, carved wooden crucifixes were usually draped with loincloths of fabric soaked in plaster. Under the cloths, no sexual members were carved — as none were painted in typical Trecento

Fig. 146. Donatello School, *Crucifix.*

scenes of Christ baptized. But on 15th-century crosses intended for similar public displays, the genitals, even though they were to be covered by plaster-soaked fabric, were fully rendered. Margrit Lisner cites examples by Michelozzo, Desiderio, Giuliano da Sangallo, and the young Michelangelo, and she observes *en passant* that these 15th-century crucifixes have carved genitalia as "an interpretation of the human nature of Christ." (Lisner, "The Crucifix from Santo Spirito," p. 813; to Lisner's examples we add the Donatellesque crucifix [Fig. 146] published both with and without its added loincloth, in Baldini/dal Poggetto, *Firenze restaura,* figs. 64, 65.)

A striking instance of later date is a crucifix after Giambologna (c. 1600). In the catalogue of the Giambologna exhibition held in London and Vienna (1978, no. 107a), the loincloth was described as a contemporary addendum ("Lendentuch eine wohl zeitgenössische Hinzufügung"). Catalogued again for a remarkable ex-

hibition at the Liebighaus, Frankfurt (*Dürers Verwandlung in der Skulptur,* 1981, no. 161), the work elicited the observation that "the meaning [of these naked crucifixes] has not been explored"; and that the novelty here is "not the representation of the nude, but the possibility of exposing the pudenda."

In painted representations of the Crucifixion—a subject in which Duccio and Giotto had introduced the diaphanous loincloth—a number of 14th- and 15th-century artists risk representing full nakedness, and they do so invariably in works of exceptional poignancy. (Figs. 38, 149. See also the *Crucifixions* in the Holkham Hall Bible, cited above, n. 31; Van Eyck's *Crucifixion* panels in Berlin, Fig. 147, and New York, The Metropolitan Museum of Art; Giovanni Angelo di Antonio, *Christ on the Cross,* Venice, Fondazione Cini, reprod. in Zampetti, *Paintings from the Marches,* fig. 72. For 16th-century examples, see Burgkmair's woodcut, our Fig. 148, and Dürer's *Large Calvary,* a

Fig. 147. Jan van Eyck (?), *Crucifixion,*
c. 1430.

Fig. 148. Hans Burgkmair, *Christ on the
Cross,* 1515.

drawing of 1505 in the Uffizi, copied both
in sculptured relief and engravings,
reprod. in *Dürers Verwandlung,* cat. 97.)
Roger van der Weyden invents the motif
of a breeze-driven sheet, not tied to the
body, but loosely floated against the loins,
as if by a sudden gust (Fig. 100).

Turn to images of the Flagellation.
From the early 15th-century onward,
they begin to show Christ totally naked.
(Examples: the Rohan Hours, Paris,
Bibliothèque Nationale, ms. lat. 9471,
fol. 214; Master of Marguerite d'Orléans,
Book of Hours, c. 1450, New York, Pierpont Morgan Library, ms. 190, fol. 50v;
a *Flagellation* panel by a 15th-century Lim-
bourg master, forming the painted wing
of a sculpted *Deposition* altarpiece, Paris,
Musée de Cluny; a Holbein school canvas
in the Kunstmuseum Basel.) The shock of
these works has hardly abated.

In scenes of the Lamentation, too, from
about 1400, the nakedness of the corpse
may be newly dramatized (Fig. 149).
Sometimes a mourner appears in the act

Fig. 149. Illumination from the Grandes
Heures de Rohan, *Lamentation,* c. 1420–25.

Fig. 150. Wolf Huber, *Lamentation*, 1524.

cency and the need to "follow the naked Christ." Perhaps this conflict explains why some painters, modest enough to keep the loins of Christ covered, will yet include a disturbing incipience of pubic hair, as if to say — if there must be concealment, let that which is hidden at least be confessed (see Antonello da Messina's *Man of Sorrows* in Madrid, Prado, and Rosso's *Dead Christ with Angels,* Boston, Museum of Fine Arts).

No motive now on the books justifies these phenomena. They project a religious vision unwilling to compromise with decorum — as we find it again in Crashaw's poem "On our crucified Lord Naked, and bloody": "Th' have left thee naked Lord, O that they had: / This garment too I would they had deny'd Thee. . . ."

XIII. Baptism and required dress

of drawing a cloth over Christ's loins (Figs. 107, 108; cf. also Meiss, *French Painting,* figs. 646, 648 for variants of this theme); or the Virgin, holding the deposed body, covers it by the vehement throw of a mantled arm (Pseudo-Jacquemart, c. 1400, ibid., fig. 216). In 16th-century German art, as in some Hans Baldung engravings, or in Wolf Huber's *Lamentation* (Fig. 150), the nakedness of the corpse is not uncommon. An outstanding example of a stark naked Christ is Rosso Fiorentino's *Pietà* in the Louvre. A rare later instance is Cavaliere d'Arpino's *Entombment* of c. 1606 (*Il Cavalier d'Arpino,* exh. cat., Rome, 1973, no. 41). D'Arpino is one of a handful of artists who carry the theme of the naked Christ into the 17th century.

Finally, post-Passion Christs often appear totally nude (e.g., Campin's *Mass of St. Gregory,* Friedländer, *Early Netherlandish Painting,* II, pl. 100, nos. Add. 150 and 73a); each work seeks an original resolution of the conflict between common de-

As a pictorial subject, Baptism presented artists with a delicate problem, since the sacrament was understood as a new birth. "In Baptism," wrote Theodore of Mopsuestia (c. 350–428; quoted in Danielou, *The Bible and the Liturgy,* p. 49), "the water becomes a womb for him who is born"; and such radical symbolism was not easily reconciled with the wearing of garments. Even the white raiment worn ritually over the naked body betokened ideal nudity, for Bishop Theodore says further: "Since you came up from Baptism, you are clad in a vestment that is all radiant. This is the sign of that shining world . . . to which you have already come by means of symbols. When indeed you receive the resurrection in full reality and are clothed with immortality and incorruptibility, you will have no further need of such garments" (ibid.). So also St. Gregory of Nyssa (c. 330–c. 395) speaks of the "robes of light," lost through the sin of Adam, to which the Christian is restored in the baptismal sacrament, wherein Christ has "taken away the fig-leaves, that garment of our misery, and clad us once more with a robe of glory" (ibid., p. 50).

Whatever the degree of actual nudity prescribed in Early Christian performances of the rite, in representations of Jesus baptized, he often appears wholly naked (Fig. 151). Until the end of the 6th century, this "unembarrassed type," as I would call it, preserves the antique habit of nude figuration. But it was the requisite Christian symbolism that allowed the habit to linger—in the exceptional instance of Baptism—before Christian interdiction took root.

The growth of a puritanical ethos in Early Christian art is traceable in the legend of the "Nude Crucifix of Nar-

Fig. 151. Byzantine mosaic, *Baptism of Christ,* c. 500, detail.

bonne," ably discussed by K. Wessel ("Der nackte Crucifixus von Narbonne"). The story comes to us through Gregory of Tours (c. 540–594) in his *Eight Books of Miracles* (*Miraculorum libri VIII,* I, 23). It tells of a priest named Basileus, who receives three nocturnal visitations from Christ. Terrible of aspect, the apparition demands that the painted image in the local cathedral, wherein he, Christ, appears girt with only a linen cloth, be decently covered over. Twice Basileus forgets; and is whipped for his negligence. Finally, he apprises his bishop, who orders the image veiled, to be exposed thereafter only for brief devotional exercises; whereupon the apparitions cease.

We do not know when the story first came to be told—Wessel points out that Gregory of Tours may have transcribed a legend more than a century old. But he reconstructs the likeliest circumstances under which such a legend would have arisen: presumably, during the 6th century, a picture of the Crucified in the Church of Narbonne was normally veiled by a curtain, and it would be this custom which the legend undertakes to explain. Wessel concludes that a traditional earlier (mid-5th-century?) image of the near naked Christ began to give umbrage in the course of the latter 5th and early 6th centuries. To demonstrate an analogous retreat from earlier nudity—first in the Eastern Empire, then in the West—he traces changes in representations of Daniel.

But we have a more direct index in representations of Christ's Baptism. From the 7th century on, artists having to cope with the subject faced an awkward dilemma: its natal and resurrectional symbolism called for full nudity, and the dignity of the protagonist demanded frontality; yet modesty forbade the display of his sex. (See Schiller, *Iconography,* I, figs. 376, 374, for two rare instances of evaded

136

frontality: a 12th-century stone relief on the Parma Baptistry portal, and an illumination from a Lower Saxon manuscript, c. 1200, in Trier Cathedral. Such attempts to escape the dilemma are instantly recognized as falling outside the tradition.)

Medieval artists tended to meet the difficulty in one of two ways: either by piling the baptismal water up to waist level and rendering it opaque with dark pigment or texture—and this I call the "embarrassed type" (see the 9th- and 10th-century examples in Schiller, figs. 366–71); or else, if the water was left transparent, by simply stripping the loins of genitalia (9th century [Schiller, fig. 372] through the late Gothic period, our Fig. 152). The choice was between hiding or nothing to

Fig. 152. Byzantine illumination, *Baptism of Christ,* 14th century.

hide. After about 1400, both these expedients—embarrassed and disembarrassed, respectively—were gradually discarded. And for good reasons: for even if, according to pious faith, it was the contact with Christ that purged the Jordan and so fitted it for its baptismal task, nevertheless, darksome water as a cleansing agent is an infelicitous medium; and the obliteration of the pudenda must have appeared no less offensive. Hence the emergence of two compromise solutions, of which the earlier (1200 to the mid-15th century) resorts to a gesture of modesty recalling that of the antique *Venus pudica:* the left hand covers the groin, the other, crossing the chest, rises in blessing. We are given a novel type, a *Christus pudicus,* or, in terms of our chronological sequence, a Christ re-embarrassed (Figs. 153–55; later examples are Simon Bening's *Baptism* of 1525–29 in the Prayerbook of Albrecht of Brandenburg, fol. 58v, now in the J. Paul Getty Museum, and the *Baptism* relief, 1531, on the choir screen of Amiens Cathedral). One-handed modesty gestures in scenes of Baptism are occasionally found earlier (Schiller, figs. 357, 379, 380). They become common again around 1400 (our Figs. 156, 157; Meiss, *French Painting,* figs. 98, 168, 229).

The final and definitive compromise consists in adapting to scenes of Baptism the loincloth that had been standard in Crucifixion imagery since the 5th century. Renaissance painting has made this motif so banal that we accept it unquestioningly, like a bathing suit at the beach. Yet Christian art had resisted this concession—the recourse to even a minimal garment at the baptismal moment—for almost a thousand years. It was adopted at last only when other alternatives to stark nudity were felt to have failed. In the judgment of Renaissance artists, tinctured water to effect intransparency must

Fig. 153. English enamel, *Baptism of Christ,* c. 1200.

have appeared naive, and the omission of a man's sex, simply monstrous.

The chronology of these developments leads to a surprising conclusion. Jesus' loins in Renaissance painting are draped; but the retirement of his genitalia behind shamefast gesture or breechcloth takes on a new meaning, the opposite of the obvious. We discover that the action of covering up, whether by hand or garment, is not imputed to Christ as a reflex of modesty, comparable to the posture of Adam possessed by the shame of pudenda. On the contrary, Renaissance *Baptisms* resort to the covering in order to remedy a dispossession of genitalia ascribed to

Christ's body in older pictures; they protest against the prior negation. In short, the loincloth that becomes standard attire in Renaissance *Baptisms* and for ever after was initially charged, like the foregoing pudicity gesture, to reverse an intolerable deprivation. Its function was to affirm the presence of what was concealed. Without

Fig. 154. Limoges School, *Baptism of Christ,* c. 1250.

Fig. 155. Roger van der Weyden (copy), *Baptism of Christ,* after c. 1450.

Fig. 156. Illumination from the Très Belles Heures de Notre-Dame, *Baptism of Christ*, c. 1390.

Fig. 157. Flemish, *Baptism of Christ*, c. 1400.

offense to propriety, it gave assurance that the Incarnate was complete in every part of a man. I close this Excursus with a passage from a French Passion play of the early 16th century, presumably based on an earlier tradition:

JESUS
Baptize me, if you will!
SAINT JOHN
Baptize you?

. . .

You who come to save us all.
JESUS
Good knight, do not speak such
   words.
We must now, between us,
Humbly fulfill
All righteousness.
SAINT JOHN
Oh, precious, holy flesh,
I would not dare to touch you.
Naked must I see you, my Lord.
To begin the New Law.

Jesus disrobes. Then let the dove descend
   near Jesus.

JESUS
Now I am naked; baptize me
Without further protest.

Let SAINT JOHN, *pouring the water,*
   say in a loud voice
Sanctify me, good Jesus,
Sanctify me, my savior!

. . .

Then let Jesus put on his clothes.

GOD THE FATHER *to his angels*
This is my beloved son
Who has initiated baptism.
He has ended circumcision.

(*The Baptism and Temptation of Christ: The First Day of a Medieval French Passion Play,* trans. John R. Elliott, Jr., and Graham Runnalls, New Haven and London, 1978, pp. 77–79.)

XIV. The virginity of Christ

The phrase from Tertullian (c. 160–230) cited in the text is taken from his *De monogamia*, 5: "This more perfect Adam, Christ—more perfect because more pure—having come in the flesh to set your infirmity an example, presents Himself to you in the flesh, if you will but receive Him, a man entirely virginal" (*Treatises*, p. 80). The St. Methodius passage that precedes the title "Archvirgin" reads: "What then did the Lord, the Truth and the Light, accomplish on coming down to the world: He preserved His flesh incorrupt in virginity with which He had adorned it. And so let us too, if we are to come to the likeness of God, endeavor to aspire to the virginity of Christ. For becoming like to God means to banish corruptibility . . ." (*Symposium*, Logos I, 5, p. 47).

The St. Jerome quotations in the text are taken from Epistles XXII, 19 and XLIX (*Letters*, p. 151, and Kelly, *Early Christian Doctrines*, p. 189). Elsewhere, Jerome writes, intending to include married couples: "All those who have not remained virgins, following the pattern of the pure chastity of angels and that of our Lord Jesus Christ himself, are polluted" (*Against Jovinian*, I, 40; quoted in Pelikan, *Christian Tradition*, I, p. 289).

For the Photius passage, see his Homily VII, 6, p. 145.

The tradition runs from the Apocalypse (14:4)—"Who were not defiled with women, for they are virgins. These follow the Lamb . . ."—to Jean Gerson: "Jesus Christ as a virgin is married to the Holy Church, similarly a virgin . . ." (*Considérations sur S. Joseph*, 1413, in *Oeuvres complètes*, ed. P. Glorieux, Paris, 1966, VII, p. 64). But it was St. Bernard who, in his forty-seventh sermon on Canticles (*Song of Songs*, p. 7), encapsulated the doctrine in the most elegant pun ("a virgin shoot sprung from a virgin"): *virgo virga virgine generatus*.

XV. Potency under check

"It is necessity that makes another a eunuch, my own choice makes me so," writes the proud St. Jerome (Epistle XXII, 19; *Letters*, p. 150). For some of the orthodox Fathers, notably St. Methodius, voluntary chastity is the test of man's likeness to God (Musurillo, introd. to *The Symposium*, p. 7). Askesis here is indissociable from the exercise of free will. For it was in the faculty of volition that man, before the Fall, was made in God's image; and that faculty is supremely demonstrated in man's ability to choose chastity—not on occasion, but in sustained continence.

Christ's commendation of those who make themselves eunuchs for heaven's sake was taken literally by Origen, the 3rd-century Father. Son of a Christian martyr, he had in his youth committed the "headstrong act" of castrating himself—a notorious error which he later repudiated. (The story and its consequences are recounted in Eusebius, *History of the Church*, VI, 8, p. 247.)

If the connection between commendable chastity and free will seems somewhat obvious, the point of it still escaped the great Edward Gibbon. A footnote in chapter 69 of the *Decline and Fall* lifts from Hume's *History of England* the following account of the cruelty of Geoffrey Plantagenet, father of Henry II: "When he was master of Normandy the chapter of Seez presumed, without his consent, to proceed to the election of a bishop: upon which he ordered all of them, with the bishop elect, to be castrated, and made all their testicles be brought him in a platter."

Gibbon comments: "Of the pain and danger they might justly complain; yet, since they had vowed chastity he deprived them of a superfluous treasure."

Fine English wit; wretched theology. Geoffrey's victims had more to complain of than pain and danger: they had been robbed of the merit of volitional abstinence in imitation of Christ.

XVI. Concerning Michelangelo's *Risen Christ*

The longer one dwells on the theological grounds for genital shame, the more imperative that Christ be therefrom exempted. This exemption, overruling propriety, must be the Christian meaning of the nakedness of Michelangelo's *Risen Christ* in the church of the Minerva in Rome. But on this point, our professional literature is distracted. The undress of the statue still impels Michelangelo scholars to discover its cause outside Christianity. "Michelangelo has conceived the Man of Sorrows as a naked hero of antiquity," wrote Herbert von Einem (*Michelangelo* [1959], London, 1973, p. 127). And Wolfgang Lotz: "Michelangelo's creation reflects rather the antique conception of the god who appears among men in supreme earthly beauty, than the post-antique conception of the 'spiritualized,' crucified and resurrected Son of the transcendent God" ("Zu Michelangelos Christus in S. Maria sopra Minerva," p. 148). Near the close of his article, Lotz cites the nudity of the statue as one reason for its proven unsuitability as a religious cult image. He points out that all preserved replicas, the earliest of which dates from the 1580s, show the figure with a loincloth, even though the nudity was stipulated in the original contract: "un Cristo grande quanto al naturale, ignudo, ritto, con una croce in braccio." (The word

"ignudo" need not mean total nudity; in common parlance even penitents stripped to the waist were called "nude," and the Roman signatories to the contract may have gotten more nudity than they expected.) But Lotz adds this significant sentence: "For Michelangelo this nudity must have been an essential part of the work's 'spiritual content'" ("Sie [die Nacktheit] muss für Michelangelo ein wesentlicher Teil des 'geistigen Gehaltes' gewesen sein," p. 149). He did not stay to define the spiritual content that would have been served by an *ostentatio genitalium;* Wolfgang Lotz died in October 1981.

Meanwhile, modern Michelangelo monographs continue to cling to aestheticism:

The nature of this Christ is ambiguous and the reasons for its total nudity are obscure. . . . We see here Michelangelo's unabashed love, even hunger, for the beauty of the nude figure, which from the rear could be in every sense a pagan work. It is ultimately this conflict between pagan nude and the Man of Sorrows of Christian iconography that has placed Michelangelo's Christ in a special limbo, separate from all his other works (Howard Hibbard, *Michelangelo,* New York, 1974, pp. 168–69).

As my text argues, the "conflict" here is not between the rival attractions of Christian iconography and pagan nudism. The conflict inheres in the Christian content, caught between the competing claims of morality and the exemptive nature of the body of Christ. Of course, the normal alternative of a Christ figure modestly draped is no less justifiable. Leagued with the moralist, even the theologian might agree that Christ needs a loincloth, not to conform to his own proper nature, but in concession to ours—so that lewd ogling not be encouraged. But that, in 1514–20, was not Michelangelo's worry. He would have shrugged and approved Calvin's quote from Augustine: "If you receive carnally, it does not cease to be spiritual, but it is not so for you" (Calvin, *Institutes of the Christian Religion,* IV, xiv, 16).

The dictates of carnal decorum became compelling before the end of the 16th century. And by 1630, the nudity of Michelangelo's statue at the Minerva furnished the subject of an apocryphal anecdote told by the Sicilian chronicler Francesco Baronio (*De Panormitana majestate libri IV,* Leiden, [1630], III, 96, p. 102):

> When Michelangelo Buonarroti, in Rome, had carved a Christ our Lord and had made him with his male parts unencumbered [laid bare or set free — *humanis partibus absolvisset*], it befell that when he placed the statue on view . . . a certain man, indignant at seeing Christ Jesus covered by no human garment, girded him with a linen cloth, so that he might not seem indecorous. Michelangelo, unable to endure this, snatched it away. The man put another back; again he [the artist] in vain tore it to pieces. . . .

Baronio's contentious fable is ill-conceived. Michelangelo's statue was not carved in Rome; it was shipped unfinished from Florence, and the sculptor did not attend its installation; nor did the mature Michelangelo at any time show the least interest in work once delivered. But the very improbability of the invention (recalling the 6th-century legend about the crucifix at Narbonne; see Excursus XIII) betrays the quandary which Christians found so hard to resolve wherever the vision of the *nudus Christus* had to be faced, not as a metaphorical trope (like *nuda veritas*), but in earnest.

XVII. Of the nudity of the Christ Child

Two great medievalists — Emile Mâle and Millard Meiss — gave thought to the phenomenon of Christ's nudity. Under the head "Aspects nouveaux du groupe de la Mère et de l'Enfant," Mâle wrote this important passage (*L'Art religieux,* p. 147):

> In the 12th century, the Son of God, seated on the lap of his mother, is robed in the long tunic and the philosophers' pallium; in the 13th, he wears a child's dress; in the 14th, he would be entirely naked did not his mother wrap his lower body in a fold of her mantle. This nudity of Christ is, as it were, the mark of his humanity; he now resembles the children of humankind. He resembles them further in his whims, his lovable infant capers [*aimables enfantillages*], whether caressing his mother's chin, or at play with a bird. He resembles them, finally, in his subjection to nature [*par les fatalités de la nature*]: the Son of God feels hungry, and the artists show the Virgin giving him suck.

These, when first published, were pioneering insights. Mâle saw correctly that the Child's nakedness serves 14th-century painters as an index of its humanity; that the Infant is ranked with other nurslings even in its hunger for milk. But in perceiving only a process of humanization, Mâle mistook the boy's caress of the Virgin's chin, or his clutching a bird, for playful sport that could have been any baby's. He ignored the appellant gaze of the Child while at the breast, and would not see that the mother's mantle, seeming to cloak the Child's *bas du corps,* might be an unveiling. The mystery of humanation which the artists projected by way of a naturalism fraught with symbol, scandal, and paradox, was demystified, as though the sole impulse had been to render the Infant lifelike and run-of-the-mill.

Meiss' chapter on the evolution of the nude image of Christ (*French Painting,* pp. 125–30) proceeds similarly without regard to the theological motive. He observes "the decision to allow the Child to appear quite nude at the ceremonial occasion of the homage of the Magi"; finds this decision taken in 14th-century painting in Alsace and Bohemia, and widely diffused by the end of the century. But he adds at once that it was "not only the Christ Child when adored by the Magi whom certain centers in the later fourteenth century wished to see nude"—"there are a few other very unusual nude figures that suggest a broader concern with the unclothed body." Of this "broader concern" the first example cited is a stark naked Christ in a Catalan *Crucifixion* of c. 1355–60 (Fig. 38 left). But in this altarpiece, the thieves flanking the central cross wear ample aprons, so that here again, in Meiss' prime exhibit, the "broad concern" is, in fact, narrowly focused on the nakedness of the Christ. (The distinction between a wholly or nearly nude Christ and well-aproned thieves is made elsewhere, as in the Holkham Hall Bible, fol. 32 [see n. 31 above], and again in the Rohan Hours, Paris, Bibliothèque Nationale, ms. lat. 9471, fol. 27.)

Meiss discovers a "more startling instance of nudity" in a *Nativity* scene from a Tyrolese altarpiece of c. 1370: the Virgin abed—"at the moment of parturition"—appears nude from the waist up, "rendered with the tender sensuousness of a Renaissance Venus." This work and a comparable *Birth of the Virgin* from Lombardy (c. 1383; his figs. 557, 558) are said to reflect "the habit of sleeping without clothes." Perhaps so; but if the author had

information about a change in Tyrolean sleeping habits around 1370, he chose not to share it. He did not wonder whether a woman would dress for sleep "at the moment of parturition"; nor consider the hierarchic distinction between upper and lower body (discussed below, Excursus XVIII); nor the special dignity of Mary's, or of her mother's, bosom. He was positing a general concern with the unclothed body so as to undistinguish the special undress of the Child initiated in cult images half a century earlier. The Christ Child's nakedness was to be not a symbolic value but a "manifestation of nudism," introduced because "infancy [was] associated on naturalistic grounds with both nudity and nursing."

Reflecting on the general evolution of nudity in the Trecento, Meiss found the great Tuscan centers "conspicuously absent from this development"—until Masaccio in the 1420s based his nude Christ Child on antique models. "Evidently," he wrote, "the nudity of the Christ Child was acceptable to the Florentines only when it assumed a classical, indeed pagan form—a rather paradoxical situation."

To us the facts look somewhat different, since we find the Child's total nudity, the "altogether," less interesting than the anxiety to achieve it. In this enterprise, Florence, in the century before Masaccio, is fully engaged—witness the standing Child, nude under all-showing gossamer, in the panels by Maso di Banco and Nardo di Cione (Figs. 32, 36). And we see even this as a denouement, following the gradual unveiling that began c. 1260 with the hoisting, parting, and thinning of the Child's dress (see Excursus XIX). As for classical models, their entrance is tardy: it was only when nudity, or a close approximation of it, had been achieved that antique forms became relevant as correctives and paradigms. But nudity was not initially visited on the image of

Christ "on naturalistic grounds," or through pagan influence; it flowered within the devotional subject, fostered by a determination to see Christ naked.

Yet the urge to explain the precocious nakedness of the Child in 14th-century art without crediting Christian motives remains strangely persistent. And it has led at least one modern art historian to adopt a socio-economic model. He proposes to read our 14th-century icons as social protests conceived somewhat in the spirit of Käthe Kollwitz, with the Infant's nakedness pleading the neediest cases: I quote from a recent issue of *Kunstchronik:*

> Mary with the nude Child in the 14th century. The Child is truly a child, and it was then (as it still is) contrary to custom to display a noble child naked. What decisive events and experiences lie behind this? I surmise: the terrible hardships suffered during the 14th century, when crop failures, famine, and epidemics created great labor shortages far and wide. The nude Christ Child in its indigence is a cry for help directed to God: "Let our children live!" [Das nackte Jesuskind in seiner Bedürftigkeit ist ein Hilferuf an Gott: "Lass unsere Kinder leben!"] (*Kunstchronik,* 36 [January 1983], p. 54, summarizing a public lecture delivered by Rudolf Zeitler in Kassel, September 23, 1982).

The author seems not to have noticed how often the nudity of the 14th-century Christ Child is artfully managed by the shunting of precious fabrics, and amid gifts of gold, frankincense, and myrrh. One would take his pleading for a burlesque of neo-Marxist historiography, but the context forbids.

XVIII. The body as hierarchy

The human body as a hierarchical system is a conceit of Late Antiquity, if not older. According to Artemidorus, "many dream interpreters think that the feet signify menials" (*Oneirocritica,* or *Interpretation of Dreams,* p. 40). Inevitably, such or similar rank ordering was applied to the Incarnation; head and feet respectively polarized the divine and the human. Thus Eusebius: "The nature of Christ is twofold; it is like the head of the body in that He is recognized as God, and comparable to the feet in that for our salvation He put on manhood as frail as our own" (*History of the Church,* I, 2, p. 33). The 7th-century Byzantine theologian St. Maximus Confessor taught as follows: "Whoever says that the words of theology 'stand at the head' because of the deity of Christ, while the words of the dispensation 'stand at the feet' because of the Incarnation, and whoever calls the head of Christ his divinity, and the feet his humanity, he does not stray from the truth" (*Liber ambiguorum, Pat. Gr.,* 91, col. 1379).

Simon the New Theologian (d. 1022) assigns distinct functions to the members of the body of Christ conceived as a figure of the Church. Among these members the "thighs" stand for "those who bear within themselves the generative power of the divine ideas of mystical theology and who give birth to the Spirit of salvation on earth" (*Ethical Orations,* I, 6; quoted in Pelikan, *Christian Tradition,* II, p. 256).

The notion of the God-man's body as a rank-ordered system appears in the West in St. Bernard's restatement: "If it seemed right to St. Paul to describe Christ's head in terms of his divinity (I Cor. 11:3), it should not seem unreasonable to us to ascribe the feet to his humanity" (*Song of Songs,* Sermon VI, 6, p. 35). Cf. the French text, apparently 17th century, quoted (as usual without source) in Anna Jameson's *Legends of the Madonna* (ed. London, 1903, p. 47): "Dieu montre par ses pieds nus qu'il a pris le corps de l'homme." The topos is discussed by Ernst Kantorowicz (*The King's Two Bodies,* pp. 70–75) with emphasis on St. Augustine's exegesis of Psalms 90 and 91, whose drift Kantorowicz summarizes as *pedes in terra, caput in coelo*—feet on earth, head in heaven. He adduces the familiar image of the Ascension, wherein Western artists, from Ottonian times to the Cinquecento, depicted a "disappearing Christ," whose "feet alone—the symbol of the Incarnation—remain as a visible token of the historical fact that the Incarnate has migrated on earth." (For the iconography of the "Disappearing Christ," see Meyer Schapiro in *Gazette des Beaux-Arts,* 85 [1943], p. 147.)

The symbolism is ancient only in origin. Renaissance artists continued to take it for granted, so that we recognize the trope "feet on earth, head in heaven" even in the naturalistic staging of Leonardo's *Last Supper;* see L. Steinberg, "Leonardo's *Last Supper,*" *The Art Quarterly,* 36 (1973), p. 388, n. 32. In a nearly contemporaneous image, Mazzolino's *Nativity* of 1510 in the Ferrara Pinacoteca, the idea is spelled out with quaint literalness: the Christ Child inhabits a body-sized bubble halo that excludes only the loins and legs. The Christ of Michelangelo's *Last Judgment* still honors this ancient tradition.

We must add that the symbolism is fluctuant. Feet, thighs, lower body, and genitalia are treated as interchangeable, depending on context. Marvin H. Pope (*Anchor Bible,* p. 381) points out that "'feet' is a standard biblical euphemism for genitalia"—St. Jerome appropriates it for the harlot who "opens her feet to every one that passes by" (Epistle XXII, 6; Jerome, *Letters,* p. 139). The 12th-century poet Bernardus Silvestris (Economou,

The Goddess Natura, p. 158), conceives the human body in three major divisions—head, breast, and loins, the lower appendages being comprised under the last. Within the inferior region, further differentiation would serve no useful symbolic purpose; what matters is the contrast to the superior dignity of head and breast. The topos is recognizable in King Lear's "But to the girdle do the gods inherit," and again in Goethe's assertion that "all ethical expression pertains only to the upper part of the body" ("Jeder sittliche Ausdruck gehört nur dem oberen Teil des Körpers an"; see "Über Leonardo da Vincis Abendmahl zu Mailand," 1817). The feet themselves may be menial or humble, or may simply signify the whole lower stratum, summarily identified with the generative function. Thus Pico della Mirandola, in the closing paragraph of the *Heptaplus or Discourse on the Seven Days of Creation* (1489), analyzing the body on the lines of Bernardus Silvestris, finds it "astonishing how beautifully and how perfectly" the three parts of man—head, neck-to-navel, and navel-to-feet—"correspond . . . to the three parts of the world. The brain, source of knowledge, is in the head; the heart, source of movement, life, and heat, is in the chest; the genital organs, the beginning of reproduction, are located in the lowest part" (*Heptaplus,* p. 113).

Given the prevalence of these metaphors, it should not astonish us to see artists responding to the spirit of incarnational theology by focusing on Christ's lower body and denuding the Child from the feet upward. They were confronting a system whose major divisions carried specific symbolic values.

XIX. 14th-century nudity

The hieratic Byzantine image of the Madonna and Child allowed the Child's nakedness only in unshod feet—left bare perhaps from that same symbolic consideration which we discern in the later works of the West. For the latter, this token nudity no longer sufficed; the garment recedes to expose the knees (Figs. 29, 158, 159, 163; comparable examples are: the Florentine panel of the *Madonna and Child,* c. 1270, at the Yale University Art Gallery; a *Madonna and Child with Saints* by the Magdalen Master [art market]; Guido da Siena's *Maestà,* Siena, Palazzo Pubblico, and the *Madonna and Child Enthroned,* by his shop, Florence, Galleria Accademia; the *Madonna and Child* panel by a Cimabue follower in Turin, Galleria Sabauda; Master of the Fogg Pietà, *Madonna and Child Enthroned,* Assisi, San Francesco, Lower Church; three panels of the *Madonna and Child* by Deodato Orlandi [Pisa, Museo Civico, and two in private collections]; Giuliano da Rimini, *Madonna and Child with Saints,* Boston, Isabella Stewart Gardner Museum).

Two more examples of total nudity in 14th-century Bohemian art are reproduced in Karel Stejskal, *European Art in the 14th Century,* London, 1978: an *Adoration of the Magi* panel in the Pierpont Morgan Library, c. 1355, fig. 38; and a wood statue of the *Madonna and Child,* c. 1360, Karlstein Castle, Prague, fig. 90. In at least two further instances, the Child's gesture of covering or indicating the genitals assures us that the objective of this total nudity is the *ostentatio genitalium:* a drawing by Master Oswald of the *Madonna and Child with St. Wenceslas,* c. 1360, Stockholm, Royal Library, fig. 101; and a *Nativity,* in a historiated initial of the Liber Viaticus of John of Středa, Prague, Národní Galerie, before 1360, fig. 48.

Fig. 158. Guido da Siena, *Madonna and Child Enthroned,* 1262.

Fig. 159. Cimabue (?), *Madonna and Child with Two Angels,* c. 1300.

146

The token covering of the Child's nudity by transparent garments or veils is a motif common throughout the Trecento. For the transparent chemise, see also Figs. 160–62; and the *Madonna and Child* panel by Simone dei Crocefissi in Bologna, Pinacoteca Nazionale.

Surprisingly frequent is the accent on the Child's groin by the action of the Madonna's hand (Figs. 33–35, 163, 164). In later painting the motif of indication, whether assigned to the Virgin or to the Child, becomes more overt; see Figs. 4, 42, 45, 196, etc.; as well as Andrea di Giusto's polyptych of the *Madonna and Child Enthroned with Saints,* 1435, Prato, Galleria Communale; the Master E.S. engraving of 1467 (Lehrs 76); and Cranach's *Madonna and Child with Sts. Catherine and Barbara* at Erfurt, c. 1522.

Fig. 161. Maso di Banco, *Madonna and Child,* c. 1340.

Fig. 160. Lippo di Benivieni, *Madonna and Child,* c. 1330 (?).

Fig. 162. Lippo Dalmasio, *Madonna del Velluto,* c. 1400.

Fig. 163. Master of the Magdalen, *Madonna and Child Enthroned,* c. 1280.

Fig. 164. Sienese (Duccio?), *Madonna and Child Enthroned,* c. 1290–1300.

XX. "Swags of gossamer about the hips"

Among the vanities that kindled the righteous bonfires of Savonarola, George Eliot distinguished "transparent veils intended to provoke inquisitive glances" (*Romola,* chap. 59). To such gear, writers modern and ancient, Christian and pagan, have generally brought stern disapproval, or at least irony — one hears of the filmy gowns of Tarentum, of flesh-flattering silks brought in from Cos, or "imported at vast expense from nations unknown even to trade" (Seneca). Lucian described "clothes of a tissue as fine as a spider's web [which] pass for clothes so as to excuse the appearance of complete nakedness." Seneca deplored "silken raiments — if that can be called raiment, which provides no protection for the body, or indeed modesty, so that, when a woman wears it, she can scarcely, with a clear conscience, swear that she is not naked." (Seneca, *De beneficiis,* VII, 9, in *Moral Essays,* II, trans. John W. Basore, Cambridge, Mass., 1935, pp. 478–79; Lucian, *Amores,* XLI, trans. M. D. Macleod, Cambridge, Mass., 1967, pp. 212–13). The stated objection is not so much to undress, as to the falsehood of fabrics that pretend otherwise. Transparent weaves over bare skin strike ancient censors as instruments of deceit and seduction. And yet, when such fabrics surface again in the Trecento, it is the flesh of the Christ Child they celebrate.

The fine cloths reproved by the moralists still served as garments, however inadequate. We do not hear of them being manipulated for erotic effect — as we see them dandled by the Renaissance *Venuses* of Antico, Lorenzo Costa, Lorenzo di Credi, Hans Baldung, and Lucas Cranach (Figs. 165–67); or by Lucas van Leyden's *Fortuna* (Fig. 168). These veils charming a woman's flanks were meant to delight. And what we need to explain is the prior appearance of just such paraphernalia and of similar provocation in 14th- and 15th-century images of the young Christ (Fig. 169; see also Excursus XXI). Perhaps we must rank the striptease with the drama, the dance, and the oratorio as another cultural form whose deep roots are religious.

Fig. 165. Lorenzo Costa, *Venus,* c. 1500.

Fig. 166. Lucas Cranach, *Venus and Cupid,* 1531.

Fig. 167. Lucas Cranach, *Venus,* 1532.   Fig. 168. Lucas van Leyden, *Fortuna.*

Fig. 169. Jean Bellegambe (?), *Holy Family,* c. 1520, detail.

XXI. Exposure as revelation

Fig. 170. Fiorenzo di Lorenzo. *Madonna and Child with St. Jerome,* detail.

Fig. 171. Piero di Cosimo, *Madonna and Child Enthroned with Saints,* c. 1515.

Fig. 172. Francesco Pesellino, *Madonna and Child with St. John,* c. 1455.

Fig. 173. Zanobi Machiavelli, *Madonna and Child,* c. 1460.

Fig. 174. Francesco del Cossa, *Madonna and Child,* detail from the Pala dei Mercanti, 1474.

Fig. 175. Giovanni della Robbia, *Madonna and Child,* c. 1490–1500.

Fig. 176. Titian, *Madonna and Child,* c. 1510–20.

Fig. 177. Francesco Pesellino, *Madonna and Child with Six Saints,* c. 1445–50.

Fig. 178. Sebastiano Mainardi, *Madonna and Child with St. John,* c. 1490.

Fig. 180. Correggio, *Madonna del Latte,* c. 1525.

Fig. 179. Bramantino, *Madonna Trivulzio,* c. 1512.

Fig. 181. Botticelli School, *Madonna and Child with Pomegranate,* c. 1495.

Fig. 182. Giovanni Dalmata, *Madonna and Child,* c. 1471–77.

Fig. 183. Imitator of Antonio Rossellino, *Barney Madonna.*

Figs. 170–82 reproduce select further instances of uncensored showings. These should be mentally supplemented by innumerable works whose original genital emphasis has been suppressed and dissembled by subsequent overpainting (see Excursus XXXI).

Fig. 183 is a special case. It reproduces a marble relief of the *Madonna and Child,* formerly attributed to Antonio Rossellino, but condemned by John Pope-Hennessy as the work of an unknown forger of the second half of the 19th century. The author is the best authority in the field of Italian Renaissance sculpture, and one would be inclined to believe him even if he offered no arguments for his opinion. But Pope-Hennessy had the courtesy to state his grounds as follows: "That this [relief] dates from the nineteenth century is not open to doubt; the angels which overlap the moulding, the cherub head which is inserted on the left, the carving of the Virgin's head and the throne with a full-length putto on an arm, all prove de-

cisively that that is so. One of the hallmarks of this sculptor is the fact that he first dresses up the Child, and then, in a rather muddled fashion, undresses him" ("The Forging of Italian Renaissance Sculpture," *Apollo,* 99 [April 1974], p. 252).

The closing argument is the most fully stated, but it is not entirely clear. Is it only the "muddled fashion" that betrays the hand of the forger, or the very fact that the Child is undressed after being "dressed up"? If the latter is meant, then we have been given something to think about, irrespective of the status assigned to the relief. We have learned that the widespread phenomenon I am discussing, the frequent arrangement of "fabrics fussed so as not to hinder the showing," has not been decisively registered even by the most attentive observer. Our anonymous 19th-century forger becomes the first modern to recognize that the purposeful dressing up to undress had been a characteristic Quattrocento motif.

XXII. A Digression on the "Stone of Unction"

The supposed relic on which the body of Christ was anointed for burial is a pious fraud, first fabled in 12th-century Constantinople, lost sight of after the Fourth Crusade (1204), and produced again in the early 19th century for permanent installation at the Church of the Holy Sepulcher in Jerusalem. The modern literature on the subject has cultivated confusion ever since 1860, when the young Charles Jean Melchior, Marquis de Vogüé, published his *Les Eglises de la Terre Sainte.* Vogüé's errors were magnified in 1916 by Gabriel Millet, amplified subsequently by others, and remain to this day uncorrected. An attempt to expose some of the current falsehoods was made in my (unpublished) convocation address to the College Art Association Conference in Washington, D.C., in January 1975. Since the corrective material bulks too large for the present occasion, I confine myself to a note concerning one major painting whose symbolism is too eloquent to be needlessly muddled.

To qualify as the legendary Stone of Unction, the platform supporting the deposed Christ in a painting (or embroidered aer) must satisfy several conditions: (1) it must be, as originally described, a movable slab of red, white-veined stone; (2) it must be wept over by the Madonna; (3) as a minimal reference to the rite, it must at the very least show an ointment jar ready for use; (4) its surface must be reserved for the revered body and may never be trampled on. Not one of these conditions is met in the famous picture now chiefly associated with the Unction Stone—Caravaggio's *Entombment* of 1602–04. Here the huge plinth supports a half dozen figures; and the corpse, carried leftward to where the entrance of the sepulcher looms, is not being laid upon it. (People don't step upon a bench or a tabletop if they mean to lay something on it.) Therefore, the object that so blatantly juts from the picture out is no Stone of Unction. But this disqualification does not degrade it. On the contrary, the huge, hovering base underpropping the compressed cluster of mourners becomes more tremendous, more fundamental, when we see that it must be the slab destined to seal the rectangular opening of the sepulcher. (In the original painting in the Vatican Pinacoteca, this opening was only faintly visible before recent cleaning. It shows well in Guattani's engraving [1784] and in old painted replicas—even in the ruined copy in the Fogg Art Museum at Cambridge.)

Caravaggio gave the supporting slab extraordinary dramatic presence. He dignified it by the touch of Christ's fingers and the caress of the shroud. At bottom right, in its shadow, he engloomed a dejected plant to contrast with the fresh growth under its lighted face; propped it on cobbles as though to facilitate lifting; and honed its extruded angle to perfect congruence with the right-angled entranceway of the tomb. The stone's thickness, sufficient to carry the weight of all, shows it infrangible and resistant to penetration, an unbreakable seal. Thus is foreshown the wonder of the Resurrection, when the risen Christ passes through—not in spirit but bodily; passing through as in his miracle birth, without breaking the barrier. Preachers had stressed the sheer physicality of the miracle: "He issued forth from the sepulcher without removing the stone; and thus there were two bodies at the same time in the same place. O you philosophers, what say you now? This effect is altogether contrary to your philosophy: two bodies at once in the same place" (Savonarola, *Predica sopra Giobbe,* ed. Roberto Ridolfi, Predica XLIV

[Easter sermon], Rome, 1957, II, p. 376).

This, I believe, is the promised marvel which Caravaggio's vision holds out. This is why a finger of Christ's right arm (the veins of which are engorged as a dead man's are not) pointedly touches the stone—a pledge not lost on the watchful St. John. And it is fitting that the stone's salient corner be brightest lit, beetling over the altar. Caravaggio's impassable block is the port designate of the Resurrection.

For the Stone of Unction, meanwhile, we look elsewhere. Its earliest, most impressive and accurate representation is the lapidary support of Mantegna's foreshortened *Dead Christ* in the Brera (Fig. 58).

XXIII. The eighth day

For the Church Fathers the phases of eschatological time were as the days of the week; they saw the present world figured by the seven days of Creation, the world to come by the eighth. "The day of the Lord," writes St. Basil, "is the future age, the eighth day which is beyond the cosmic week" (Danielou, *The Bible and the Liturgy,* p. 266). St. Methodius (fl. 270–309) sees the first five days corresponding to the period of the Temple, of ritual law, and of man's progress from incest to monogamy. The sixth day marks the period of the Church in the world. The seventh signifies the millennium consequent upon the general resurrection—to be superseded at last by the eighth day which, following upon shadow and image, brings the reality of heaven, of immortality in eternity (Musurillo, introd. to *Symposium,* p. 35).

Eight hundred years later, Hugh of St. Victor explained that "because of the five senses, the number five aptly represents natural men. . . . The number six suits spiritual persons. . . . The number seven, signifying rest, is proper to the souls who rest in . . . anticipation of the glory of the resurrection. The number eight, which signifies beatitude, fits those who, having already received back their bodies, rejoice in blessed immortality" (*Noah's Ark,* I, 16, p. 70). That this system reflects the primordial hebdomad Hugh takes for granted: "Seven denotes this present life which runs through seven days; eight, which comes after seven, signifies eternal life. . . . Let wisdom grow, then, through seven and eight. Let it begin with seven and attain its perfection through eight." The same periodization still appears in Voragine's *Golden Legend* (p. 37) and determines the structure of Hartmann Schedel's enormously popular *Nuremberg Chronicle* of 1493 and 1497. This *Weltchronik,* or *Liber Chronicarum,* plots the world's history through six eons down to the coming of the Antichrist in the seventh age, to close at world's end with the Last Judgment, when God sets a term to death in the institution of immortality.

Of almost equal persistence is the association of Circumcision with Resurrection by way of the number eight. Circumcision on the eighth day typifies baptism, which signifies participation in the Resurrection of Christ on the day after the Sabbath. On this point, we have a wealth of patristic texts, assembled by Danielou. Thus Justin Martyr (c. 100–c. 165): "The precept of circumcision, commanding that children be circumcised on the eighth day, is the type of the true circumcision . . . by Him Who rose from the dead on the first day of the week. . . . For the first day of the week is also the eighth" (*The Bible and the Liturgy,* p. 66). Similarly, Asterius of Amasea (d. aft. 341): "Why did circumcision take place on the eighth day? Because during the first seven, the child was wearing swaddling clothes, but on the eighth, freed from these bonds, he received circumcision, sign of the seal [*sphragis*] of the faith of Abraham. And this also typified the fact that, when we have carried the seven days of life, that is to say, the bonds of sin, we should, at the end of time, break these bonds and, circumcised by death and resurrection, as if on the eighth day embrace the life of the angels" (ibid., p. 65). See, further, Danielou's chapter 16, "The Eighth Day," with exposition of St. Basil's thought upon "the first day of the week, that on which light was created, on which the Savior rose from the dead, of which the Sunday of each week is the liturgical commemoration . . . the cosmic day of creation, the biblical day of circumcision, the evangelical day of the Resurrection, the Church's day of the Eucharistic celebration, and, finally, the eschatological day of the age to come" (p. 266).

Danielou proceeds to summarize the relevant speculations of St. Gregory of Nazianzus, who finds "the contrast between the hebdomad and ogdoad" in this cryptic text of Ecclesiastes 11: "Cast thy bread upon the running waters, for after a long time thou shalt find it again. Give a portion to seven, and also to eight. . . ." In expounding this verse, Danielou points out, the Church Fathers followed a rabbinical tradition, the rabbis being "the first to see in this text of Ecclesiastes the figure, not of the Sabbath and of the Sunday, but of the Sabbath and the circumcision. . . . What the Fathers did was merely to apply this idea to the Sunday" (p. 268).

For an excellent introduction to the general subject of arithmology, see Hopper, *Medieval Number Symbolism,* from which I quote a portion of his summary of pertinent Augustinian texts (p. 85): "Since the universe is constituted in 7, 8 is the number of Immortality. It returns to Unity as the first day of the second week, or in the eighth sentence of the Beatitudes, which repeats the first. It is the number of resurrection and circumcision

and the number of those who did not perish in the flood. It is taken as the eighth age of Eternal Salvation. . . ."

XXIV. Resisting the physical evidence of circumcision

In view of the infinite merit which Christian doctrine attached to the Circumcision of Christ, the refusal of Renaissance art to acknowledge its visual effect remains an unexplained puzzle; and Renaissance scholarship has evaded the problem, though the blatant uncircumcision of that other true son of Abraham, Michelangelo's *David,* causes even tourists to wonder (see L. Steinberg, "Michelangelo and the Doctors," *Bulletin of the History of Medicine,* 56 [Winter 1982], p. 552).

It has been suggested that Renaissance artists perhaps did not know and simply could not conceive the lineaments of a circumcised penis. This seems unconvincing, if only because in 15th-century Italy Muslim slaves of both sexes were near ubiquitous. The evidence is presented in Iris Origo's masterly essay, "The Domestic Enemy"; and it raises the question: were the bodies of deceased slaves never anatomized? We must assume that dissections, practiced with increasing frequency by physicians and artists from the late 15th century on, were performed not only on bodies of executed criminals, but as well on circumcised slaves. For the mid-16th century, the practice is, in fact, documented in Condivi's Michelangelo *vita* (1553). Condivi reports that the anatomist-surgeon Realdo Colombo sent the artist, for purposes of dissection and study, "the body of a Moor, a very fine young man, and very suitable. . . . On this corpse Michelangelo showed me many rare and recondite facts, perhaps never before understood" (Condivi, pp. 81–82). Of course, the young Moor, whose cadaver the aged Michelangelo studied, could have been captured in childhood, before his circumcision in early teen-age. Nevertheless, his case cautions us against laying contented ignorance on generations of studious artists engrossed in the subject of the male nude.

Perhaps the grounds for their resistance should be sought rather in an unresolved conflict of attitudes: I mean the perception of circumcision as both deliverance and deprivation, riddance and loss. A God-framed sacrament, vouchsafed of old to cleanse man of the odium of Original Sin, was yet a "despoiling of the body" (Col. 2:11), an embarrassing defect. The honorific seal of a compact between man and God was manifestly a shameful scar. Between these conflicting positions the gulf was unbridgeable—deeper than the theological issue, wide as the divergence between, say, Hellenic sculptor and biblical prophet. Where the twain finally meet in Christianity they collide in a culture shock never quite overcome.

In the Old Testament, circumcision, once instituted, becomes instantly metaphorical. The God of Deuteronomy (10:16) pleads with his people to "circumcise the foreskins of their hearts," and Jeremiah berates the unrepentant who cannot hear because their "ears are uncircumcised" (6:10). Thus, too, St. Stephen: "You stiffnecked and uncircumcised in heart and ears, you always resist the Holy Ghost" (Acts 7:51). And St. Paul: "He is a Jew, that is one inwardly; and the circumcision is that of the heart, in the spirit, not in the letter" (Rom. 2:29).

This tropological vein, wherein "circumcision" represents any form of spiritual purgation, is followed thereafter by thousands of Christian preachers. The Venerable Bede wants man's every sense circumcised. "They are uncircumcised in taste whom the Prophet confutes, saying

'Woe unto them that are mighty to drink wine, . . . uncircumcised are they in smell and touch, who are steeped in unguents . . . who pursue the embraces of harlots. . . . And those who preserve their hearts in all due care . . . have been circumcised by the stone [knife] of spiritual exercise" (*In die festo circumcisionis domini,* col. 57). In medieval preaching, the figurative tradition persists even to the censure of idle chatter: "Therefore we must be circumcised in the tongue, that is, speak few and only necessary things" (Pseudo-Bonaventure, *Meditations,* p. 45).

The habit here is that of wordplay, of voice to ear, the habit of rhetoric and sermon. The verbal trope does not dwell among forms of vision, is not meant to be eyed—and "circumcision" is not beheld, but understood as a figure for the sloughing of rank encumbrance, the removal of any morally crippling impediment. And against this aural tradition stands the conviction of the unhoodwinked eye, which perceives this same circumcision as an injury, an impairment, the marring of a primordial perfection. And this too is Christian, since "the faith has turned away from circumcision back to the integrity of the flesh, as it was from the beginning" (Tertullian, *De monogamia,* 5, in *Treatises,* p. 79).

No wonder that the word "mutilation" comes to the mind of a mid-16th-century author, discussing the incidence of circumcision among the ancient Egyptians; I am speaking of Pierio Valeriano's *Hieroglyphica* (Book VI, p. 47) in its original Latin. But the Italian edition published in 1602 translates "mutilation" as "pruning" ("scapezzare la pellicina della verga all'uomo"), substituting the metaphor of beneficent, life-giving care for the author's abhorrence of maiming (Pierio Valeriano, *Ieroglifici,* trans. Scipion Bargagli, Venice, 1602, p. 93). In this instance, the immediate subject is anti-

quarian, antedating the Christian super-
session of circumcision in baptism. Yet
even here translator and author separate
in a characteristic polarity, of which both
terms are inherently Christian — one homi-
letic, the other concrete; one respectful, the
other repelled.

That Renaissance artists took an unequivocal stand on this matter is a fact
recorded in all their pictures and
sculptures. Depicting the nude infant
Christ at whatever age, they willingly
paid the price of inaccuracy to spare the
revered body the blemish of imperfection.

So much for the conspicuous anomaly
of a Christ (or a David) uncircumcised.
Since the topic does not seem to have
entered Renaissance writings on art, the
proposed explanation remains hypothetical. But the silence of art-oriented period
texts reflects only the restraints governing
that genre of literature: it is not in the
character of humanist authors to refer to
the genitalia of Christ. The artists,
however — those who were celebrating
these genitalia — had other connections,
other strains of culture to draw on. During the centuries under review, the piety of
believers dwelt on the details of the Incarnate's physical being more freely than was
permissible under the inhibitions of polite
letters. We are addressing that Christian
culture which enabled St. Catherine of
Siena (d. 1380) to claim the Lord's foreskin mystically as her betrothal ring; a
world in which the supposed relic of the
prepuce of Christ was owned competitively
by several churches, most eminently by
St. John Lateran; a theological climate
wherein it was proper to speculate whether
or not the foreskin was reassumed in
Christ's risen body — some arguing that "it
ought to be resurrected with him as per-
taining to the truth and integrity of his
human nature" (Carvajal, *Oratio in die circumcisionis,* fol. 9). Under such focused attention, the aspect of the uncircumcised

member in Renaissance images of the
Christ Child at an age well past the eighth
day of life is not attributable to ignorance
or indifference. The reason for the Child's
apparent uncircumcision must lie in the
artists' sense of the body's perfection.
Here they would not infringe, any more
than they would deprive Eve of a navel,
no matter what the learned might say.

XXV. Attitudes to sermons

What the word "sermon" sets off in a
secular modern mind is told in *Webster's
Third International* under definition 3b; and
more eloquently in Joyce's account of
young Stephen's wanderings through
Dublin slums: "He examined all the book-
stalls which offered old directories and
volumes of sermons and unheard-of
treatises at the rate of a penny each or
three for twopence" (*Stephen Hero,* Episode
XXII). We hardly need to be told that no
purchase was made.

But even where sermons resound in
their proper place, i.e., from the pulpit,
our sympathies are likely to fall on the
side of inattention, as when we read, for
example, how the consistory of the church
at Arnstadt, in February 1706, repri-
manded their young organist, one J. S.
Bach, because "he went to a nearby
wineshop during the sermons." Or when
O'Malley tells us that in Renaissance
Rome "a proclivity for talking during the
sermons delivered in the papal chapel
seems to have been almost ineradicable";
in which matter "the cardinals themselves
were not above reproach" (*Praise and
Blame,* pp. 20–21).

I remember being struck by the "In-
troductory Note" to a neat Oxford edition
of *Evelyn's Diary* (London, 1959). The
editor, E. S. de Beer, had previously
published the corpus complete in six

volumes (1955), and my demotic version—a convenient 1300-page tome—had been slimmed to one-third its bulk. How this reduction was compassed, the editor explains as follows: "The principal class of omissions is Evelyn's reports of the contents of the sermons he heard between the Restoration (29 May 1660) and the end of 1705. Only a very few fragments of these are retained, either for their general historical significance or for Evelyn's express emotional responses to them."

The effect of such systematic omission is to leave the modern reader, who finds all the Evelyn he needs in the epitome, with the false notion that the diarist scanted "the contents of the sermons he heard"; which makes the man's mental world that much more secular. We have here a type of retroactive secularizing imposed alike on the modern perception of, say, Newton, Kepler, Leonardo da Vinci, or indeed, the entirety of Renaissance culture. It takes some effort of historical imagination to reinstate the institution of public preaching where that culture maintained it—near the center of its intellectual, moral, and social life.

XXVI. The blood hyphen

Painters of Christ on the cross who respect nature's laws (e.g., Velázquez in his *Crucifix* at the Prado) depict the blood flow from the side wound moving in down-right trickles upon the right thigh. Where the flow is diverted into the groin, we are apprised that the determinant is a force other than gravitational. Now last and first wound are connected, as though the graph of Christ's lifelong Passion were traced on the chart of his body. The motif appears conspicuously in French painting shortly before 1400, and it remains for more than a century a ready symbol. We

Fig. 184. Jean de Beaumetz and Shop, *Crucifixion with Carthusian,* 1390–95.

need not assume the operation of symbolism whenever the blood of the Crucified deflects from side to center. One has to allow for imitators who deploy a given motif because it looks right or familiar, without rethinking its original meaning. But that the genital reference in the motif could be fully intended seems confirmed by a startling juxtaposition of images on a page in the Rohan Hours (Fig. 185). Folio 237 displays a large *Crucifixion* and, as its typological parallel, a small Old Testament scene adjoined. The latter depicts the incident told in Numbers 25: 7–8, where the priest Phineas dispatches an Israelite fornicator and his Midianite harlot by piercing the man and the woman together with a single thrust of his lance—"in locis genitalibus," says the Vulgate (Douay: "in the genital parts"). In the Rohan miniature the accompanying legend reads in Old French: "S'y fery l'un et l'autre parmy leurs natures"—the word "nature" being the common latinate

Fig. 185. Illumination from the Grandes Heures de Rohan, *Crucifixion* with *Phineas Punishing the Adulterous Couple*, c. 1420–25.

Fig. 186. Middle Rhenish, *Lamentation,*
c. 1450.

Fig. 187. Hans Pleydenwurff Shop, *Deposition,*
1465.

euphemism for the pudenda ("Nature
. . . Parties du corps humain servant à la
generation"; A. J. Greimas, *Dictionnaire de
l'ancien français,* Paris, 1968, p. 433, def.
3). Remarkable here is the pairing of a
coup de lance inflicted on genitalia with a
Crucifixion wherein the first wounding of
the "nature" of Christ is recalled in a copi-
ous effusion of blood at the groin.

(In the original 13th-century *Bible
moralisée,* the New Testament parallel to
the Phineas scene is not the Crucifixion,
but the punishment of monks who break
their vows of chastity; see A. de Laborde,
La Bible moralisée. . . , Paris, 1911–27, fol.
83v of the Oxford manuscript. Further-
more, though the Phineas scene in the
Rohan Hours is copied from the 14th-
century Angevin *Bible moralisée* [Paris,
Bibliothèque Nationale, ms. fr. 9561, fol.
97], the latter manuscript does not draw
the typological parallel with the Crucifixion.)

XXVII. The calendrical style of the Circumcision

A learned friend suggests an intriguing
possibility: as the reckoning of our era
refers to the Nativity, could our reversion
to the ancient Julian calendar in placing
the year's beginning on January 1 refer to
the Circumcision? I have been unable to
confirm the hypothesis, but the following
considerations are pertinent.

(1) January 1, from its association with
pagan revels, was held in contempt by the
early Fathers and was therefore considered unfit to introduce the Christian
year. "On this day," writes St. Augustine,
"the Gentiles celebrate their festival with
worldly joy of the flesh, with the sound of
most vain and filthy songs, with banquets
and shameless dances. If what the Gen-

tiles do in celebrating this false feast does not please you, then you will be gathered from among the Gentiles" (Sermon XVII [Ben. 198]; *Sermons,* p. 149). For subsequent ecclesiastical prohibitions of Christian participation at such rejoicings — documented for Italy, Spain, and Gaul — see K. A. Heinrich Kellner, *Heortology: A History of Christian Festivals . . . ,* London, 1908, pp. 163–64. As late as 742, St. Boniface (the "Apostle of Germany," 680–754) spoke with "horror of the heathen rites with which, as he heard, it was customary at Rome to celebrate the New Year on 1 January" (Poole, *Studies in Chronology and History,* p. 10). So long as paganism was vital, the Christian shudder at its excesses may explain why (I quote Poole's conclusion, p. 26) "the Church steadily opposed the observance of 1 January as the beginning of the year," even though that date was accepted for calendrical purposes.

(2) "New Year" continued to mean January 1, even when, after the 7th century, the civil year was made to begin at other dates. Thus the Byzantine year began on September 1. In the Carolingian Empire, under the authority of St. Boniface, it began with the Nativity. Other polities reckoned from the Annunciation, i.e., not from December 25, but from March 25; others again from Easter. "It was natural," writes Poole, "to choose for the beginning of the year a day which was associated only with Christian observances." And it was not until the High Middle Ages that the "Style of the Circumcision," coincident with the old Julian calendar, became one among the competing styles.

(3) By the 6th century, if not before, January 1 was established as a festival of the Church, the Feast of the Circumcision; but with no reference in the liturgy to the beginning of the civil year. It was during the 13th century, chiefly in German lands, that this date became again the chronological landmark it had been in antiquity — a restoration which Poole attributes to the increasing use of almanacs and the study of Roman law. The coincidence was not lost upon the author of the *Golden Legend* (late 13th century): he finds it fitting that the Circumcision of Christ, "the head of the Church," was "established in the head and beginning of the year" (Voragine, *Golden Legend,* p. 34).

(4) I have found no indication that the decision to appoint January 1 as the gateway of the year was at any time influenced (or justified *ex post facto*) by symbolic considerations. And on this point Poole is silent. We can only say that the coincidence of the two events — the year's beginning and the "beginning of our salvation" in the Circumcision (see p. 62) — offered itself to association. A German document of 1513 quotes St. Jerome on the pagan custom of performing no executions on New Year's day — "there is not a day in the year to which we may not ascribe more than 5000 martyrs . . . excepting only the day of the new year or Circumcision of our Lord." (Quoted in an inventory of the relics assembled at Wittenberg; see P. Kalkoff, *Ablass und Reliquienverehrung an der Schlosskirche zu Wittenberg unter Friedrich dem Weisen,* Gotha, 1907, p. 55.)

(5) In the sermon delivered in the pope's chapel on January 1, 1485, the preacher Antonio Lollio refers to the Feast of the Circumcision as "this most holy day which not unjustly is set at the head of the year." And concludes: "Let us venerate this most sacred day of the Circumcision, which we may call the gate that opens the way to paradise, even as it opens the year" (Lollio, *Oratio circumcisionis,* fol. 3v).

A quarter century earlier (1459), the Duchy of Milan had officially adopted the "Style of the Circumcision," a fact that must have made this mode of reckoning a

matter of widespread discussion. During
the 16th century, most of Western Europe
gradually followed suit. And in 1582,
almost a hundred years after Lollio's sermon, the calendrical reform of Pope
Gregory XIII (1572–85) fixed January 1
as the gateway of the Christian year for
the countries of the Roman obedience.
Yet his bull of February 24, 1582, entirely
technical and precise, makes no reference
to the concomitant feast of the Church.
Lollio's then century-old rhetorical flourish had cited the aptness of setting the
Circumcision feast at the head of the year,
not vice versa. Whether the reform of
1582 was accompanied by similar rhetoric
must await further study. (For the bull in
English translation, see Lewis A. Scott,
"Act and Bull; or, Fixed Anniversaries," *A
Paper submitted to the Numismatic and Anti-
quarian Society of Philadelphia,* Philadelphia,
1880. The gradual adoption of the reform
and abolition of alternative systems by
Protestant and other states during the
following two centuries is itemized in
A. Cappelli, *Cronologia,* 3rd ed., Milan,
1969, pp. 11–13; and Poole, p. 27.)

XXVIII. Ghirlandaio and the Adoration

In his role as discussant following the
original presentation of this material at
the Lionel Trilling Seminar in November
1981, Professor Julius S. Held offered an
alternative reading of the central action in
Ghirlandaio's tondo (Fig. 66). He suggested that the old Magus, preparing to
kiss the Child's foot, may be reaching for
the cloth so as not to be grasping the
sacred limb with bare hand. I answer:

(1) Though the proposed sequel to the
moment depicted is conceivable, it is not
visually given. What the Magus' gesture
imparts is his reverence in touching the

Fig. 188. Juan de Flandes, *Adoration of the Magi,* c. 1510.

Fig. 189. Pontormo, *Adoration of the Magi,* c. 1519–20, detail.

Fig. 190. Andrea Andreani after Aurelio (?) Luini, *Adoration of the Magi*, c. 1570.

Fig. 191. Marco Pino, *Adoration of the Magi*, 1571.

loincloth whose withdrawal makes the Child naked. This much alone are we shown.

(2) In the ritual touching of sacred objects with covered hands, the cloth used is one's own. Never is it borrowed from the center of sanctity. No wiseman would steal the Child's covering to respectfully grasp its foot.

(3) We know several *Adorations* that show the first King grasping the Infant's foot with veiled hand, possibly with intent to implant a kiss (Fig. 69; cf. also Botticelli's *Adoration* in the Uffizi). But such instances are exceptional; in the overwhelming majority of *Adorations* that depict the old King in the act of touching the Child's arm, foot, or leg, the contact is bare-handed (Figs. 67, 68, 190, 191)—significantly so, since the reality of the Child's human flesh is being verified.

(4) Even if Ghirlandaio's depicted present were spun out according to the scenario proposed by Professor Held, the import of the given moment, wherein the boy exposes his groin to the anxious curiosity of the King, would not be affected.

Dr. Joanna Lipking of Northwestern University suggests that the boy's nakedness in Renaissance Infancy scenes may need revealing to show him possessed of a navel, proving him born of woman. It is an engaging thought.

The *Adorations* reproduced here and in the text are taken from a large stock in which the genital focus of the old King's attention is unmistakable. Other outstanding examples are: the *Adoration* page in Jacquemart de Hesdin's *Petites Heures de Jean de Berry* (c. 1380–85; Meiss, *French Painting*, fig. 93); the Botticini tondo in the Art Institute of Chicago; Veronese's *Adoration* in Vienna. In numerous instances, the focus is effectively blurred by overpainting at the Child's groin. This appears to be the case in the *Adorations* of Vincenzo Foppa and Bruegel (Fig. 192), both at the London National Gallery; in the Van Scorel at Bonn (Fig. 68), etc.; see also Excursus XXXI.

Fig. 192. Bruegel, detail of Fig. 71.

XXIX. The protection motif

To the works reproduced in Figs. 74–78 and 193–201, I add a short list of further examples that seem particularly expressive: Andrea di Giusto's polyptych of 1435 in Prato (cited in Excursus XIX); Jacopo Bellini's *Madonna and Child* in Bergamo, Accademia Carrara; Jacopo del Sellaio's *Madonna and Child* tondo in Vaduz, Liechtenstein Collection; a Crivelli panel of the *Madonna and Child Enthroned* in the Arthur Lehman Collection, and another in the Metropolitan Museum of Art, Robert Lehman Collection; Bramantino's *Madonna and Child,* also in the Metropolitan Museum; Lorenzo di Credi's *Madonna and Child with Saints* in the Louvre; Antonio da Viterbo's *Madonna and Child* panel in Bergamo, Accademia Carrara; Lorenzo Costa's *Holy Family with Sts. Jerome and Francis,* Budapest, Museum of Fine Arts; Pontormo's *Sacra Conversazione* in Florence, SS. Annunziata; Perino del Vaga's *Holy Family with St. John and St. Anne,* Rome, Galleria Borghese; Parmigianino's *Madonna della Rosa* in Dresden; Gerolamo Bassano's *Madonna and Child* of c. 1600 in the Museo Civico, Bassano del Grappa. Remarkable Northern examples of the protection motif, dating again from the 15th and 16th centuries (supplementing Figs. 11, 30, 49) include: the *Adoration* page by the Bedford Master, c. 1430–35, New York, The Pierpont Morgan Library, M. 359, fol. 52v; Stefan Lochner's *Adoration* altarpiece in the Cologne Cathedral; Hans Memling's Donne Triptych in the Devonshire Collection, Chatsworth; Cranach's panel of the *Madonna with the Child Holding Grapes* in the Louvre; Lucas van Leyden's *Madonna and Child* in the Oslo National Gallery, and Lucas' engravings, *The Adoration of the Magi,* 1513 (Hollstein 37), and the *Holy Family,* c. 1530 (Hollstein 27).

Fig. 193. Bohemian, *Madonna of Strahova*, c. 1350.

Fig. 194. Master of St. Severin, *Adoration of the Magi*, c. 1500.

Fig. 195. Battista di Gerio, *Madonna and Child,* c. 1410.

Fig. 196. Sassetta, *Madonna and Child with Angels,* 1437–44.

Fig. 197. Mantegna School, *Sacra Conversazione,* c. 1465, detail.

Fig. 198. Botticelli, *Madonna dei Candelabri,* c. 1476.

Fig. 199. Giovanni Bellini, *Madonna and Child with Saints,* c. 1490.

Fig. 200. Raffaellino del Garbo, *Madonna
and Child Enthroned,* 1500.

Fig. 201. Domenico Puligo, *Madonna and
Child Enthroned with Saints,* c. 1515.

XXX. Images of self-touch and of Infant erection

Fig. 202. Titian (?), *Sacra Conversazione,* before 1511.

Fig. 203. Sodoma, *Holy Family,* c. 1525.

Fig. 204. Veronese Shop, *Holy Family*, c. 1600.

Fig. 205. Gian Antonio Guardi after Veronese, *Holy Family*, c. 1750.

None but the God-man may.

A drawing by Ludovico Carracci (Fig. 206) displays the supine, naked Christ Child touching himself with his left hand, while his right points rhetorically toward an angelic messenger. Long attributed to Annibale, the drawing is probably a study for a lost painting, of which several copies are mentioned in a 1631 inventory of the collection of Ludovico's patron, Bartolommeo Dulcini. One such copy, as well as a reproductive engraving, is preserved in the Bologna Pinacoteca. For attribution and documentation, see Leonora Street, "La vendita Ellesmere di disegni di Carracci," *Arte Illustrata,* 5 (September 1972), pp. 356–57 and fig. 14.

While the motif of the self-touch seems fairly rare, that of the Christ Child's erection must have been common, though presumably painted out in most cases. The earliest instance I know is a *Madonna and Child with Four Angels* by Giovanni di Marco dal Ponte (Florentine, c. 1385–1437) in the De Young Museum, San Francisco (61.44.5): the Child reaches for the Madonna's veil and exposes his lower body. In the *Madonna* pictures of Cima da Conegliano, erection is normal; e.g., his *Madonna and Child with Sts. Jerome and John* in the Washington National Gallery; a *Madonna and Child* in the Bologna Pinacoteca; another (in addition to Fig. 84) in the National Gallery, London. See also Perugino's *Madonna and Child* of c. 1500 in the Detroit Institute of Arts; Francesco Francia's *Madonna and Child with Sts. Jerome and Francis,* The Norton Simon Foundation; Marco Palmezzano's *Madonna and Child* panel in Bologna, and the same artist's *Holy Family with the Infant St. John* in the Phoenix Art Museum; and a *Holy Family with St. John* by a Perino del Vaga follower in the Galleria Doria, Rome (1982 catalogue, fig. 56). In Parmigianino's *Vision of St. Jerome* (London,

Fig. 206. Ludovico Carracci, *The Dream of St. Joseph,* c. 1605.

Fig. 207. Antonio Carneo, *Holy Family Adored by Lieutenants and Deputies,* 1667, detail.

Fig. 208. Vivarini, detail of Fig. 82.

National Gallery), the Child's member may not be erect, but it casts a long shadow.

XXXI. Bowdlerism

The assault on art in the name of propriety is one mode of iconoclasm. But a general history of the iconoclastic impulse in action remains to be written. As I see it, such a work would reveal the preservation of art as an embattled cause, intermittently threatened by waves of anti-art feeling.

The modalities of iconoclasm are various, as are the objects of its execration. The grounds may be doctrinal (as in the classic Byzantine phase); or socio-political (as in the destruction of royalist imagery by revolutionists); or ideological (as in the proscription of "decadent" art under Hitler and Stalin); or moralistic (as in the

zeal of the censor); or entrepreneurial (as in site clearing for urban development and renovation); or gustatory, the deadliest ground of all, since nothing endangers a work's survival more than a recent aversion of taste.

In the past, works of art have been destroyed by avarice or sudden need, as when the production of goldsmiths was melted down for the metal, or bronzes were cast into cannon. And always, in past times as now, there is the attritional work of neglect presiding over the crumbling of structures that need care to survive. The dispassion of cold indifference is a prime killer, like Baudelaire's *ennui*. More positive passions come into play periodically: a rage against art as evidence of the unconscionable luxury of the rich; fear of the magic of images—which accounts for eyes gouged out on painted figures; or the sheer exhilaration of vandalism. It seems to me that mankind's commerce with art is a yes/no affair, of which standard art history gives a lopsided picture.

Add to all the above the animus felt by those who are making art now against those who formerly made it. "Images are symbols of a deposed ruling class, . . . or of a hated one," writes David Freedberg in a fundamental work on the subject ("The Structure . . . of Iconoclasm," p. 167). But images are symbols as well of a deposed ruling style. And this explains what Freedberg calls the "surprising participation of artists themselves" in outbursts of art destruction. He documents such participation for the 16th century, then quotes Stanley Idzerda's "Iconoclasm during the French Revolution" (*The American Historical Review,* 60 [1954], p. 21): "No group seemed more anxious to join the iconoclastic crusade than the artists themselves." Not really surprising if one remembers that students of Jacques-Louis David would toss rotten eggs at Watteau's *Embarkation for Cythera*—a picture which from the vantage of a stout Davidien must have seemed an absurd confection. A century later, the Italian Futurists paraded under the slogan "Burn down the museums!"

What one ought to dislike in Duchamp's suggestion to use a "Rembrandt as an ironing board" is ultimately the provincial banality of the project: it's been done. Were not the *Belvedere Torso* and the reliefs of the Pergamon frieze used for building stones? Were not the *Unicorn Tapestries* brought out annually to protect stored potatoes from frost? Did not 15th-century prints serve later bookbinders as paper stuffing? I once bought a pack of Old Master engravings out of a junk dealer's cellar; I had found them wrapped in a large paper sheet that turned out to be Callot's *Temptation of St. Anthony* in the third state; no charge for the wrapper. Arts out of fashion decline readily into

raw material and Duchamp's famous ploy would have been braver, less arch, had he suggested a household use for the *Demoiselles d'Avignon* or Matisse's *Red Studio.* The proper response to his proposed waste of a Rembrandt is—"not again?!"

Or think of Miró's *Portrait of a Man in a Late Nineteenth Century Frame* in New York (see William Rubin, *Miró in the Collection of the Museum of Modern Art,* New York, 1973, pp. 84–85). Judging from what remains after Miró's mayhem (1950), he worked over a perfectly good academic 19th-century portrait—scraping away and superimposing his own devices. The day may not be far distant when some enterprising Ph.D. candidate identifies the anonymous artisan of the vandalized portrait; and then those modern graffiti may begin to lose their appeal.

Miró's overframed palimpsest is eloquent of the destructive energy of most modernism. Living art needs elbow room, the glib successes of foregoing art stand in the way. The young who now crave attention resent ancestor worship. Their indifference to senior art can be chilling, their antagonism implacable. And this is why engaged artists swell the ranks of those other zealots who form the wreckers' procession. In the book I envisage, the destruction of works of art would emerge as an ongoing cultural enterprise, pursued at all times with a sense of enormous accomplishment: remove the blight and the world will be the better for it. Iconoclasts jubilate like angelic hosts at the Church's burning of heretical books.

The mode of iconoclasm which is called censorship does not necessarily take the form of direct assault or removal. Its cunning consists in denying its own operation and leaving no scars. Even in cases of outright destruction for decency's sake, the proceedings tend to be conducted (like Ruskin's burning of Turner's erotic drawings) in secret, the offending art being refused the protection of *habeas corpus,* of publicity, or open trial.

Usually, where serious art is arraigned, the censor's hand spares the whole on condition of partial smothering or mutilation; examples of which may be studied in any public museum, but most instructively on the surface of the world's greatest fresco, the Sistine Chapel's *Last Judgment,* punctuated throughout by the fuss of loinbibs and underwear. As a grudging alternative to total destruction, Michelangelo's nudes were twice painted over in his own century—to be further overpainted in the 18th.

It is indeed the early 18th century that initiates one of iconoclasm's busiest moments. It was then that Bandinelli's nude statues of Adam and Eve were withdrawn (two hundred years after their installation) from the Cathedral of Florence; that Michelangelo's *Times of Day* in the Medici Chapel became serious candidates for fig leaves; and that Gian Antonio Guardi produced the reformed version of the Veronese discussed above (Fig. 205); while the emasculating of lesser-known works of art became a steady sub-industry in all public collections.

But we are not well informed about the chronology of these practices. Montaigne (*Essays,* III, 5) cites the "many beautiful and antique statues" which were being "castrated" in Rome during his youth by "that good man," meaning Pope Paul IV (1555–59). This gives us a date for some of those mutilations. But who knows by whose hand the *Playing Children* in the Amadeo relief in the Colleoni Chapel at Bergamo had their genitals docked? (see Pope-Hennessy, *Italian Renaissance Sculpture,* pl. 115). Who knows when the marble penis of Michelangelo's *Risen Christ* in the Minerva was broken, and whether that action was prompted by private enterprise or official decree?

The losses borne by our masterpieces are largely handmade, but of a making rarely dignified by historical record. When a major Massachusetts museum exhibits a Renaissance marble roundel of the *Madonna and Child* with the Child's sexual member carefully chiseled off, we cannot tell which of the last two or three centuries deserves credit for the improvement. When the recent cleaning of a glazed terracotta relief at the Metropolitan Museum of Art restores the Christ Child to its intended nudity (Figs. 209, 210), we remain ignorant whether the deceptive drapery of painted plaster, now consigned to the store rooms, had been put on in the Enlightenment, or by benighted Victorians, or in our own century with an eye to the American market. And what is the date of that lavender veil coiled about the smiling Christ in Domenico Veneziano's *Madonna and Child* in the Washington National Gallery (Kress Collection)? The museum files preserve letters from Bernard Berenson, Roberto Longhi, and others, assuring the prospective purchaser of a perfect surface, free of all overpaint. Yet a frank look discerns what even old X-ray pictures confirm: that this loincloth is a poisonous interference botching Domenico's color, compositional rhythm, textural consistency, and symbolic purpose. Some day, when the picture's extensive areas of overpainting are swept away, we shall behold a major religious icon of the Florentine Quattrocento in a pristine state that would have made it unexhibitable in the United States when the Kress Collection was formed. But whether that silken rag was painted on in the 1930s or two hundred years earlier may never be known.

August 7, 1826: A Virginia lady on a pleasure trip to New York scurries past certain plaster casts at the American Academy of Fine Arts (she cites the *Apollo Belvedere,* the *Venus de'Medici,* the *Three*

Figs. 209, 210. Luca della Robbia, *Madonna and Child,* c. 1440–60, terracotta, before and after 1977 cleaning.

Graces, etc.) and records in her diary: "The room containing the statues I took a very hasty view of: there is something revolting to the nature of a female to see so much nudity" ("New York City in 1826," unpublished diary of a Virginia lady, quoted in *The American Magazine of Art,* 9 [December 1917], p. 66).

Most gravely affected by the reign of such attitudes were American artists, John Trumbull being a case well documented. Eager to match the Old Masters on their own ground, he had, during a sojourn in London in 1801, painted an *Infant Savior and St. John.* Twenty-seven years passed before the picture was exhibited at the Boston Athenaeum, and a year later Trumbull wrote to Warren Dutton Esq. in Boston: "Understanding you to say last year that an acquaintance of yours would have purchased my picture of the Saviour & St. John, playing with a Lamb: but for the entire nudity of

the former:—upon my return here I began a Copy, in which the objection should be obviated. . . . It is more finished and is altogether quite equal to the original:—be so good as to let it be seen by the person in question. . . ." (The letter, datelined "New York May 27th 1829," is preserved in the Huntington Library, San Marino, California. For text and collateral information, I am indebted to Helen A. Cooper of the Yale University Art Gallery. See also her *John Trumbull: The Hand and Spirit of a Painter,* exh. cat., New Haven, Yale University Art Gallery, 1982, esp. p. 204 and nn. 10, 11.)

Two versions of Trumbull's *Infant Savior* survive. The one at Yale has the Child decently covered; but, Trumbull's claim notwithstanding, it is sadly inferior to the Wadsworth Atheneum version of 1801—upon which, at a date uncertain, a broad loincloth was smeared. It is not

Fig. 211. Mantegna, *Madonna and Child with the Magdalen and St. John,* c. 1500, detail.

known whether the overlay was applied by the repentant painter himself, or (I am changing the subject) by that hundred-handed anonymous who, throughout the past century, decked thousands of master-works with fig leaves and loincloths—including even Mantegna's enthroned *Madonna and Child* in the London National Gallery. This radiant altarpiece was purchased for the British nation in 1855, cleaned in 1957, and soon after described as "in exceptionally good condition"; the dismal imposition at the Child's loin receiving no comment (Fig. 211; see Martin Davies' catalogue of *The Earlier Italian Schools,* London, 1961, p. 329).

But the times change. Museum culture has entered upon its deciduous season, a kind of autumnal shedding and falling of fig leaves throughout the civilized world, wherever livings are to be made by restorers (Figs. 212–15). Many Renaissance paintings are stripped of false loincloths already; dismantling awaits many more; and when these moral coils have all been shuffled off, a generation of museum goers will face anew the immodesty of high art—even in Philadelphia. For there, in the Johnson Collection, hangs an early 15th-century *Madonna and Child* attributed to Battista di Gerio (Fig. 195). The panel has suffered the addition of an extra loincloth under the mother's left hand, a patchwork so maladroit in tone, color, and texture that it all but emphasizes the artist's original meaning; the Child's exposed member was presented between the Madonna's index and middle finger. (My thanks to Mrs. Marigene Butler, Conservator, Philadelphia Museum of Art, for lending her skill and judgment to our preliminary investigation. And while I am in parentheses, let me cite two further instances of Renaissance works recently disencumbered: Francia's *Gambaro Madonna* at Yale, from which cleaning in 1959 removed "earlier repaints . . . including

Figs. 212, 213. Barent van Orley, *Holy Family,* 1521, before and after 1980 cleaning.

Figs. 214, 215. Bronzino, *Holy Family*,
c. 1540–42, before and after 1980 cleaning.

a veil over the Christ Child's genitals"
[Seymour, *Early Italian Paintings,* p. 222];
and the Ghiberti School terracotta of the
Virgin and Child, Florence, Ognissanti
[Baldini/dal Poggetto, *Firenze restaura,*
figs. 203, 204]).

The question returns — when were
these cover-ups perpetrated, these aggres-
sions under the aegis of purity? We are
not ready yet to produce a reliable periodization of Western prudishness in its
subtler iconoclastic effects. But it does appear that resistance to the freedoms of art
is diachronic. The virtuous disfigurement
of so much Renaissance painting and
sculpture cannot be blamed simply on recent Comstockery, or on Victorianism, or
on 18th-century etiquette, or Calvinist
Puritanism, or the bigotry that prevailed
after the Council of Trent. The affront
from which these successive ages recoiled
was deep enough to have given offense in
some quarters even while these works
were created. I draw attention to one

paradigmatic instance, dating from the
period which has been our chief preoc-
cupation, the second half of the Quattrocento.

About 1455 Fra Filippo Lippi created
his immensely successful *Madonna and
Child with Two Angels* (Uffizi) — a thought-
laden compound of mystic symbols in
Renaissance dress. The Christ Child is
shown arriving on the hands of two ro-
guish angels, one of whom, a winged
gamin with a grin on his face, lets us in on
a happy secret, God's espousal of human
nature. In a ritual gesture of marital ap-
propriation, Lippi's heavenly Bridegroom
lays a hand on the shoulder of his bride-
mother (see Steinberg, "Metaphors,"
p. 255, and Lavin, "The Joy of the
Bridegroom's Friend"). Yet his lower
body, as the symbolic locus of Christ's
humanity, attests his sex. The exposure is
minimal, for what matters to Lippi is not
how much, but that the showing be understood as the patent of God's humanation.

For Lippi's copyists, however, even this discreet token was overmuch. In the dozen-odd variants and replicas of the Uffizi picture that survive from the latter Quattrocento—in every one of them, the Child is copiously draped. Evidently, Lippi's way of declaring the coincidence of divine spousehood with manhood was unacceptable to the copyists and their patrons. One is led to suspect that the great Renaissance masters tapped symbolic resources too radical or too intimate for wide comprehension. Confronted by the undress of the Child, most viewers, even in Lippi's day, seem to have seen only a breach of decorum. And though they withheld their hands from the original, they circulated Lippi's *concetto* in expurgated editions. (Following is a list of nine copies or adaptations of Lippi's design. Four more are cited without reproductions and as privately owned in Lionello Venturi, "Nella collezione Nemès," *L'Arte,* 34 [1931], pp. 263ff., nos. 2, 3, 7, 8. Some of these may since have passed into the public collections cited here. [1] Lippi School, Florence, Ospedale degli Innocenti, c. 1465; [2] Lippi follower, New York, The Metropolitan Museum of Art, 29.100.17; [3] Botticelli studio, Washington, National Gallery of Art, 714; [4] early Botticelli[?], Naples, Museo di Capodimonte, 46; [5] Botticelli follower, London, National Gallery, 589; [6] Pseudo Pier Francesco Fiorentino or Pesellino follower, Budapest, Museum of Fine Arts, 50.752; [7] Botticelli[?], Ajaccio, Musée Fesch; [8] Paris, Musée Jacquemart-André; [9] Florentine, London, National Gallery, 2505.)

Figs. 216 and 217—one pair to stand for hundreds—illustrate the principle of corrective copying in works other than Lippi's.

The censorship wreaked by publishers of art books is another chapter; it is ex-

Fig. 216. Jan van Hemessen, *Madonna and Child,* c. 1540.

Fig. 217. After Jan van Hemessen, *Madonna and Child.*

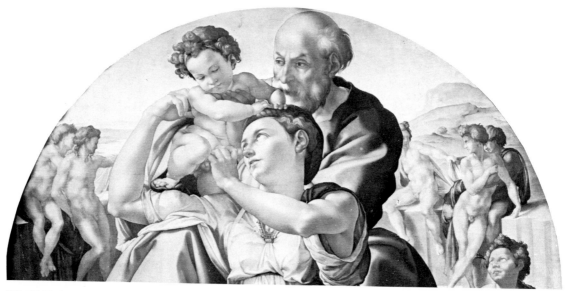

Fig. 218. Michelangelo, *Doni Madonna*, 1506, detail.

Fig. 219. Achille Jacquet engraving after Michelangelo's *Doni Madonna*, 1876.

Fig. 220. Retouched photograph of the *Doni Madonna*, published in Symonds' *Life of Michelangelo*.

emplified in two of the finest Michelangelo monographs produced in the latter 19th century: the 1876 quatercentenary volume of the *Gazette des Beaux-Arts* (vol. 13, 2ème pér., *L'oeuvre et la vie de Michel-Ange*), and the *editio princeps* of John Addington Symonds' *Life of Michelangelo*, London, 1893. In both works, the illustration of the *Doni Madonna* is retouched to forestall the offense of sexual exposure (Figs. 218–20). In another reproductive engraving in the 1876 *Gazette des Beaux-*

Arts volume, Michelangelo's nude allegory of *Dusk* in the Medici Chapel is given a loincloth (pl. aft. p. 102); and so, needless to say, is his *Risen Christ* (p. 261).

But it appears that even Anderson/Alinari, long the venerable purveyors of photographic documentation to students of Renaissance art, are, or were, in complicity with the censor. We gaze in dismay at their photograph, just received, of Giovanni Bellini's *Madonna and Child* in Bergamo (cf. Figs. 221 and 53): the golden strait between Mary's blue mantle and the Christ Child's white tunic has been stained to the devil's color, black gray—as though St. Jerome's warning "the power of the devil is in the loins," pursued even here.

Fig. 221. Giovanni Bellini, *Madonna and Child* (Fig. 53), retouched Anderson/Alinari photograph.

XXXII. "A peculiar notion"

Professor Held met my observations concerning phallism in Heemskerck's paintings with steadfast skepticism; and since disbelief on this score is a near universal reaction, I adduce his argument in full along with rejoinders:

That there is a noticeable bulge in the loincloths Heemskerck painted in three examples of the Man of Sorrows no one could deny. What it may indicate, I submit, is the presence of a sizeable male member, proportionately related to the markedly athletic appearance the artist gave to his figure of Christ (and let us remember that this happened precisely at a time when fashion glorified male virility with the so-called codpiece, a piece of clothing which suggested size but surely was not meant to indicate a permanent state of erection).

The answer to the above parenthesis is that often enough "a permanent state of erection" is exactly what the 16th-century codpiece was meant to indicate; see the examples cited in n. 90, above.

Held continues:

At best, Heemskerck's pictures could be explained as part of the iconography of *ostentatio vulnerum*, referring back to the first blood shed by Christ; and it is perhaps not accidental that in one of these paintings the blood from the wound in Christ's side runs down to the groin. To finish this point, I should like to introduce a penitent *St. Jerome* [Lisbon] painted by Jan van Hemessen, a contemporary of Heemskerck, where the saint's loincloth shows a similar bulge [Friedländer, *Early Netherlandish Painting,* XII, no. 215A]; it would add a rather peculiar notion to Jerome's penance if this suggested a connection between his self-abasement and sexual arousal.

Since there is little profit, and less dignity, in debating whether Van Hemessen's "similar bulge" is in fact sufficiently similar, I shall address myself instead to that "peculiar notion" which, Held believes, a sign of sexual arousal would add to Jerome's penance.

Suppose we ask what it is that makes Jerome penitent; and let us allow that the question occurred to the painter. Was it remorse over one dire misstep, like St. Peter's denial; or over a misguided career, like the Magdalen's harlotry? Was it the guilt Jerome felt over his early absorption in Cicero that makes him so beat his breast that even his lion weeps? Does the artist depict Jerome's penance because he thinks the hermit saint has a specific transgression to expiate, or because he attributes to him a consciousness of sin so grounded inward that a lifetime's contrition will not expunge it? Suppose Van Hemessen conceived Jerome confessing himself here like St. Paul (Romans 7:22–25): "I am delighted with the law of God, according to the inward man: But I see another law in my members, fighting against the law of my mind, and captivating me in the law of sin, that is in my members. Unhappy man that I am, who shall deliver me from the body of this death?"

St. Augustine had this Pauline passage in mind when he confessed that concupiscence "intrudes where it is not needed, and it agitates even the hearts of the faithful and of the saints with importune and nefarious desires" (*C.S.E.L.*, vol. LXXXVIII, Vienna, 1981, p. 36). In the words of Van Hemessen's contemporary, Conrad Braun (see n. 17, above): "Man, disobedient to God, feels his disobedience in his very members." Both authors, Augustine and Braun, were speaking specifically of sexual shame. They incriminated the phallus, rebellious member *par excellence,* as the exponent of man's captive condition.

And we have certain saints' legends —how they repelled the onslaught of sexual temptation: St. Benedict by flinging himself naked into a thicket of briars and nettles and rolling in it till the blood flowed; the young Thomas Aquinas by laying a fiery brand to his flesh. These heroes became and remained—as St. Jerome said of himself—eunuchs by their own choice. Through instant, ever-vigilant renunciation, they contained that "disobedience" which exemplifies the indwelling law of sin.

Tennyson's St. Simeon Stylites, who after thirty years of painful expiation atop a pillar still cries out, "Have mercy, Lord, and take away my sin"—he indeed may be more sorely threatened by pride ("Show me the man hath suffered more than I") than by sexual arousal; the sin encrusting him "from scalp to sole" is not localized by his Victorian hagiographer at the crotch. But a Catholic artist of Van Hemessen's erotic temper, painting in the age of the boastful codpiece—if he, in 1531, sought to project upon his penitent's body the mark of rebellious flesh, why not precisely at the loincloth? I therefore find it less improbable than does Professor Held that this artist would forge a perceptible link between the saint's carnal propensity and his self-flagellation. The terms connect as attack with defense, sickness with remedy. In short, the "rather peculiar notion" which the sexual symptom adds to the penance of Van Hemessen's St. Jerome would be the Christian doctrine of Original Sin. But in a risen Christ, the similar sign would convert to a new meaning, as the resurrected flesh itself is converted in the glorified body.

XXXIII. On the afterlife of Boccaccio's jest

Novella III, 10 of the *Decameron* tells how the monk Rustico taught guileless Alibech the proper way to put the devil in hell. The line I have quoted — recalled by my colleague Professor Paul Watson — is unforgettable. But it has not fared well at the hands of translators. The first Modern Library edition (New York, 1930, trans. John Payne) was prefaced by Morris Ernst with the good news that the *Decameron* had at last passed the United States censors; but at the onset of that devilish passage in the novella, the text reverts (with footnote apology) to the Italian. We find the same tedious ploy in the J. M. Riss edition (privately printed, London, n.d., I, p. 252). Verbatim: "Then, having divested himself of his scanty clothing, he threw himself stark naked on his knees, as if he would pray; whereby he caused the girl, who followed his example, to confront him in the same posture. E così stando, essendo Rustico più che mai nel suo desidero acceso per lo vederla così bella, venne la resurrezion della carne, la quale riguardando Alibech e maravigliatasi, disse. . . ." A weasel note adds: "No apology is needed for leaving, in accordance with precedent, the subsequent detail untranslated." Apology is due rather from the Random House edition, where our sentence is rendered as "then his flesh grew stiff," the translator dropping the pun and the blasphemy to preserve only the lewd.

An old German edition I happen to own (by D.W. Soltan, Berlin, 1860) is remarkable in another way. Here again, the translator, like the Random House man, supposed that Boccaccio had been merely coy in referring to his hero's erection; and that therefore any updated leer about the sizeable angle formed by an electrometer with the horizon would do as well. ("Indem nun der Eremit alle Reize des jungen Mädchens vor Augen hatte, . . . wirkte das alles so mächtig auf ihn, dass bei ihm der Elektrometer anfing, einen beträchtlichen Winkel mit dem Horizont zu machen. . . .") In sum, all four translators shied at the given intersection of wit and sex with religion; and no doubt they thought themselves pious. But I suspect that when religion ceases to furnish matter for jokes such as Boccaccio's, or for strong oaths, such as "Zounds," it has already departed this life.

One hears echoes of Boccaccio's metaphor in the amatory poetry of the 16th and 17th centuries. Since Elizabethan verse habitually wrote "dying" for orgasm, and since its expiring swains normally "dye and rise," the analogy with resurrection may have become too banal, as well as too blasphemous, for plain iteration. But consider Mercutio's conjuring speech, designed to raise up Romeo ("the ape is dead") by sexual innuendo (*Romeo and Juliet,* II, 1). Or (at John Hollander's suggestion) Thomas Nashe's "The Choise of Valentines." Here the male member, lying dead, fears "To dye ere it hath seene Ierusalem"; then receives treatment "That maie availe to his recoverie"; and is at last raised "from his swoune." The blasphemy skirted remains uncommitted.

But it surely survived in tavern talk and black humor. (I read recently that Albert Camus' favorite Algiers café had in one corner "a skeleton equipped with a phallus that stood erect when jerked by a string"; Frederick Brown in *The New York Review of Books,* November 18, 1982, p. 10.) It would be strange indeed if there were no intermediaries between Boccaccio's finesse and the vulgarity of D. H. Lawrence's *The Man Who Died* (1928): "He crouched to her, and he felt the blaze of his manhood and his power rise up in his loins, magnificent. 'I am risen!'"

XXXIV. Sesostris' hieroglyph

Chief witness for the Sesostris story to which Casali's sermon refers is Herodotus, II, 102: "When those that he met were valiant men and strove hard for freedom, he set up pillars in their land whereon the inscription showed his own name and his country's, and how he had overcome them with his own power; but when the cities had made no resistance and been easily taken, then he put an inscription on the pillars even as he had done where the nations were brave; but he drew also on them the privy parts of a woman, wishing to show clearly that the people were cowardly." (Trans. A. D. Godley, Cambridge, Mass., 1920, I, p. 391. The text was well known in the Renaissance. A Latin translation by Lorenzo Valla, prepared in the 1450s at the request of Pope Nicholas V, was printed in 1474. By 1510 it had gone through three more editions. The first Italian translation was made by the poet Matteo Maria Boiardo [1441–94].)

The second reference to Sesostris' commemorative inscriptions occurs in the *Philippica* of Diodorus Siculus (I, 55, 7–8; 1st century B.C. The Latin translation by Poggio Bracciolini, produced again in the 1450s and dedicated to Nicholas V, was published in 1472; by 1515 it had been printed five times.) Our passage reads: "And he fashioned the stele with a representation, in case the enemy people were warlike, of the privy parts of a man [note that Herodotus had mentioned no sign for the male member], but in case they were abject and cowardly, of those of a woman, holding that the quality of the spirit of each people would be set forth most clearly to succeeding generations by the dominant member of the body" (trans. C. H. Oldfather, Cambridge, Mass., 1933, p. 195). In Poggio's Latin version, the last words translate "by the more powerful member of the man" (*ab potiori hominis parte*).

These texts, then, were widely available. But when Casali in 1512 retold the Sesostris story as part of his sermon on the Feast of the Circumcision, his direct informant is likely to have been Pierio Valeriano, then already at work on the *Hieroglyphica* (published at the end of a long life in 1556). Valeriano's youthful studies in Greek and Latin had been pursued under renowned masters in Venice. In 1509, aged thirty-two, he settled in Rome and soon won the favor of Julius II, before whom Casali's sermon was read. Valeriano's reference to the Sesostris story falls within a general discussion of phallic symbolism, where we read as follows under the rubric of "Magnanimity":

Let this be the primary signification of the male organs which, incised on so many pillars, marked on so many obelisks, and carved on so many other monuments of the ancients, display the great and lofty spirit of the strong man [*magnum et erectum viri fortis animum ostentarint*]. There still exist some fragments of columns erected in honor of Sesostris, inscribed with Egyptian letters, in which are discerned the sculpted natural parts [*naturae*] of both sexes . . . . Therefore, wherever you see the male pudenda on columns or obelisks set up by him, understand [them to mean] warlike, strong, and magnanimous men whom he conquered by arms (*Hieroglyphica*, XXXIV, p. 246).

And how did this curious lore stray into Casali's sermon? It is introduced by way of explaining why God had excluded women from the sacrament of circumcision. Casali's answer—retrojecting masculine hardihood to week-old infants—

explains that the ordeal of circumcision called for the strength of men, rather than the softness of women. Sesostris' hieroglyphs are brought in to clinch the argument.

The question remains how the symbolic equation of phallus with power would sit with an audience of monks and prelates— men who, in Jesus' phrase, had "made themselves eunuchs for the sake of the kingdom of heaven." I think the answer lies ready-made in the doctrine of victorious chastity. They would have answered that the male member is not disqualified as an emblem of strength for being sexually unemployed. On the contrary: in sexual exercise the martial male organ conquers no more than the "cowardly" female parts; whereas continence, the exercise of self-discipline, subdues the strong.

Does such an answer seem sophistical and outlandish? We hear its echo as late as 1854: "The generative energy, which, when we are loose, dissipates and makes us unclean, when we are continent invigorates and inspires us. Chastity is the flowering of man." The lines were written by our own Henry Thoreau in *Walden,* chap. 11.

XXXV. Wings of excess

Fig. 222. Lucas Cranach, *Crucifixion,* 1538.

Fig. 223. Lucas Cranach, *Christ on the Cross,* before 1502.

Fig. 224. Dürer and assistant, *Crucifixion*, c. 1500.

In the hands of the German Renaissance masters, the loincloth, or perizonium, luxuriates like the mantling of an escutcheon, yet even more broadcast, resplendent, and irrepressible. We read in John 3:8 that "the wind bloweth where it listeth." In the works reproduced below, it chooses to blow selectively about Christ's naked loins. And there are times when only a steady gust keeps the otherwise unattached fabric in place.

More may be said on the subject of the loincloth of Christ—because artists have made more of it than a study in drapery. Even the central knot, as tied by Mantegna (Copenhagen) or Cosimo Tura, deserves thinking about, for even here metaphor is at work. Are there readers who doubt that a cloth can be knotted to allude to the phallus? or who suspect that only a mind misled by modern jargon about symbolic displacement would sport such fantasies? Let them turn again to Montaigne (*Essays,* III, 5): "In my neighborhood [i.e., around Bordeaux] the married women twist their kerchief over their forehead into the shape of [a phallus], to boast of the enjoyment they have out of it; and when they become widows, they turn it behind them and hide it under their coif." Whether this is indeed what the tied kerchiefs of those Bordelaise women denoted, or whether Montaigne interpreted them in an *esprit mal tourné* may be open to question; either way he has proved the thought thinkable in his century. But let the pictures suffice.

Fig. 225. Hans Baldung Grien, *Crucifixion,* 1512.

Fig. 226. Cosimo Tura, *Dead Christ Supported by Angels,* c. 1474.

Fig. 227. Dürer and assistant, *Lamentation,* c. 1500.

XXXVI. Not other than willed

In a *Crucifixion* panel by Guido da Siena (Utrecht, Archiepiscopal Museum; reprod. in Meiss, *Black Death,* fig. 122), a light-footed Christ climbs the rungs of a ladder to mount his cross. Such literalism in symbolizing eagerness for Crucifixion is rare—it almost annuls the root of sufferance in the word "Passion." But Guido's image was intended to visualize one term of a paradox: that Christ in his dual nature instigates as he suffers, undergoes nothing but what he wills. This is why the Trinity's Second Person is said, in the active voice, to enter the Virgin's womb, and to emerge from it nimbly, as a bridegroom issues forth from the bridal chamber. In the words of St. Augustine's Epiphany sermon: "The Son of God was born of his own free will" (Sermon XVIII, 3 [Ben. 199]; *Sermons,* p. 157). This is why St. Bernard assures us that the eight-day-old Infant could easily have repelled from its flesh the knife of the circumcision—he who even in death kept corruption away (see p. 54). And this is why, in one of the most persistent metaphors of the Christian tradition, the outspread arms nailed to the cross are received by the faithful as a tendered embrace. The very doctrine of the Incarnation demands it: it requires that everything done to Christ be attracted, that it be suffered and at the same time elicited or commanded, so that passive and active concur in unison with Christ's concurrent natures. Thus the task before Renaissance artists who were choreographing the Passion was to project physical motions that would be at once contradictory and convincing.

Few, admittedly, had Michelangelo's imaginative resources in making a deposed Christ seem both expired and vital. But in Renaissance painting almost every dead Christ on the cross averts his head from the bad thief; the lifeless droop still renders a judgment. And every artist understood that no member of the cruci-fied body rests or falls except by the acquiescence of Christ's other nature.

In his formal response to my paper (November 1981), Professor Held wondered "if the word 'gesture' can really be applied to a corpse." The dead Christ's hand on his groin, he remarked, "can only result from an act of piety, imputed by the artist to the mourners who had laid out the dead body." I answer: Even if it were piety to dispose dead men's hands at the crotch (they often are folded over the lower abdomen) no such intervention by the mourners is shown. The self-touching hand of the deposed Christ is gestural after all — no need to acquit the corpse by inculpating the mourners. Where a dead Christ's hand is cupped over the genitals, as it is unmistakably in scores of monuments, our task is not to exonerate the deceased, but to search the artist's intention in choosing so stark a symbol.

XXXVII. The un-dead hand on the groin

Fig. 228. Flemish, *Entombment,* c. 1380–1400.

Six further instances of the groin-touching motif in multi-figured scenes of Lamentation or Entombment are reproduced in Figs. 228–33. These are followed by five images of the *Pietà*, remarkable for the *ostentatio genitalium*, as discussed on p. 104 (Figs. 234–38). (Among striking examples not reproduced are Giovanni Mansueti's panel at Bergamo, Accademia Carrara, and Piero di Cosimo's *Pietà with Saints* in Perugia, Galleria Nazionale dell'Umbria.)

Fig. 229. Flemish, *Mary Magdalen* (?) *Supporting the Dead Christ*, c. 1490.

Fig. 231. Andrea Solario, *Lamentation*, 1504–07.

Fig. 230. German, *Lamentation*, 1481–1504.

Fig. 232. Mattia Preti (?), *Dead Christ with Angels*.

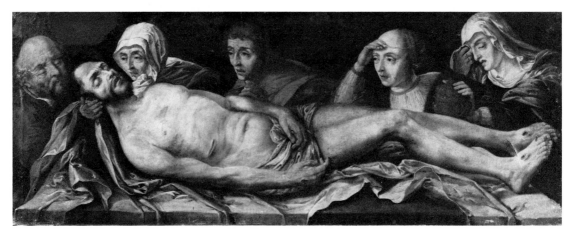

Fig. 233. David Kindt, *Lamentation*, 1631.

Fig. 234. Master of the St. Lucy Legend,
Pietà, c. 1475.

Fig. 236. Lower Rhenish, *Pietà,* c. 1480.

Fig. 235. Lower Rhenish, *Pietà,* 15th century.

Fig. 237. German, *Pietà,* c. 1490–1500.

Fig. 238. Westphalian, *Pietà,* 1550.

XXXVIII. In imitation of Christ

Professor Julius Held has questioned the necessity of my interpretation of the groin-touching gesture. He rightly remarked: "If the pose were restricted to the dead body of Christ, the hypothesis might be acceptable that, with Christ's Passion completed, the motif points back to its beginning, i.e., the Circumcision. Yet as it is encountered in different contexts— even in renderings of women—another explanation may have to be found. Could it be the symbolic expression of the fact that the organs of procreation have now ceased their function? Or might it be meant as a last, though purely wishful, defense against putrefaction which begins (or was believed to begin) in these parts? Or may it, after all, be a final sign of modesty?"

Fortunately, there is little disagreement between us—only a need for clarifica-

tions. In the 16th-century tombs cited by Held, imputed shame is unquestionably a factor. Montaigne tells of the Emperor Maximilian's modesty—"carried to such a pitch of superstition, that in his will he expressly ordered that after death his parts should be hidden by drawers" (*Essays,* III, 5). Just such posthumous modesty is monumentalized in the French royal *gisants* at Saint-Denis. These nude marble effigies, though of the dead, are represented bunching fistfuls of shroud at the pubis, as if fearful of being uncovered (Fig. 239). But no risk of shameful exposure threatens the figure of Christ in Deposition scenes or Entombments. There the body is almost invariably draped, wearing a loincloth securely tied and so adequate as to make any modesty gesture redundant. If, in such presentations, the dead Christ nevertheless lays his hand on his groin, if he keeps pointing to what is in no danger of showing, the will that directs the hand must be mysterious, the motive must be other than shame of body. And this conclusion is strengthened by the physical character of the gesture: in scores of instances it takes form as a vigorous clasping, grasping, or cupping—more likely a symbol of continence than a covering up.

Yet I am grateful to Professor Held. For if the sculptured cadavers he cites engage, in his words, in "symbolic expression," or evince posthumous modesty, or by their gesture seek to ward off decay, he has already conceded enough. The threshold of metaphor has been crossed, and the gesture we are considering will be understood as a trope. Now of his three proposed explanations for the self-touch in these figures, I am inclined to doubt only the first, which would refer the gesture to the cessation of procreative function. The remaining two—genital shame and the imminence of decay—do not exclude, but rather intensify one another.

Fig. 239. Germain Pilon, Tomb effigies of Henry II and Catherine de' Medici, 1565–70.

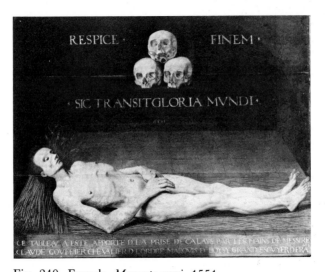

Fig. 240. French, *Memento mori,* 1551.

The warding hand in these effigies may well have been motivated by the belief that "putrefaction begins in these parts"; though perhaps the gesture should be understood less as a futile, wishful defense against corruption, than as indicating where corruption begins—"corruption" to be understood in the word's double meaning, moral and physical, comprehending the effect of both sin and death. And this is why for these 15th- and 16th-century effigies, the groin-touching gesture as an allusion to shame *and* decay seems an acceptable explanation.

But since Christ's body does not suffer corruption, and since in the works discussed his hand lays demonstrative stress on well-draped loins that need no further covering, the meaning of his gesture must be *sui generis,* whatever the reason for its subsequent assignation to other dead (Fig. 240). That these others, when their tombs come to represent them as naked, follow the example of him who had died a thousand deaths naked in earlier images — that these Christian dead in their nudity put on the uniform of their Lord — seems to me hard to deny. If their tomb effigies, from whatever motive, enact so private a gesture, they can do so because the dead Christ had performed it three days before his Resurrection, and their hope reposes in following Christ.

The dependence on the example of Christ may be confirmed by the fact that the earliest funerary monument to exhibit the self-touching motif in a mortal other than Christ is the tomb of Guillaume de Harcigny, a man who had practiced medicine at Laon, where he died in 1393. This "très vaillant et sage médecin" (Froissart) had repeatedly treated King Charles VI. It is likely that he would have had knowledge of the marble *Entombment* relief of c. 1330 (Fig. 109) housed in the royal chapel, the Sainte-Chapelle, Paris. Far more improbable that he would re-invent such a shocking motif for his personal tomb in ignorance of Christ's effigy in the king's chapel.

(For biographical data on Harcigny and the dating and provenance of the *Entombment,* see *Les Fastes du Gothique: Le siècle de Charles V,* exh. cat., Paris, Grand Palais, 1981, nos. 18, 93. The Harcigny tomb, now in the Musée Archéologique at Laon, is reproduced as fig. 1 in Kathleen Cohen, *Metamorphosis of a Death Symbol: The Transi Tomb in the Late Middle Ages and the Renaissance,* Berkeley and Los Angeles, 1973 — along with a representative selection of later tomb effigies. The motif of the self-touch is not discussed in her work, nor, so far as I know, elsewhere in the literature.)

Further in response to Professor Held, I must rectify a misunderstanding. In discussing the hand-on-groin gesture of a

Fig. 241. Dirc van Delf, illumination, *Animation of Adam,* c. 1404.

dead Christ, I do not mean to refer it exclusively to the Circumcision. I would say rather that the crucified God, in that token gesture, indicates his sacrificial humanity, of which Circumcision and stigmata together are the symbolic form.

The groin-touching gesture occurs in two other contexts. In 15th-century iconography it is occasionally found in images of Adam, either at his creation or that of Eve, or in his death. (See Fig. 241 and the contemporaneous Netherlandish *Bible historiale,* Paris, Bibliothèque de l'Arsenal, ms. 5057, fol. 7, reprod. in Erwin Panofsky, *Early Netherlandish Painting,* Cambridge, Mass., 1953, II, fig. 57. At the *Creation of Eve,* the gesture appears in the Bible of Borso d'Este, 1455–61, Modena, Biblioteca Estense, VG. 12, I, fol. 6, reproduced in J. J. G. Alexander, *Italian Renaissance Illuminations,* New York, 1977, pl. 20. The gesture appears again in Giovanni Dalmata's *Creation of Eve* relief from the dismantled tomb of Pope Paul II in the Grotte Vaticane (Fig. 242). In the illumination for the Office of the Dead in the Limbourgs' *Belles Heures* of Jean de Berry, the corpses of both Adam and Eve are shown shielding their groins; New York, The Metropolitan Museum of Art, The Cloisters Collection, fol. 99.)

Fig. 242. Giovanni Dalmata, *Creation of Eve,*
c. 1471–77.

Finally, a word concerning the hand-
on-groin gesture in secular representations of corpses. Only two instances of the
motif have come to my attention so far,
both dating from the latter 16th century.
One is a panel from the atelier of Antoine
Caron. It represents the *Funeral of Amor.*
The nude child god, laid out on a bier,
crosses his hands in his lap (Musée National du Louvre, *Peintures: École française
XIVe, XVe et XVIe siècles,* Paris, 1965, pls.
163–65). The other is an engraving after
Theodore Barendt by Jan Sadeler (Hollstein 451). It is one of a set representing
"The Four Last Things." The image of
"Death" shows an old man's corpse fully
shrouded, extended across the foreground,
lamented by next-of-kin. The left hand
shields the pudenda in a gesture clearly
adapted from imagery of the Holy Grave.

XXXIX. The Throne of Grace

The type of the seated Father sustain-
ing the corpse of the Son in upright position, while the Son points to his wound,
appears to be Robert Campin's invention
(see the Leningrad panel and the Frankfurt grisaille in Friedländer, *Early Netherlandish Painting,* II, figs. 60 and 65). But
what now concerns us is that modification
of the type which directs the Father's hand
to the Son's groin. The motif seems to
originate in a painting, no longer extant,
which once exerted a powerful influence,
giving rise to numerous adaptations and
copies (Figs. 122, 243–45). Whether this
modification was introduced by Campin
or, as I incline to believe, by Roger van
der Weyden, cannot yet be decided with
certainty. The literature concerning the
problem of attribution is not helpful since
the specific gesture which modifies the

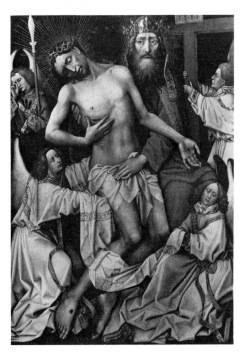

Fig. 243. After Campin (?) or Roger,
Throne of Grace.

198

Fig. 244. South Netherlandish, *Throne of Grace,* 1450.

Fig. 245. Brabant School, *Throne of Grace,* 15th century.

Campin type has not been discussed.

The motif of the Father's hand on the Son's groin is found again in a later compositional type of German provenance: oblong, multi-figured woodcarvings, known to me in two monumental examples (Figs. 123, 246). Whether this variant type is an independent invention, or derives the paternal gesture from the Campin-Roger design, is at present unclear.

(Since images of the *Trinity* that include the groin-touching gesture are rare, I list four further copies and adaptations of the Rogerian type: the medallion of an embroidered cope, Berne, Historisches Museum, Friedländer, *Early Netherlandish Painting,* II, pl. 99, no. 71A; a panel by the Master of St. Sang in Brussels, and another by Colin de Coter in Paris, ibid., IXb, no. 201 and IV, no. 90; and the engraving by the Master of the Banderoles, Lehrs 83. A variant form of the composition, showing the Son's groin touched by himself, appears in the *Throne of Grace* illumination in the Breviary of Philip the Good, c. 1454, in The Hague; see V. Leroquais, *Le Bréviare de Philippe le Bon,* Brussels, 1929, pl. 66.)

Fig. 246. Lübeck School, *Throne of Grace,* c. 1510 (?).

XL. Postscript by John W. O'Malley, S.J.

The following comments, published here with the author's consent, were delivered at the first presentation of the foregoing text in its original brevity (Lionel Trilling Seminar, Columbia University, November 1981). They were not addressed to the present expanded version. Where O'Malley's references to Renaissance sermons on the Circumcision seem to overlap mine, it should be remembered that it was he who brought these sermons to light; to have deleted his remarks as "repetitious" would have been robbery on my part. I have, however, taken the liberty to delete one or two sentences for their ad hominem *character. For the rest, I am proud to have furnished the context for O'Malley's first public avowal of an "outrageous thesis," which he is about to expound more fully elsewhere.*

When I was invited several months ago to comment on this evening's lecture, I was apprehensive. I was not sure that I wanted to be involved in a public discussion or, more probably, public controversy on "the sexuality of Christ." Curiosity, however, overcame cowardice, and I accepted the invitation.

I was invited, as I understand it, not simply because I am a Renaissance historian but because my specific interest is Renaissance theology and religious culture. It is in that capacity that I will comment on the lecture.

Let me affirm straightaway that as soon as I read Steinberg's lecture any misgivings that I entertained about participating in this evening's event disappeared. . . . A topic that could easily have been sensationalized is, instead, treated with such a high degree of theological sophistication that it naturally leads to larger issues about the nature of Renaissance culture and religion. I will try to correlate some of those issues with tonight's lecture.

What was "Renaissance theology," for instance, and what was there about it that might allow or compel us to see it as a distinctive moment in the long tradition of reflection upon the mysteries of the Christian faith? Those are the complex questions that historians are only now beginning to address. Erasmus is the Renaissance theologian who has received the most attention in the last twenty years, and we now perceive how poorly served he has been through the centuries by interpreters who dismissed him as merely a poor match for Luther. But the studies by historians like Charles Trinkaus, Salvatore Camporeale, and others have demonstrated that there were Italian antecedents to Erasmus that were just as fascinating and that have consistently been deprived of their rightful place in the history of theology. Rome has been not only neglected but especially denigrated in that history. Yet I, for one, am now on the verge of proposing the outrageous thesis that it was in Rome in the seventy-five years before the outbreak of the Reformation that the most original and creative theological work was being done in all of Europe. Whatever the merits of that thesis, there is no question that "Renaissance theology" in general was severely damaged, perhaps in large part destroyed, by

the bitter controversies sparked by the Reformation and Counter Reformation, and even the memory of it was almost obliterated. Part of the merit of Steinberg's paper is to help revive that memory.

One of the most striking characteristics of Renaissance theology was, in my opinion, its treatment of the mystery of the Incarnation. I have gone so far as to call it an "incarnational theology" and to try to detail the implications of that term. For our purposes this evening it will suffice to say that the mystery of the Incarnation tended to be seen as the central truth of Christianity and as being identified with the mystery of the Redemption. This was no novel idea. It was the basis for the theology of many of the Greek Fathers and is found also in Thomas Aquinas. But the idea was revived with a new emphasis in the Renaissance and tended in effect to place as much, if not more, redemptive efficacy on the moment of the incarnation in the Virgin's womb as in the suffering and death of Jesus on the cross. Humanity was saved, redeemed, at least inchoately, at the moment the Godhead assumed human flesh and became one with us.

The reasons why this mystery so specially engaged Renaissance thinkers are complicated and still need study. In my opinion, however, the emergence of a new emphasis on the Incarnation was intimately related to the revival of the *studia humanitatis* and to the application of those *studia* to the Christian concerns that preoccupied many of the men and women of the Renaissance. Within the *studia humanitatis,* the revival of epideictic rhetoric was crucial. This was the rhetoric of panegyric that, in its pure form, rehearsed the life and deeds of its heroes. It was, therefore, essentially biographical or historical in its perspective. Sometime around the year 1400 it was applied to the saints, then to funeral eulogies, and, finally, in a bold move, to sermons on Christ. It easily correlated, therefore, with an older and independent tradition that developed with Bernard in the 12th century and with the Franciscans in the 13th and 14th that loved to meditate on the humanity of Christ.

The well-known "weakness for general ideas" that has characterized the rhetorical tradition from its beginnings in ancient Greece also factors into this Renaissance phenomenon. Renaissance humanists, in this instance, wanted to avoid the hair-splitting and the theological byways of their scholastic counterparts, and wanted, as well, to be faithful to the most venerable, secure, and central traditions of the Church. The Creeds and the controversies of the patristic era were their guides, and they thus turned their attention to the Trinitarian and Christological issues that shook the patristic era and, presumably, were settled once and for all at that time. The Trinity was difficult to deal with in popular discourse and could hardly be treated without the use of sophisticated philosophical terminology. That was much less true about the way the patristic era resolved the Christological controversies. Here the results could be stated in commonsense terms: true God, true man.

This abstract truth of the Creed then had to be turned, according to the principles of rhetoric, to the advantage of the audience. It had to be utilized to lift that audience to lofty sentiments that would then animate behavior worthy of a Christian. It is at this juncture that the rhetoric evokes and promotes the theme of the "dignity of man." What better way could there possibly be to drive home the truth of the dignity of human nature than to insist that God himself had not disdained to assume it and had, indeed, become man —truly man.

You must recall, moreover, that the liturgy of the Roman Rite prescribed that the celebrant and the entire congregation fall to its knees at only one point during the recitation of the ancient Creed—*"et incarnatus est ex Maria Virgine, et homo factus est."* The next phrase—*"crucifixus etiam pro nobis"*—followed almost as an afterthought, a corollary, once the assembly had again returned to its feet. This dramatic rubric must have impressed any artist sensitive to the religious subjects he was called upon to paint.

That is, in general terms, the Renaissance context into which Steinberg's lecture must be placed. He has been at pains to show that the theological underpinnings for his interpretation of the nude Christs fit into the general tradition of Christian theology. He is correct. But the immediate tradition of the religious culture of the Renaissance is even more confirmatory of his findings. The "dignity-of-man" theme, it seems to me, inspires, with a paradoxical bravado, the *ostentatio genitalium* that Steinberg has called to our attention.

The Incarnation took place, of course, at the moment of conception in the Virgin's womb—during the Annunciation, that scene so common to Renaissance art; but Renaissance thinkers were too subtle and supple to restrict the event so narrowly. The Incarnation was manifested—"revealed"—only later, when the Child was manifested to the world at his birth, held in his mother's arms, shown to the Magi for their adoration, and most unmistakably of all when he was subjected to the rite of circumcision.

There was no better occasion for Renaissance preachers to capitalize on the wonderful paradox of true-God-true-man than in sermons on the Circumcision. You must remember that January 1 was a holy day on which people were obliged to go to Mass and, often enough, to hear a sermon. I have examined a number of these sermons. Faithful to the Gospel text of the day, the sermons generally dealt with two things: the physical act of circumcision (and its possible mystic meaning as well), and the giving of the Name, JESUS—that is, savior. MAN-GOD, if you will.

There is an earthiness and concreteness in some of these sermons on the Circumcision that would surely offend our contemporary tastes. I would mention, for example, the sermon by Bernardino Carvajal, 1484, in St. John Lateran that contains a discussion about the authenticity of the foreskin of Christ held in that Church's collection of relics. Even more pertinent to the lecture this evening are the lines from the sermon to the papal court by Francesco Cardulo, about 1495, in which he argues the humanity of Christ by the, quite literally, palpable reality of the male member that "is fondled, taken in the hand, receives a wound, feels pain"—*"quod attrectatur, quod sumitur in manus, quod plagam recipit, quod sentit dolorem."* I might note that *attrectare* is not a particularly respectable word and sometimes has the erotic connotations of our equivalent, "fondle."

At this point I would even venture to develop further a suggestion Steinberg makes about the draperies that often seem to be deliberately removed from the infant's genitals in many of the scenes we have seen. I suggest that here we might have a deliberate play on the idea of "revelation." *Velum* is a veil, while *revelare* means to unveil, just as epiphany means to show and to make manifest. This God, in other words, is unveiled, *revealed,* in these scenes as truly and fully man.

I will venture an even less easily substantiated suggestion for interpreting the nude infant. The poverty issue that racked the Franciscan order was still very much alive in the 15th and 16th centuries. Could there, at least in some instances, be a vague allusion to the prophetic, radical impulse articulated in the evocative slogan

so popular in the late Middle Ages—*"Nudum sequi nudum Christum."* In other words, might there be an ascetical and reform overtone even to the seemingly comfortable scenes of nude infancy?

This suggestion is perhaps more applicable to the paintings of the Man of Sorrows, to the Crucifixion, Deposition, and Burial than to the scenes of childhood. I must admit that where there is question in these scenes of an erection, howsoever veiled or revealed, I am truly surprised and at a loss to find a correlation with Catholic theology. Steinberg's suggestions for resolving this problem are ingenious rather than traditional, but I have to admit that I welcome them because I know no place else to turn.

When the hand of the dead Christ simply covers the genitals there is much less of a problem, and the simplest explanation is perhaps to take this gesture as a sign that there was, indeed, something there to cover—and, hence, to take the gesture as a sign of the genuine humanity of the one who died and as a symbol of modesty by the one who had been so immodestly stripped. Or the gesture very well may be meant, as Steinberg proposes, to point to the first wound and first shedding of blood for our redemption. There is, in fact, a clear literary text to support this interpretation in the sermon on the Circumcision by the noted humanist, Gasperino Barzizza, written sometime before 1431.

In summary: Steinberg, as an art historian using artistic evidence, has arrived at certain conclusions about one aspect of Renaissance religious art. Working independently and with quite different evidence, I have arrived at some conclusions that easily correlate with his. I believe some of my colleagues have done the same. It seems to me that we may be on the threshold of seeing the Renaissance as a more integrated cultural reality than has heretofore been the case — or, better, as integrated in a way different from what we have sometimes been led to believe. We know, of course, that there was in the Renaissance a rivalry between artists and men of letters, and they did not always move in the same company. Nonetheless, they both were products and creators of a common culture, and, as such, had more impact on each other than even they may have been ready to admit and able to perceive.

BIBLIOGRAPHY

Ambrose, St., *Letters* (The Fathers of the Church, 26), New York, 1959.

Aquinas, St. Thomas, *Summa theologiae,* Blackfriars ed., London, 1964.

Ariès, Philippe, *Centuries of Childhood,* trans. Robert Baldick, New York, 1962.

Artemidorus, *Oneirocritica,* trans. Robert J. White, Park Ridge, New Jersey, 1975.

Athanasius, St., *Contra Gentes and De Incarnatione,* trans. Robert W. Thompson, Oxford, 1971.

Augustine, St., *Harmony of the Gospels,* ed. Philip Schaff (A Select Library of the Nicene and Post-Nicene Fathers of the Christian Church, 6), Grand Rapids, Michigan, n.d.

———, *On Marriage and Concupiscence,* in *Anti-Pelagian Writings,* ed. Philip Schaff (A Select Library of the Nicene and Post-Nicene Fathers of the Christian Church, 5), Grand Rapids, Michigan, 1956.

———, *Sermons for Christmas and Epiphany,* trans. Thomas Comerford Lawler (Ancient Christian Writers, 15), Westminster, Maryland, and London, 1952.

Bagnariis, Ludovicus de, *Oratio de nomine Iesu,* Rome (E. Silber?), 1486.

Baldini, Umberto and Paolo dal Poggetto, *Firenze restaura: il laboratorio nel suo quarantennio,* exh. cat., Florence, Fortezza da Basso, 1972.

Bede, St., *A History of the English Church and People,* trans. L. Sherley-Price, Harmondsworth, 1955.

———, *In die festo circumcisionis domini, Homiliae genuinae,* lib. I, hom. X, *Pat. lat.,* 94, cols. 53–58.

Berenson, Bernard, *Italian Pictures of the Renaissance. Florentine School,* London, 1963; *Central Italian and North Italian Schools,* London, 1968.

Bernard, St., *Oeuvres de St. Bernard,* trans. M. Armand Ravelet, Bar-le-Duc, 1890.

———, *On the Song of Songs,* trans. Kilian Walsh and Irene Edmonds, 4 vols., Kalamazoo, Michigan, 1971–80.

Bettenson, Henry, ed., *Documents of the Christian Church,* New York and London, 1947.

Bonaventure, St., *The Breviloquium,* trans. José de Vinck (The Works of Bonaventure, 2), Paterson, New Jersey, 1963.

———, *The Soul's Journey into God. The Tree of Life,* trans. E. Cousins, New York, 1978.

Bougerol, J. Guy, *Introduction to the Works of Bonaventure,* Paterson, New Jersey, 1963.

Bultmann, Rudolf, *Kerygma and Myth: A Theological Debate* (1948), ed. Hans Werner Bartsch, New York, 1961.

Campano, Giovanni Antonio, *De circumcisione oratio,* in *Opera a Michaele Ferno edita,* Rome (E. Silber), 1495.

Cardulus, Franciscus Narniensis, *Oratio de circumcisione,* Lucca, Biblioteca Capitolare, cod. 544, II, fols. 86v–90v.

Carvajal, Bernardino, *Oratio in die circumcisionis,* Rome (S. Plannck), 1488–90.

Condivi, Ascanio, *The Life of Michelangelo* (1553), trans. Charles Holroyd, London and New York, 1903.

Danielou, Jean, *The Bible and the Liturgy,* Notre Dame, Indiana, 1956.

Denzinger, Henry, *The Sources of Catholic Dogma,* trans. Roy J. Deferrari, St. Louis and London, 1957.

Economou, George D., *The Goddess Natura in Medieval Literature,* Cambridge, Massachusetts, 1972.

Eusebius, *The History of the Church,* trans. G. A. Williamson, New York, 1966.

Freedberg, David, "The Structure of Byzantine and European Iconoclasm," in *Iconoclasm,* eds. Anthony Bryer and Judith Herrin, Birmingham, England, 1975, pp. 165–77.

Friedländer, Max J., *Early Netherlandish Painting,* 14 vols., New York and Washington, D.C., 1967–76.

Hopper, Vincent F., *Medieval Number Symbolism,* New York, 1969.

Hugh of St. Victor, *Noah's Ark,* in Hugh of St. Victor, *Selected Spiritual Writings,* London, 1962.

Jerome, St., *The Letters of St. Jerome,* I, trans. Charles Christopher Mierow (Ancient Christian Writers, 33), New York, 1963.

Kantorowicz, Ernst, *The King's Two Bodies: A Study in Medieval Political Theology,* Princeton, 1957.

Kelly, J. N. D., *Early Christian Doctrines,* New York, etc., 1958.

Lavin, Marilyn Aronberg, "The Joy of the Bridegroom's Friend: Smiling Faces in Fra Filippo, Raphael, and Leonardo," in *Art the Ape of Nature: Studies in Honor of H. W. Janson,* eds. Moshe Barasch and Lucy Freeman Sandler, New York, 1981, pp. 193–210.

Lisner, Margrit, "The Crucifix from Santo Spirito and the Crucifixes of Taddeo Curradi," *The Burlington Magazine,* 122 (1980), pp. 812–19.

Lollio, Antonio, *Oratio circumcisionis dominicae,* Rome (S. Plannck), 1485 (?).

Lotz, Wolfgang, "Zu Michelangelos Christus in S. Maria sopra Minerva," in *Festschrift für Herbert von Einem zum 16. Februar 1965,* eds. Gert von der Osten and Georg Kauffmann, Berlin, 1965, pp. 143–50.

Mâle, Emile, *L'Art religieux de la fin du moyen âge en France* (1908), 5th ed., Paris, 1949.

Marrow, James H. and Alan Shestack, *Hans Baldung Grien: Prints & Drawings,* exh. cat., Washington, D.C., National Gallery of Art, 1981.

Meiss, Millard, *French Painting in the Time of Jean de Berry: The Late Fourteenth Century and the Patronage of the Duke,* London and New York, 1969.

————, *Painting in Florence and Siena after the Black Death,* Princeton, 1951.

Methodius, St., *The Symposium: A Treatise on Chastity,* trans. Herbert Musurillo (Ancient Christian Writers, 27), New York, 1958.

Molanus, Johannes, *De historia ss. imaginarum et picturarum* (1570), ed. Louvain, 1771.

The Nag Hammadi Library in English, trans. Thomas O. Lambdin, New York, 1977.

Norden, Eduard, *Die Geburt des Kindes: Geschichte einer religiösen Idee* (1924), Darmstadt, 1958.

O'Malley, John W., "The Feast of Thomas Aquinas in Renaissance Rome: A Neglected Document and Its Import," *Rivista di storia della Chiesa in Italia,* 35 (1981), pp. 1–27.

————, *Praise and Blame in Renaissance Rome: Rhetoric, Doctrine and Reform in the Sacred Orators of the Papal Court, c. 1450–1521,* Durham, North Carolina, 1979.

————, "Preaching for the Popes," in *The Pursuit of Holiness in Late Medieval and Renaissance Religion,* eds. Charles Trinkaus and Heiko A. Oberman, Leiden, 1974, pp. 408–43.

————, "The Vatican Library and the School of Athens: A Text of Battista Casali, 1508," *Journal of Medieval and Renaissance Studies,* 7 (1977), pp. 271–87.

Origen, *On First Principles,* trans. G. W. Butterworth, New York, 1966.

————, *The Song of Songs: Commentary and Homilies,* trans. R. P. Lawson (Ancient Christian Writers, 26), Westminster, Maryland, and London, 1957.

Origo, Iris, "The Domestic Enemy: The Eastern Slaves in Tuscany in the 14th and 15th Centuries," *Speculum,* 30 (1955), pp. 321–66.

Pelikan, Jaroslav, *The Christian Tradition: A History of the Development of Doctrine.* I: *The Emergence of the Catholic Tradition (100–600);* II: *The Spirit of Eastern Christendom (600–1700),* Chicago, 1971, 1974.

Perella, Nicolas J., *The Kiss Sacred and Profane,* Berkeley and Los Angeles, 1969.

Photius, *The Homilies of Photius, Patriarch of Constantinople,* trans. Cyril Mango, Cambridge, Massachusetts, 1958.

Pico della Mirandola, *Heptaplus or Discourse on the Seven Days of Creation,* trans. Jessie Brewer McGaw, New York, 1977.

Poole, Reginald L., *Studies in Chronology and History* (1934), Oxford, 1969.

Pope, Marvin H., *The Anchor Bible: Song of Songs,* Garden City, New York, 1977.

Pope-Hennessy, John, *Italian Renaissance Sculpture,* 2nd ed., London, 1971.

————, "The Virgin with the Laughing Child" (1957), in *Essays on Italian Sculpture,* London, 1968, pp. 72–77.

Pseudo-Bonaventure, *Meditations on the Life of Christ,* trans. Isa Ragusa and Rosalie B. Green, Princeton, 1961.

Reinach, Salomon, "Le rire rituel," *Revue de l'Université de Bruxelles,* 6 (1910–11), pp. 585–602.

Ringbom, Sixten, *Icon to Narrative: The Rise of the Dramatic Close-up in Fifteenth-Century Devotional Painting,* Åbo, 1965.

Schiller, Gertrud, *Iconography of Christian Art,* 2 vols., Greenwich, Connecticut, 1971–72.

Seymour, Charles, *Early Italian Painting in the Yale University Art Gallery,* New Haven and London, 1970.

Steinberg, Leo, "Leonardo's *Last Supper,*" *The Art Quarterly,* 36 (1973), pp. 297–410.

————, "The Metaphors of Love and Birth in Michelangelo's Pietàs," in *Studies in Erotic Art,* eds. Theodore Bowie and Cornelia V. Christenson, New York, 1970, pp. 231–335.

Tertullian, *Treatises on Marriage and Remarriage,* trans. William P. Le Saint (Ancient Christian Writers, 13), New York, 1951.

Valeriano, Pierio, *Hieroglyphica* (1556), ed. Basel, 1567.

Voragine, Jacopo da, *The Golden Legend or Lives of the Saints as Englished by William Caxton* (1483), ed. London, 1900.

Wentzel, Hans, "Die ikonographischen Voraussetzungen der Christus-Johannes-Gruppe und das Sponsa-Sponsus-Bild des Hohen Liedes," *Heilige Kunst: Jahrbuch des Kunstvereins der Diözese Rottenburg,* Stuttgart, 1952, pp. 6–21.

Wessel, K., "Der nackte Crucifixus von Narbonne," *Rivista di archaeologia cristiana,* 43 (1967), pp. 333–45.

Zampetti, Pietro, *Painting from the Marches: Gentile to Raphael,* London, 1971.

LIST OF ILLUSTRATIONS

Where no medium is indicated, the work is in oil or tempera on canvas or panel. Dimensions are given in centimeters, height preceding width.

Fig. 22. Roger van der Weyden, *Madonna and Child,* c. 1460 (49 × 31). Caen, Musée des Beaux-Arts; Mancel Collection.

Fig. 23. Antonio Rossellino, *Virgin with the Laughing Child,* c. 1465–75, terracotta (ht. 48.3). London, Victoria and Albert Museum.

Fig. 24. Vitale da Bologna, *Madonna and Child,* c. 1345, detached fresco. Bologna, Pinacoteca Nazionale.

Fig. 25. Gentile da Fabriano, *Madonna and Child with Sts. Nicholas and Catherine,* c. 1415 (131 × 113), detail. Berlin, Gemäldegalerie.

Fig. 26. Filippo Lippi, *Madonna and Child,* c. 1445 (75.5 × 52.3). Baltimore, Walters Art Gallery.

Fig. 27. Antoniazzo Romano, *Madonna and Child with Sts. Paul and Francis,* 1488 (166 × 155), detail. Rome, Galleria Nazionale, Palazzo Barberini.

Fig. 28. Michelino da Besozzo, illumination, *Christ Crowning Duke Giangaleazzo Visconti in Heaven,* 1403. Paris, Bibliothèque Nationale, ms. lat. 5888, fol. 1.

Fig. 29. Coppo di Marcovaldo, *Madonna del Bordone,* 1261. Siena, Sta. Maria dei Servi.

Fig. 30. Bohemian illumination, *Adoration of the Magi,* c. 1360–70. Prague, Cathedral Library, Cim VI, fol. 32.

Fig. 31. Bohemian, *Madonna and Child with Emperor Charles IV and Saints,* 1371 (181 × 96), detail. Prague, Národní Galerie.

Fig. 32. Maso di Banco, *Madonna and Child Enthroned,* c. 1350 (54.1 × 19.1), detail. The Brooklyn Museum; Gift of the Heirs of Frank L. Babbatt.

Fig. 33. Giotto Shop, *Madonna and Child Enthroned,* c. 1320. Whereabouts unknown.

Fig. 34. Taddeo Gaddi, *Madonna and Child Enthroned,* 1355 (154 × 80). Florence, Galleria degli Uffizi.

Fig. 35. Andrea di Bartolo, *Madonna and Child with Fourteen Saints,* c. 1405–10 (87.6 × 67). New Haven, Yale University Art Gallery; Bequest of Maitland F. Griggs.

Fig. 36. Nardo di Cione, *Madonna and Child with Four Saints,* c. 1355 (195 × 98). The New-York Historical Society; Bryan Collection.

Fig. 37. English illumination from the Holkham Hall Bible, *Crucifixion,* c. 1325–30. Holkham Hall, Earl of Leicester, fol. 32v.

Fig. 38. Master of St. Mark (Catalan), *Crucifixion* panels from a polyptych, 1355–60. New York, The Pierpont Morgan Library.

Fig. 39. Westphalian, *Disrobing of Christ,* c. 1490, detail from an *Anna Selbdritt* panel (46.5 × 38). Cologne, Wallraf-Richartz-Museum.

Fig. 40. Jacopo Bellini, *Madonna of Humility with Donor,* c. 1441 (60.2 × 40.1). Paris, Musée du Louvre.

Fig. 41. Antoniazzo Romano, *Madonna and Child with Donor* (Gaetani Triptych), 1474–79 (147 × 71). Fondi, S. Pietro.

Fig. 42. Cosimo Rosselli, *Madonna and Child with St. Anne and Four Saints,* 1471 (163 × 163). Berlin (East), Gemäldegalerie.

Fig. 43. Filippino Lippi, *Mystic Marriage of St. Catherine,* 1501 (202 × 172). Bologna, S. Domenico.

Fig. 44. Burgundian, *Madonna and Child,* c. 1490 (78.1 × 54.6). University of North Carolina at Chapel Hill, The Ackland Art Museum; Burton Emmett Collection.

Fig. 45.   Benedetto da Maiano, *Madonna and Child,* c. 1480–90, terracotta (dia. 104.1). Boston, Isabella Stewart Gardner Museum.

Fig. 46.   Domenico Ghirlandaio (?), *Madonna and Child* (78.7 × 55.5). Paris, Musée du Louvre.

Fig. 47.   Hans Baldung Grien, *Nativity,* 1523 (92 × 55). Frankfurt, Städelsches Kunstinstitut.

Fig. 48.   Hans Baldung Grien, *Venus and Cupid,* 1525 (208.3 × 84). Otterlo, Rijksmuseum Kröller-Müller.

Fig. 49.   Jan van Hemessen, *Madonna and Child,* 1543 (135 × 91). Madrid, Museo del Prado.

Fig. 50.   Andrea del Verrocchio, *Madonna and Child,* c. 1470 (84.5 × 64). Frankfurt, Städelsches Kunstinstitut.

Fig. 51.   Verrocchio Shop, *Madonna and Child,* c. 1470 (66 × 48.3). New York, The Metropolitan Museum of Art; Bequest of Benjamin Altman.

Fig. 52.   Roger van der Weyden, *Madonna and Child,* c. 1460 (49 × 31). San Marino, California, The Henry E. Huntington Library and Art Gallery.

Fig. 53.   Giovanni Bellini, *Madonna and Child,* c. 1470 (47 × 34). Bergamo, Accademia Carrara.

Fig. 54.   Bramantino, *Madonna and Child with Sts. Ambrose and Michael,* c. 1518 (122 × 157), detail. Milan, Pinacoteca Ambrosiana.

Fig. 55.   Martin Schongauer, *Christ Child as Salvator Mundi,* c. 1480, engraving (8.8 × 6.1). Lehrs 31.

Fig. 56.   Alsatian, *Madonna and Child with St. Anne,* 15th century (34 × 24). Paris, Musée du Louvre.

Fig. 57.   Francesco Bonsignori, *Virgin Adoring the Sleeping Child,* 1483 (65 × 52). Verona, Museo di Castelvecchio.

Fig. 58.   Andrea Mantegna, *Dead Christ,* before 1506 (66 × 81). Milan, Pinacoteca di Brera.

Fig. 59.   Joos van Cleve, *Holy Family,* c. 1515–20 (49 × 36.5). London, National Gallery.

Fig. 60.   Jacob Jordaens, *Holy Family,* c. 1620–25 (123 × 93.9). London, National Gallery.

Fig. 61.   Piero di Cosimo, *Madonna and Child with St. Margaret and the Infant St. John,* c. 1520 (dia. 135). Tulsa, Oklahoma, Philbrook Art Center; Samuel H. Kress Collection.

Fig. 62.   Andrea Mantegna, *Circumcision,* c. 1470 (86 × 42.5). Florence, Galleria degli Uffizi.

Fig. 63.   Jean Malouel, *Pietà,* c. 1400 (dia. 52). Paris, Musée du Louvre.

Fig. 64.   Henri Bellechose, *Retable of Saint Denis,* 1416 (162 × 211). Paris, Musée du Louvre.

Fig. 65.   Dijon School, *Entombment,* c. 1400 (32.8 × 21.3). Paris, Musée du Louvre.

Fig. 66.   Domenico Ghirlandaio, *Adoration of the Magi,* 1487 (dia. 172), detail. Florence, Galleria degli Uffizi.

Fig. 67.   Tyrolean, *Adoration of the Magi,* c. 1440 (87.5 × 71). Kunstmuseum Basel.

Fig. 68.   Jan van Scorel, *Adoration of the Magi,* c. 1530–35 (86 × 69). Bonn, Rheinisches Landesmuseum.

Fig. 69. Botticelli, *Adoration of the Magi,* c. 1470 (50 × 136), detail. London, National Gallery.

Fig. 70. Mantegna School, *Adoration of the Magi,* c. 1475–80, engraving (39 × 28.2). Bartsch 9.

Fig. 71. Pieter Bruegel, *Adoration of the Magi,* 1564 (111 × 83.5). London, National Gallery.

Fig. 72. Giovanni Cariani, *Madonna and Child with Donor,* 1520 (56 × 75). Bergamo, Accademia Carrara.

Fig. 73. Sebastiano del Piombo, *Holy Family with Saints and Donor,* c. 1505–10 (95 × 136). Paris, Musée du Louvre.

Fig. 74. Giovanni Bellini, *Madonna and Child,* c. 1475–80 (78 × 58). Venice, Accademia.

Fig. 75. Cosimo Rosselli, *Madonna and Child with the Infant St. John.* New York, The Metropolitan Museum of Art; Robert Lehman Collection.

Fig. 76. Lorenzo Lotto, *Holy Family with Donors,* c. 1526–30 (88.9 × 114.3). Malibu, California, The J. Paul Getty Museum.

Fig. 77. Palma Vecchio. *Holy Family with the Magdalen,* c. 1516–17 (80 × 117). Florence, Galleria degli Uffizi.

Fig. 78. Adriaen Isenbrandt, *Rest on the Flight into Egypt,* c. 1515 (48 × 33.5). Private collection.

Fig. 79. Bruges School illumination, *Adoration of the Magi,* c. 1480–1500 (16 × 11.5). Book of Hours, New York, The Pierpont Morgan Library, M. 493, fol. 58v.

Fig. 80. Paolo Veronese, *Holy Family with St. Barbara and the Infant St. John,* c. 1560 (53 × 63). London, Christie's, June 26, 1970 (replica of painting in the Uffizi).

Fig. 81. Paolo Veronese, *Presentation of the Cuccini Family to the Madonna,* 1571 (167 × 416). Dresden, Gemäldegalerie.

Fig. 82. Alvise Vivarini, *Madonna and Child with Saints,* 1504 (89 × 129). Leningrad, Hermitage.

Fig. 83. Perino del Vaga, *Holy Family,* c. 1520 (dia. 85.5). Vaduz, Liechtenstein Collection.

Fig. 84. Cima da Conegliano, *Madonna and Child,* c. 1500–10 (69.5 × 57). London, National Gallery.

Fig. 85. Perugino, *Madonna and Child,* c. 1500 (70 × 51). Washington, D.C., National Gallery of Art; Samuel H. Kress Collection.

Fig. 86. Correggio, *Madonna of the Basket,* c. 1523–25 (33 × 25). London, National Gallery.

Fig. 87. Raffaellino dal Colle, *Madonna and Child with the Infant St. John,* c. 1530 (125 × 85.4). Baltimore, Walters Art Gallery.

Fig. 88. Correggio, *Madonna di S. Giorgio,* 1530–32 (285 × 190), detail. Dresden, Gemäldegalerie.

Fig. 89. Jan van Scorel, *Madonna and Child with Donors,* c. 1527–29 (55 × 76). Castagnola, Thyssen-Bornemisza Collection.

Fig. 90. Jacques de Gheyn, *Madonna and Child with the Infant St. John,* c. 1590–93, engraving (dia. 18.3). Hollstein 334.

Fig. 91. Willem Key, *Pietà,* after 1530 (127 × 99.5). Staatliche Kunsthalle

Karlsruhe (replica of the painting in Munich, Alte Pinakothek).

Fig. 92.   Jacques Bellange, *Pietà*, c. 1615, etching (30.7 × 19.7). Robert-Dumesnil 86.8.

Fig. 93.   Flemish, *Christ as Victor over Sin and Death*, c. 1590–1600. Bruges, Memling Museum.

Fig. 94.   Ludwig Krug, *Man of Sorrows*, c. 1520, engraving (11.8 × 7.8). Hollstein 8.

Fig. 95.   Maerten van Heemskerck, *Man of Sorrows*, c. 1525–30 (77.5 × 54.6). Greenville, South Carolina, Bob Jones University Collection.

Fig. 96.   Maerten van Heemskerck, *Man of Sorrows*, 1532 (90 × 65). Ghent, Museum voor Schone Kunsten.

Fig. 97.   Maerten van Heemskerck, *Man of Sorrows*, 1525 (120 × 95). Whereabouts unknown.

Fig. 98.   After Maerten van Heemskerck, *The Trinity with Christ Resurrected*, glass (40 × 26.5). Amsterdam, Rijksmuseum.

Fig. 99.   Robert Campin (?), *Crucifixion*, c. 1420–40 (77 × 47). Berlin, Gemälde-galerie.

Fig. 100. Roger van der Weyden, *Crucifixion*, c. 1450 (103 × 70). Berne, Kunst-museum; Abegg-Stiftung.

Fig. 101. Lucas Cranach, *Crucifixion*, 1503 (138 × 99). Munich, Alte Pinakothek.

Fig. 102. Albrecht Dürer, *Christ on the Cross*, 1505, drawing (31.5 × 21.5). Vienna, Graphische Sammlung Albertina.

Fig. 103. Master D.S., *Crucifixion*, c. 1505–10, woodcut (44 × 31.1).

Fig. 104. Hans Baldung Grien, *Christ on the Cross*, c. 1515, drawing (ht. 25.2), detail. Prayerbook of the Emperor Maximilian I, Besançon, Bibliothèque Municipale.

Fig. 105. Moretto da Brescia, *Ecce Homo*, c. 1550. Brescia, Pinacoteca.

Fig. 106. Rimini School, *Lamentation*, c. 1330 (c. 35 × 37), detail. Rome, Galleria Nazionale, Palazzo Barberini.

Fig. 107. Illumination from the Petites Heures of Jean de Berry, *Entombment*, c. 1380–85 (21.5 × 14.5). Paris, Bibliothèque Nationale, ms. lat. 18014, fol. 94v.

Fig. 108. French illumination, *Lamentation*, c. 1400. Book of Hours, Paris, Biblio-thèque Nationale, ms. lat. 1364, fol. 105v.

Fig. 109. French, *Entombment*, c. 1330, marble (ht. 49). Paris, Musée du Louvre.

Fig. 110. Alberto di Betto da Assisi, *Lamentation*, c. 1421, wood. Siena, Cathedral.

Fig. 111. Guillaume Vrelant (?), illumination, *Entombment*, c. 1454. Book of Hours, The Hague, Koninklijke Bibliotheek, ms. 76, fol. 7.

Fig. 112. Fouquet Shop illumination, *Lamentation*, c. 1470. Book of Hours, New York, The Pierpont Morgan Library, M. 834, fol. 21 (copy of the *Lamentation* in Fouquet's Hours of Etienne Chevalier).

Fig. 113. Master of the Žebrák Lamentation (Bohemian), *Lamentation*, c. 1505, wood. Prague, Národní Galerie.

Fig. 114. Jan van Scorel, *Lamentation*, c. 1535–40 (45.5 × 67). Utrecht, Centraal Museum.

Fig. 115. Jusepe de Ribera, *Entombment*, c. 1630 (127 × 182). Paris, Musée du Louvre.

Fig. 116. French, *Entombment*, c. 1450–1500, stone (life-size). Avignon, Saint-Pierre.

Fig. 117. Germain Pilon Shop, *Entombment,* c. 1540–54, stone (ht. c. 152). Verteuil, Church.

Fig. 118. French, *Pietà,* c. 1400, alabaster (109 × 45). Saint-André-de-Cubzac (Gironde), Church.

Fig. 119. French, *Pietà,* 15th century, stone. Montluçon, Notre-Dame.

Fig. 120. Upper Bavarian, *Pietà,* c. 1490, terracotta (ht. 106). Munich, Bayerisches Nationalmuseum.

Fig. 121. Flemish, *Pietà,* c. 1510–20, wood (ht. 66). Liège, Saint-Denis.

Fig. 122. After Roger van der Weyden, *Throne of Grace,* 1443 (100 × 45). Exterior wing of Edelheer Triptych, Louvain, Saint-Pierre.

Fig. 123. Swabian, *Throne of Grace with Saints,* c. 1480, wood. Boston, Isabella Stewart Gardner Museum.

Fig. 124. Egyptian relief, *Ramses III and Concubine,* XIX Dynasty. Medinet Habu.

Fig. 125. Archaic Greek shield relief, *Priam before Achilles,* 600–550 B.C. Olympia, Archaeological Museum.

Fig. 126. Drawing after Archaic Greek vase painting, *Theseus Wooing Ariadne,* 700–650 B.C. Heracleion, Museum.

Fig. 127. French mirror case, *Lovers Riding to the Hunt,* c. 1320–40, ivory (dia. 10). London, Victoria and Albert Museum.

Fig. 128. Cologne School, *Madonna with the Sweet-pea Blossom,* c. 1410. Cologne, Wallraf-Richartz-Museum.

Fig. 129. Upper Rhenish illumination, *Death of the Virgin,* 1250–1300 (28.4 × 20.4). Munich, Staatliche Graphische Sammlung, 40 259.

Fig. 130. French, initial "O" from a Canticles manuscript, *Christ and Ecclesia as Bridegroom and Bride,* c. 1200. Paris, Bibliothèque Nationale, ms. lat. 17645, fol. 112v.

Fig. 131. Master of Heiligenkreuz, *Madonna and Child,* c. 1410 (72 × 43.5). Vienna, Kunsthistorisches Museum.

Fig. 132. Luca Cambiaso, *Madonna and Child,* c. 1565 (82 × 67). The Hague, Mauritshuis.

Fig. 133. Lorenzo Lotto, *Mystic Marriage of St. Catherine,* 1523 (172 × 134). Bergamo, Accademia Carrara.

Fig. 134. Cesare Magni, *Madonna and Child with Sts. Peter and Paul,* c. 1530 (148.6 × 146.1). Cambridge, Massachusetts, Fogg Art Museum, Harvard University; Gift of Dr. Arthur K. Solomon, in memory of Susan Pulitzer Freedberg.

Fig. 135. Style of Joos van Cleve, *Christ Child Eating Grapes,* c. 1515 (dia. 40.5). Cologne, Wallraf-Richartz-Museum.

Fig. 136. Quentin Massys, *Madonna and Child,* c. 1500 (130 × 86). Brussels, Musées Royaux des Beaux-Arts.

Fig. 137. Pinturicchio, *Madonna and Child with Sts. Jerome and Francis,* c. 1490–95 (42.6 × 32.5). New Haven, Yale University Art Gallery; Gift of Hannah D. and Louis M. Rabinowitz.

Fig. 138. Roger van der Weyden follower, *Madonna and Child,* after c. 1440 (55 × 34). Brussels, Musées Royaux des Beaux-Arts.

Fig. 139. Carlo di Camerino, *Madonna of Humility with the Temptation of Eve* (181.5 × 88.6). The Cleveland Museum of Art; The Holden Collection.

Fig. 140. Cima da Conegliano, *Madonna and Child,* c. 1510 (83 × 68). Amsterdam, Rijksmuseum.

Fig. 141. Bramantino, *Madonna and Child in a Landscape,* c. 1485 (46 × 36). Boston, Museum of Fine Arts; Purchased from the Picture Fund.

Fig. 142. Joos van Cleve Shop, *Holy Family,* c. 1520 (48.2 × 36.4). The Art Institute of Chicago.

Fig. 143. Jusepe de Ribera, *Madonna and Child,* 1643 (108.6 × 101). Sarasota, Florida, The John and Mable Ringling Museum of Art.

Fig. 144. Filippo Lippi, *Madonna and Child with Saints,* c. 1435–40 (196 × 196), detail. Florence, Galleria degli Uffizi.

Fig. 145. Central Italian, *Madonna and Child with Saints* (overpainted), c. 1525–50 (73.5 × 52.2). Budapest, Museum of Fine Arts.

Fig. 146. Donatello School, *Crucifix,* wood, before and after restoration. Bosco ai Frati, Convento di San Francesco.

Fig. 147. Jan van Eyck (?), *Crucifixion,* c. 1430 (43 × 26). Berlin, Gemäldegalerie.

Fig. 148. Hans Burgkmair, *Christ on the Cross,* 1515, woodcut (25.5 × 18.3). Geisberg 438.

Fig. 149. Illumination from the Grandes Heures de Rohan, *Lamentation,* c. 1420–25 (29 × 20.8). Paris, Bibliothèque Nationale, ms. lat. 9471, fol. 135.

Fig. 150. Wolf Huber, *Lamentation,* 1524 (106 × 87). Paris, Musée du Louvre.

Fig. 151. Byzantine mosaic, *Baptism of Christ,* c. 500, detail. Ravenna, Arian Baptistry.

Fig. 152. Byzantine illumination, *Baptism of Christ,* 14th century (32.3 × 22.8). Baltimore, Walters Art Gallery, W. 531.

Fig. 153. English enamel, *Baptism of Christ,* c. 1200 (5.9 × 16.5). Courtesy Sotheby's, London.

Fig. 154. Limoges School, *Baptism of Christ,* c. 1250, gilt copper (36.8 × 20.9). Boston, Museum of Fine Arts; Francis Bartlett Fund.

Fig. 155. Roger van der Weyden (copy), *Baptism of Christ,* after c. 1450 (44 × 27). Frankfurt, Städelsches Kunstinstitut.

Fig. 156. Illumination from the Très Belles Heures de Notre-Dame, *Baptism of Christ,* c. 1390 (12.6 × 11). Paris, Bibliothèque Nationale, ms. nouv. acq. lat. 3093, fol. 162.

Fig. 157. Flemish, *Baptism of Christ,* c. 1400 (36.3 × 25.9). Baltimore, Walters Art Gallery.

Fig. 158. Guido da Siena, *Madonna and Child Enthroned,* 1262 (142 × 100). Siena, Pinacoteca.

Fig. 159. Cimabue (?), *Madonna and Child with Two Angels,* c. 1300 (218 × 118). Bologna, Sta. Maria dei Servi.

Fig. 160. Lippo di Benivieni, *Madonna and Child,* c. 1330 (?) (75.3 × 56.2). Florence, Collection Count Cosimo degli Alessandri.

Fig. 161. Maso di Banco, *Madonna and Child,* c. 1340 (82 × 39). Florence, S. Spirito.

Fig. 162. Lippo Dalmasio, *Madonna del Velluto,* c. 1400. Bologna, S. Domenico.

Fig. 163. Master of the Magdalen, *Madonna and Child Enthroned,* c. 1280 (92.7 × 52.1). Sotheby's, London, March 24, 1965.

Fig. 164. Sienese (Duccio?), *Madonna and Child Enthroned,* c. 1290–1300 (30.5 × 22.9). Berne, Kunstmuseum.

Fig. 186. Middle Rhenish, *Lamentation,* c. 1450 (32.5 × 31.5). Paris, Musée du Louvre.

Fig. 187. Hans Pleydenwurff Shop, *Deposition,* 1465 (178 × 113). Munich, Alte Pinakothek.

Fig. 188. Juan de Flandes, *Adoration of the Magi,* c. 1510 (124.8 × 79.4). Washington, D.C., National Gallery of Art; Samuel H. Kress Collection.

Fig. 189. Pontormo, *Adoration of the Magi,* c. 1519-20 (85 × 190), detail. Florence, Palazzo Pitti.

Fig. 190. Andrea Andreani after Aurelio (?) Luini, *Adoration of the Magi,* c. 1570, chiaroscuro woodcut (38.5 × 27.3). Bartsch 4.

Fig. 191. Marco Pino, *Adoration of the Magi,* 1571. Naples, SS. Severino e Sossio.

Fig. 192. Bruegel, detail of Fig. 71.

Fig. 193. Bohemian, *Madonna of Strahova,* c. 1350 (94 × 84). Prague, Národní Galerie.

Fig. 194. Master of St. Severin, *Adoration of the Magi,* c. 1500 (118 × 205). Cologne, Wallraf-Richartz-Museum.

Fig. 195. Battista di Gerio, *Madonna and Child,* c. 1410 (118.5 × 64.8). Philadelphia Museum of Art; The John G. Johnson Collection.

Fig. 196. Sassetta, *Madonna and Child with Angels,* 1437-44 (207 × 118). Paris, Musée du Louvre.

Fig. 197. Mantegna School, *Sacra Conversazione,* c. 1465 (56 × 43), detail. Boston, Isabella Stewart Gardner Museum.

Fig. 198. Botticelli, *Madonna dei Candelabri,* c. 1476 (dia. 192). Formerly Berlin (destroyed).

Fig. 199. Giovanni Bellini, *Madonna and Child with Sts. John and Elizabeth,* c. 1490 (72 × 90). Frankfurt, Städelsches Kunstinstitut.

Fig. 200. Raffaellino del Garbo, *Madonna and Child Enthroned,* 1500 (200 × 144). Florence, Galleria degli Uffizi.

Fig. 201. Domenico Puligo, *Madonna and Child Enthroned with Saints,* c. 1515 (154.8 × 171). Sarasota, Florida, The John and Mable Ringling Museum of Art.

Fig. 202. Titian (?), *Sacra Conversazione,* before 1511 (84 × 111.5). Rome, Galleria Doria.

Fig. 203. Sodoma, *Holy Family,* c. 1525 (75 × 67). Rome, Galleria Borghese.

Fig. 204. Veronese Shop, *Holy Family,* c. 1600 (99.1 × 118.1). The Baltimore Museum of Art; Jacob Epstein Collection.

Fig. 205. Gian Antonio Guardi after Veronese, *Holy Family,* c. 1750 (60.6 × 68.6). Seattle Art Museum.

Fig. 206. Ludovico Carracci, *The Dream of St. Joseph,* c. 1605, drawing (27.9 × 27.3). Art market (formerly Ellesmere Collection).

Fig. 207. Antonio Carneo, *Holy Family Adored by Lieutenants and Deputies,* 1667, detail. Udine, Museo Civico.

Fig. 208. Vivarini, detail of Fig. 82.

Fig. 209. Luca della Robbia, *Madonna and Child,* c. 1440-60, terracotta (48.3 × 38.7), before 1977 cleaning. New York, The Metropolitan Museum of Art; Bequest of Susan Dwight Bliss.

Fig. 210. Luca della Robbia, *Madonna and Child* (Fig. 209), after cleaning.

Fig. 211. Andrea Mantegna, *Madonna and Child with the Magdalen and St. John the Baptist,* c. 1500 (136 × 114), detail. London, National Gallery.

Fig. 212. Barent van Orley, *Holy Family,* 1521 (107 × 87), before 1980 cleaning. Paris, Musée du Louvre.

Fig. 213. Barent van Orley, *Holy Family* (Fig. 212), after cleaning.

Fig. 214. Agnolo Bronzino, *Holy Family,* c. 1540–42 (133 × 101), before 1980 cleaning. Paris, Musée du Louvre.

Fig. 215. Agnolo Bronzino, *Holy Family* (Fig. 214), after cleaning.

Fig. 216. Jan van Hemessen, *Madonna and Child,* c. 1540 (129 × 99). Wassenaar, The Netherlands, Geertsema Collection.

Fig. 217. After Jan van Hemessen, *Madonna and Child* (140 × 109). Antwerp, Koninklijk Museum voor Schone Kunsten.

Fig. 218. Michelangelo, *Doni Madonna,* 1506 (dia. 120), detail. Florence, Galleria degli Uffizi.

Fig. 219. Achille Jacquet, engraving after Michelangelo's *Doni Madonna, Gazette des Beaux-Arts,* 1876, pl. after p. 134.

Fig. 220. Retouched photograph of Michelangelo's *Doni Madonna* as published in J. A. Symonds' *Life of Michelangelo,* London, 1893, I, pl. after p. 116.

Fig. 221. Giovanni Bellini, *Madonna and Child* (Fig. 53), retouched Anderson/Alinari photograph.

Fig. 222. Lucas Cranach, *Crucifixion,* 1538 (60 × 40.6). New Haven, Yale University Art Gallery; Gift of Hannah D. and Louis M. Rabinowitz.

Fig. 223. Lucas Cranach, *Christ on the Cross,* before 1502, hand-colored woodcut (21.5 × 15). Hollstein 28.

Fig. 224. Albrecht Dürer and assistant, *Crucifixion,* c. 1500 (63 × 45.5). Dresden, Gemäldegalerie.

Fig. 225. Hans Baldung Grien, *Crucifixion,* 1512 (151 × 104). Berlin, Gemäldegalerie.

Fig. 226. Cosimo Tura, *Dead Christ Supported by Angels,* c. 1474 (44.5 × 86). Vienna, Kunsthistorisches Museum.

Fig. 227. Albrecht Dürer and assistant, *Lamentation,* c. 1500 (63 × 45.5). Dresden, Gemäldegalerie.

Fig. 228. Flemish, *Entombment,* c. 1380–1400, alabaster (20 × 38). Namur, Musée des Arts Anciens du Namurois.

Fig. 229. Flemish, *Mary Magdalen* (?) *Supporting the Dead Christ,* c. 1490, wood. Paris, Musée de Cluny.

Fig. 230. German, *Lamentation,* 1481–1504. Görlitz, Garden of the Holy Grave.

Fig. 231. Andrea Solario, *Lamentation,* 1504–07 (117.5 × 161.5). Paris, Musée du Louvre.

Fig. 232. Mattia Preti (?), *Dead Christ with Angels* (121 × 177). Bari, Pinacoteca Provinciale.

Fig. 233. David Kindt, *Lamentation,* 1631 (57.5 × 155). Paris, Musée du Louvre.

Fig. 234. Master of the St. Lucy Legend, *Pietà,* c. 1475 (52 × 39). Amsterdam, private collection.

Fig. 235. Lower Rhenish, *Pietà,* 15th century, wood. Rheinberg, Cathedral.

INDEX OF NAMES

LEO STEINBERG was born in Moscow in 1920, spent his childhood in Berlin (1923–33), then moved to London, where he studied sculpture at the Slade School, University of London, 1936–40. He settled in New York City after World War II, working as a freelance writer and translator, and as life-drawing instructor at Parsons School of Design. He studied art history at the Institute of Fine Arts, New York University, taking his doctorate in 1960 with a dissertation on the Roman Baroque architect, Borromini.

From 1962 on, he taught at Hunter College, and in 1972 was co-founder of the Art History Department of the Graduate Center, CUNY. In 1975, he was appointed Benjamin Franklin Professor of the History of Art at the University of Pennsylvania. Steinberg has published and lectured widely on Renaissance and 20th-century art. His collected writings on modern art were published under the title *Other Criteria* (1972). His subsequent books are *Michelangelo's Last Paintings* (1975), and a revision of his earlier work on Borromini (1977). Other recent writings include studies of Leonardo, Michelangelo, Pontormo, Guercino, and Picasso.

In 1982 Steinberg delivered the A. W. Mellon Lectures in the Fine Arts at the National Gallery in Washington. He is a fellow of the American Academy of Arts and Sciences, and of University College, London. In May 1983, he became the first art historian to receive an Award in Literature from the American Academy and Institute of Arts and Letters.